Neoliberalizing the University

This collection brings together essays to address the crisis of higher education today, focusing on its neoliberalization. Higher education has been under assault for several decades as neoliberalism's preference for market-based reforms sweeps across the US political economy. The recent push for neoliberalizing the academy comes at a time when it is ripe for change, especially as it continues to confront growing financial pressure, particularly in the public sector. The resulting cutbacks in public funding, especially to state universities, led to a variety of debilitating changes: increases in tuition, growing student debt, more students combining working and schooling, declining graduation rates for minorities and low-income students, increased reliance on adjuncts and temporary faculty, and most recently growing interest in mass processing of students via online instruction. While many serious questions arise once we begin to examine what is happening in higher education today, one particularly critical question concerns the implications of these changes on the relationship of education to as yet still unrealized democratic ideals. The 12 essays collected in this volume create important resources for students, faculty, citizens, and policymakers who want to find ways to address contemporary threats to the higher education-democracy connection. This book was originally published as a special issue of *New Political Science*.

Sanford F. Schram is a Professor of Political Science and Faculty Associate at the Roosevelt House Public Policy Institute at Hunter College, City University of New York, New York, NY, USA. His latest book is *The Return to Ordinary Capitalism: Neoliberalism, Precarity, Occupy* (2015). He is the 2012 recipient of the Charles McCoy Career Achievement Award from the Caucus for a New Political Science.

Neoliberalizing the University

Implications for American democracy

Edited by
Sanford F. Schram

Routledge
Taylor & Francis Group

LONDON AND NEW YORK

First published 2016 by Routledge

2 Park Square, Milton Park, Abingdon, Oxfordshire OX14 4RN
711 Third Avenue, New York, NY 10017

Routledge is an imprint of the Taylor & Francis Group, an informa business

First issued in paperback 2017

British Library Cataloguing in Publication Data
A catalogue record for this book is available from the British Library

ISBN 13: 978-1-138-19474-8 (hbk)
ISBN 13: 978-1-138-30941-8 (pbk)

Typeset in Book Antiqua
by diacriTech, Chennai

Publisher's Note
The publisher accepts responsibility for any inconsistencies that may have arisen during the conversion of this book from journal articles to book chapters, namely the possible inclusion of journal terminology.

Disclaimer
Every effort has been made to contact copyright holders for their permission to reprint material in this book. The publishers would be grateful to hear from any copyright holder who is not here acknowledged and will undertake to rectify any errors or omissions in future editions of this book.

Contents

CONTENTS

Citation Information

The chapters in this book were originally published in *New Political Science*, volume 36, issue 4 (December 2014). When citing this material, please use the original page numbering for each article, as follows:

Introduction
The Future of Higher Education and American Democracy: Introduction
Sanford F. Schram
New Political Science, volume 36, issue 4 (December 2014) pp. 425–437

Chapter 1
Realpolitik *in the American University: Charles A. Beard and the Problem of Academic Repression*
Clyde W. Barrow
New Political Science, volume 36, issue 4 (December 2014) pp. 438–458

Chapter 2
From E Pluribus Unum *to* Caveat Emptor*: How Neoliberal Policies are Capturing and Dismantling the Liberal University*
Steven C. Ward
New Political Science, volume 36, issue 4 (December 2014) pp. 459–473

Chapter 3
Academic Governance and Democratic Processes: The Entrepreneurial Model and Its Discontents
Tracy L.R. Lightcap
New Political Science, volume 36, issue 4 (December 2014) pp. 474–488

Chapter 4
Ideology and the Reform of Public Higher Education
Jacob Segal
New Political Science, volume 36, issue 4 (December 2014) pp. 489–503

CITATION INFORMATION

Chapter 5

Resisting the Exploitation of Contingent Faculty Labor in the Neoliberal University: The Challenge of Building Solidarity between Tenured and Non-Tenured Faculty
Joseph M. Schwartz
New Political Science, volume 36, issue 4 (December 2014) pp. 504–522

Chapter 6

Contingent Academic Labor Against Neoliberalism
Vincent Tirelli
New Political Science, volume 36, issue 4 (December 2014) pp. 523–537

Chapter 7

The Web We Weave: Online Education and Democratic Prospects
Seaton Patrick Tarrant and Leslie Paul Thiele
New Political Science, volume 36, issue 4 (December 2014) pp. 538–555

Chapter 8

The Changing Democratic Functions of Historically Black Colleges and Universities
Clyde Wilcox, JoVita Wells, Georges Haddad and Judith K. Wilcox
New Political Science, volume 36, issue 4 (December 2014) pp. 556–572

Chapter 9

Open Admission and the Imposition of Tuition at the City University of New York, 1969–1976: A Political Economic Case Study for Understanding the Current Crisis in Higher Education
Douglas A. Medina
New Political Science, volume 36, issue 4 (December 2014) pp. 573–589

Chapter 10

Lowering the Basement Floor: From Community Colleges to the For-Profit Revolution
Brian Caterino
New Political Science, volume 36, issue 4 (December 2014) pp. 590–606

Chapter 11

Academic Conservatives and the Future of Higher Education
George Ehrhardt
New Political Science, volume 36, issue 4 (December 2014) pp. 607–621

Chapter 12

Transforming the Game: Democratizing the Publicness of Higher Education and Commonwealth in Neoliberal Times
Romand Coles
New Political Science, volume 36, issue 4 (December 2014) pp. 622–639

For any permission-related enquiries please visit:
http://www.tandfonline.com/page/help/permissions

Notes on Contributors

Clyde W. Barrow is a Professor of Political Science at the University of Texas, Rio Grande Valley, TX, USA. His publications include *Universities and the Capitalist State* (1990), *More Than a Historian: The Political and Economic Thought of Charles A. Beard* (2000), and *Globalisation, Trade Liberalisation, and Higher Education in North America* (2003). He has also published numerous articles on state theory and higher education policy.

Brian Caterino is an Independent Scholar who works in public media in Rochester, NY, USA. He holds an MA and a PhD in Political Science from the University of Toronto, Toronto, ON, Canada, and is the co-editor (with Sanford F. Schram) of *Making Political Science Matter* (2006), as well as a contributor in *Perestroika: The Raucous Revolt in Political Science* (2005). He has published a number of articles and reviews in a number of journals on interpretive methods and critical theory.

Romand Coles is a Professor at the Institute for Social Justice, Australian Catholic University, North Sydney, Australia. He has written many books, including *Beyond Gated Politics: Reflections for the Possibility of Democracy* (2005), *Christianity, Democracy, and the Radical Ordinary: Conversations between a Christian and a Radical Democrat* (2007) with Stanley Hauerwas, and *Visionary Pragmatism: Radical and Ecological Democracy* (2016).

George Ehrhardt is an Associate Professor of Government at Appalachian State University, Boone, NC, USA, specializing in Asian politics and research methodology, as well as being active in the conservative movement.

Georges Haddad attended the American University of Beirut, Beirut, Lebanon. He is currently a tenured Professor of Physiology at Howard University School of Medicine, Washington, DC, USA. He is nationally and internationally known for his work on the effects of alcohol on cardiomyocytes and excitation–contraction coupling. He is highly skilled in single-cell patch-clamp recordings and intracellular calcium determinations. He has been recognized for his outstanding mentoring of PhD students at Howard University.

Tracy L.R. Lightcap is a Professor of Political Science and Chair of Political Science at LaGrange College, LaGrange, GA, USA. He is the author of *The Politics of Torture* (2011) and the co-editor of *Examining Torture: Empirical Studies of State Repression* (2014). He has published articles on torture and interrogation policy, judicial administration, comparative judicial politics, and judicial decision making.

NOTES ON CONTRIBUTORS

Douglas A. Medina is a PhD candidate in the Political Science Program at the Graduate Center, City University of New York (CUNY), New York, NY, USA. His research interests include the political economy of higher education, with a focus on public institutions. He is also the Associate Director of the Baruch College Undergraduate Honors Program and has taught at the Borough of Manhattan Community College.

Sanford F. Schram teaches at Hunter College, CUNY, in the Political Science Department and the Public Policy Program at Roosevelt House, New York, NY, USA. He has published numerous scholarly articles and books, including *Words of Welfare: The Poverty of Social Science and the Social Science of Poverty* (1995) and *Disciplining the Poor: Neoliberal Paternalism and the Persistent Power of Race* (2011), co-authored with Joe Soss and Richard Fording, both of which won the Michael Harrington Award from the Caucus for a New Political Science. His most recent book is *Becoming a Footnote: An Activist-Scholar Finds His Voice, Learns to Write, and Survives Academia* (2013). His current book project is entitled *The Return to Ordinary Capitalism: Neoliberalism, Precarity, Occupy* (2015). He was the 2012 recipient of the Charles McCoy Career Achievement Award from the Caucus for a New Political Science.

Joseph M. Schwartz is a Professor of Political Science at Temple University, Philadelphia, PA, USA, where he teaches political theory and American political development and chairs its Intellectual Heritage program. He is the author of *The Future of Democratic Equality* (Routledge, 2009) and also *The Permanence of the Political* (Princeton University Press, 1995). The Future of Democratic Equality won APSA's political theory section prize in 2011 for the best book published in the past five years in political philosophy. He serves on the executive committee of his faculty union (AFT) and also serves as a national vice-chair of Democratic Socialists of America.

Jacob Segal is an Associate Professor of Political Science at Kingsborough Community College of the City University of New York, Brooklyn, NY, USA. He has published articles in *New Political Science, American Political Science Review, Contemporary Political Theory,* and other journals.

Seaton Patrick Tarrant teaches sustainability studies at the University of Florida, where he is completing dissertation research on the relationship of sustainability education to emergent theories of citizenship and democracy.

Leslie Paul Thiele teaches political theory and sustainability studies at the University of Florida, where he serves as Director of the Center for Adaptive Innovation, Resilience, Ethics and Science (UF CAIRES).

Vincent Tirelli is a visiting Assistant Professor in the Government Department at Manhattan College in Riverdale, UT, USA. He obtained his PhD from the Political Science Department of the City University of New York Graduate Center in 2007. His research interests include education policy, urban politics, American national institutions, social movements, and political theory.

Steven C. Ward is a Professor of Sociology at Western Connecticut State University, Danbury, CT, USA. His most recent book is entitled *Neoliberalism and the Global*

Restructuring of Knowledge and Education (Routledge, 2012). His work has also appeared in journals such as the *American Sociological Review, Sociology, The History of the Human Sciences, The Canadian Journal of Sociology,* and *The Journal of Cultural Economy.*

JoVita Wells received her BA from Howard University, Washington, DC, USA, and her JD from Howard University School of Law. She serves as Director of Sponsored Programs and Program Manager of the Live to Give Charitable Trust, Initiative on Civic Engagement Equity at the University of the District of Columbia, USA. She was a founding member of the National Sponsored Programs Administrators Alliance of HBCUs and served as its president in 2000. She was a Vanderbilt University (Peabody College) fellowship awardee where she studied educational leadership. She is a Woodrow Wilson National Fellowship recipient to develop improved fundraising capabilities at HBCUs. She is a recognized expert in the development of nonprofit organizations and university research and development programs.

Clyde Wilcox is a Professor of Government at Georgetown University, Washington, DC, USA. He has been teaching at the Qatar campus since 2014 and will continue until 2016. He has published many books and articles in the areas of religion and politics, gender politics, political mobilization, interest groups, social movements, and science fiction and politics. He teaches new US diplomats at the Foreign Service Institute and has provided diplomatic training for other countries. He regularly travels and lectures across the world, and consults as an expert witness.

Judith K. Wilcox (formerly Judith Gwathmey) was a Professor of Medicine and Physiology at Harvard Medical School and is now a Professor at Boston University School of Medicine, Boston, MA, USA, and currently holds adjunct appointments in the Morehouse School of Medicine and Rutgers School of Medicine. She is currently a charter member of the National Institutes of Health, Vascular Cell and Molecular Biology study section. She was founder, CEO, and CSO of Gwathmey, Inc., a preclinical research biotechnology company. She is known internationally for her research on calcium channelling and heart failure. She is also a highly sought after motivational speaker and mentor. She is the recipient of the Presidential Mentoring Award in Science, Technology, Engineering, and Mathematics, the Daniel D. Savage Award from the Association of Black Cardiologists, and the Small Business Administration Tibbetts Award for Excellence in Research.

The Future of Higher Education and American Democracy: Introduction

Sanford F. Schram
Hunter College, CUNY, USA

The economic fallout from the Great Recession of 2009 has brought a number of difficult issues to the fore. Many of them share a common root. Over the last few decades, there has been an ongoing neoliberalization of the political economy. Neoliberalism is defined variously, but one incisive definition has the marketization of the state at its core.[1] In one area after another, public policies have been restructured to operate more along market lines in order to make those programs better serve market purposes. Admittedly, conservatives led by corporate elites had, for years, focused on rolling back the welfare state. The push to roll back the welfare state has been developing ever since the New Deal of President Franklin Delano Roosevelt was rolled out as a response to the Great Depression that started in 1928. Yet, by the time of the Great Society under President Lyndon Baines Johnson in the 1960s, it was clear that the roll back was going to be no simple task. After the New Deal and then the Great Society, the Keynesian countercyclical welfare state had come to be firmly embedded in the political economy. As limited as it was in its American incarnation, people had become committed to relying on the state as a backstop to the capriciousness of capitalism. In lieu of Plan A of rolling back the welfare state, conservatives eventually turned to Plan B: if you could not roll back the welfare state, the next best thing would be to marketize it—that is, restructure it not to counter the market but to make it operate more along market lines all in the name of buttressing the market.[2]

Neoliberalism involves blurring the boundaries between the market and the state. The state gets marketized so as to come to be more focused on buttressing market actors. For instance, the ideals implicit in social welfare policy envision it as protecting citizens by counteracting the negative effects of markets. Yet, with neoliberalism, social welfare policy now "jumps tracks" to become public programs designed to further the profitability of national firms in global markets (even if it means making citizens more economically precarious).[3] Welfare programs that sheltered the unemployed and unemployable morph into

---

[1] Wendy Brown, "Neo-Liberalism and the End of Liberal Democracy," *Theory & Event* 7:1 (2003); and Wendy Brown, "American Nightmare: Neoliberalism, Neoconservatism, and De-Democratization," *Political Theory* 34:6 (2006), pp. 690–714.

[2] Jamie Peck, "Zombie Neoliberalism and the Ambidexterous State," *Theoretical Criminology* 14:1 (2010) pp. 104–110.

[3] Saskia Sassen, *Territory, Authority, Rights: From Medieval to Global Assemblages* (Princeton, NJ: Princeton University Press, 2006).

programs designed to push the poor into low-wage jobs. These jobs, more often than not, leave people poor but increase the profit margins of their employers, consistent with the underlying purpose of neoliberalism.[4] Yet, neoliberalism involves much more than welfare-to-work for the poor. Plan B moves like a juggernaut, restructuring public policy in one area after another, regardless of whether liberals or conservatives are in power. Education is no exception to this powerful trend.

Education policy has proven particularly vulnerable to neoliberalization. For years, concern about the decline of the public schools suggested the need for major market-oriented reforms.[5] These would be reforms where market actors are recruited to impose market-based solutions that would involve more economically efficient ways of delivering more market-appropriate types of education on the basis of reduced budgets. From the start, the reform agenda framed the need for education reform in a just-so crisis narrative, implying that the appropriate response was the neoliberalization of education policy.[6] At the core of this crisis narrative was the founding assumption that the country was at risk of losing out in the global economic competition if it did not reform education so as to graduate more students with the skills demanded by the globalizing economy. The United States was "A Nation at Risk," as the pivotal report of President Ronald Reagan's education reform commission put it in 1983.[7]

It did not take long for specific changes to start to be implemented.[8] The alleged failures of the schools were almost never seen as a result of declines in public funding, especially for the neediest, often nonwhite students. Instead, declines in public support were used as a pretext to turn the schools over to market actors who would impose neoliberal reforms as a way of delivering education more cheaply while often still allowing the profiteers to make money themselves. Testing was imposed on students to ensure that the system was producing the desired outcomes. The testing schemes were married to systems of market competition so the networks of schools (both public and private) would have incentives to compete in meeting the new accountability standards. Charter schools and high-stakes testing became the twin pillars of neoliberal education reform of elementary and secondary public schools. Other reforms to incentivize desired outcomes among competing schools came to include such schemes as linking teacher pay to student performance on those tests.

---

[4] Joe Soss, Richard C. Fording and Sanford F. Schram, *Disciplining the Poor: Neoliberal Paternalism and the Persistent Power of Race* (Chicago, IL: University of Chicago Press, 2011).

[5] Private foundations, such as the Gates Foundation, the Lumina Foundation, and the Walton Family Foundation have led the campaign to promote market-based education reform. See Diane Ratvich, *The Death and Life of the Great American School System: How Testing and Choice Are Undermining Education* (New York: Basic Books, 2010).

[6] Garnet Kindervater and Joe Soss, "Governing Through Crisis: How States Produce the Present in the Future Tense" (Paper prepared for presentation at the Annual Meeting of the Western Political Science Association, Seattle, WA, April 17–20, 2014).

[7] *A Nation at Risk: The Imperative for Educational Reform* (Washington, DC: US Department of Education, National Commission on Excellence in Education, April 1983), http://www2.ed.gov/pubs/NatAtRisk/intro.html>.

[8] Diane Ravitch, *Reign of Error: The Hoax of the Privatization Movement and the Danger to America's Public Schools* (New York: Knopf, 2012).

The No Child Left Behind Act of 2001 made neoliberal reform of the public schools a nationwide effort supported by both the major political parties.[9] Yet, its implementation would prove problematic. As the stakes increased, pressure grew to the point where meeting performance benchmarks became the be all and end all. Cheating scandals are matched with reductions in the quality of instruction concerning anything that is not measured by the performance standards. Nonetheless, thanks to extensive lobbying based in part on profits gleaned from the privatized system, public education now continually becomes neoliberalized in ways that have proven very profitable for some entrepreneurs, regardless of whether students are better educated.[10]

Higher education has not been immune to the pressures to introduce neoliberal reforms, though it is only most recently that neoliberalization in higher education has started to receive critical scrutiny.[11] The recent push for neoliberalizing the academy comes at a time when it is ripe for change, especially as it continues to confront growing financial pressure, particularly in the public sector.[12] Higher education has had its own particular vulnerabilities that the right could exploit by fanning the flames of anti-intellectual resentment among those already predisposed to oppose what they saw as the leftist orientation of academia. By the early 1970s, demonization of the professoriate as leftist *refuseniks* facilitated the agenda to retrench funding for higher education.[13] The resulting cutbacks in public funding, especially to state universities, led to a variety of debilitating changes: increases in tuition, growing student debt, more students combining working and schooling, declining graduation rates for minorities and low-income students, increased reliance on adjuncts and temporary faculty, and most recently, growing interest in mass processing of students via online instruction.

Under-funded public colleges and universities, like the elementary and secondary public schools before them, have come under the most pressure to respond to lack of funding. Again, the preferred neoliberal response has been to turn to market-based solutions. The thinking is that these reforms can turn education into a marketable product at reduced cost. A tipping point seems to have been reached where US institutions of higher learning are now prioritizing cost-efficiency in the provision of education as a commodity at the expense of promoting the liberal learning essential to fostering a democratic citizenry. Neoliberalism becomes its own vicious cycle. The institutions of higher education are not just mimicking the neoliberal responses of the elementary and secondary schools; they are also affected by the neoliberal reforms occurring at those levels. The pressures on institutions of higher education are compounded by the crisis in

---

[9] Jesse Hessler Rhodes, "Progressive Policy Making in a Conservative Age? Civil Rights and the Politics of Federal Education Standards, Testing, and Accountability," *Perspectives on Politics* 9:3 (2011), pp. 519–544; and Jesse Rhodes, *An Education in Politics: The Origins and Evolution of No Child Left Behind* (Ithaca, NY: Cornell University Press, 2012).

[10] Ravitch, *Reign of Error*, Chapter 32.

[11] Suzanne Mettler, *Degrees of Inequality: How the Politics of Higher Education Sabotaged the American Dream* (New York: Basic Books, 2014).

[12] Ellen Schrecker, *The Lost Soul of Higher Education: Corporatization, the Assault on Academic Freedom, and the End of the American University* (New York: New Press, 2010).

[13] Henry A. Giroux, "Higher Education Under Siege: Implications for Public Intellectuals," *NEA Higher Education Journal* (Fall 2006), pp. 63–78.

elementary and secondary public education because declining state support has made it more difficult for lower-income students, especially minorities, to get the education they need to even qualify to attend college. While many serious questions arise once we begin to examine what is happening in higher education today, one particularly critical question concerns the implications of these changes on the relationship of education to as yet still unrealized democratic ideals.[14] The articles in this Special Issue of *New Political Science* address particular aspects of the crisis in higher education with attention to its implications for American democracy. In this introduction, I first present an overview of the developments in higher education and then provide a summary of the articles that follow.

Neoliberalizing Higher Education

When President Ronald Reagan's National Commission on Excellence in Education released *A Nation at Risk* in 1983, the push for reform was focused primarily on elementary and secondary education.[15] Reform of higher education was, however, coming into focus. The introduction of the report indicated:

> The Commission's charter directed it to pay particular attention to teenage youth, and we have done so largely by focusing on high schools. Selective attention was given to the formative years spent in elementary schools, to higher education, and to vocational and technical programs. We refer those interested in the need for similar reform in higher education to the recent report of the American Council on Education, *To Strengthen the Quality of Higher Education*.[16]

At the time, reform of higher education along the same neoliberal lines as elementary and secondary education was not a topic of widespread public discussion. Yet, that would change and today the neoliberalization of higher education is more widely discussed as reform works its way across the higher education landscape. And as that happens, the criticisms are starting to accumulate.[17]

The crisis narrative championed by the reformers defined education in highly economistic terms. The value of getting an education was now more than before measured in its ability to enhance the students' human capital that makes them employable in the globalizing economy. Technical skills that employers valued took precedence over the value of education in other respects, for example as in becoming a critical-minded, thoughtful citizen who could help the country better meet its democratic ideals. The idea that mass higher education could produce a more critically minded democratic citizenry is an old one that was only starting to be realized in the post-World War II era. But now the idea of higher education propelling the US to a brighter democratic future is fading fast in the face of neoliberalization.[18]

---

[14] In particular, see Harry Boyte (ed.), *Democracy's Education: Public Work, Citizenship, and the Future of Colleges and Universities* (Nashville, TN: Vanderbilt University Press, 2014).

[15] US Department of Education, National Commission on Excellence in Education, *A Nation at Risk*.

[16] Ibid.

[17] See Henry Giroux, *Neoliberalism's War on Higher Education* (Chicago, IL: Haymarket Books, 2014).

[18] See Harry Boyte, "Higher Education and Rising Inequality," *Huffington Post*, July 19, 2014, http://www.huffingtonpost.com/harry-boyte/higher-education-and-risi_b_5602158.html▷.

One result of this shift in the value of a post-secondary education was the proliferation of vocational and technical training schools which came to be funded largely by federally-funded loans to students. Traditional colleges and universities also adjusted to the demands for change offering more career-oriented programs. The overall results have not been pretty. For instance, most students who attend for-profit colleges and universities do not graduate with jobs in their chosen fields at salaries high enough to enable them to pay off their loans.[19] Actually, many students at these schools never graduate. Nonetheless, the growing reliance on federally-funded student loans by the for-profits has been a major driver in making student debt the largest form of debt across the country, crowding out home mortgages and, as a result, slowing down economic recovery.[20] Yet, for-profit colleges and universities continue to attract students, often with false advertising and by still effectively resisting strict governmental regulation, using their profits to effectively lobby Congress.

The for-profits are heavily dependent on federally-funded student loans to sustain their operations. Their promises to provide vocationally-oriented education have attracted students who overwhelmingly finance their studies via federally-funded student loans. They represent a prime example of how neoliberalism involves blurring the boundaries of the state and the market, where education policy gets marketized and market actors are state subsidized.

The continued success of the for-profits in receiving federal support without sufficient federal oversight actually points to a key irony of neoliberalism. In fact neoliberal failure may not be failure at all because much of the marketization of education in recent years seems designed to get people to comply with market forces rather than to resist them.[21] If students fail or if a chosen school fails them, as market actors they must accept responsibility for their bad choices and work to improve their market participation in the future. This logic has spread from charter schools and for-profit colleges and universities and eventually to public schools and private non-profit colleges and universities. They now all increasingly lean toward refashioning the curriculum to attract students with promises of opportunities to learn skills directly related to specific careers.[22] Students must accept responsibility for their education choices, most especially with the need to continue to pay off their student loans even if their education leaves them without a career that can finance repayment. Education is now more than ever a commodity that one buys. If it fails to improve your human capital in the form of commodifiable skills, that is a burden you must bear on your own. This neoliberal logic makes education a risky business for students as individual consumers even as it becomes less of an asset for society as a whole. The bottom line is that the commodification of education continues apace irrespective of effects for citizenship and democracy. The marketization of education seems to be a machine that now goes by itself.

---

[19] For a searing indictment of the rise of for-profit colleges and universities, see Mettler, *Inequalities of Degrees*, pp. 87–110.

[20] Andrew Ross, *Creditocracy: And the Case for Debt Refusal* (New York: OR Books, 2014), Chapter 3.

[21] David Harvey, *A Brief History of Neoliberalism* (New York: Oxford University Press, 2007).

[22] Wesley Shumar, *College for Sale: A Critique of the Commodification of Higher Education* (New York: Routledge, 1997).

In response to the growing concern about students not being able to convert their schooling into decent paying jobs, the Obama administration has proposed tying federal aid to outcome measures such as graduation rates.[23] Yet, this is just another example of using neoliberal reforms to address the failures of neoliberalism. Frequently, we see these performance measurement schemes get repudiated only to be replaced by more ambitious measurement regimes. Performance measurement becomes a "hydra-headed monster" that comes back stronger after each beheading.[24] Further, the imposition of performance standards is likely to create more perverse measurement schemes that have counter-productive effects like we have seen with "high-stakes testing" and charter schools that focus on improving scores without necessarily ensuring students get a well-rounded education. The result is that the measurement tail comes to wag the program implementation dog.

There is then risk of a neoliberal means–ends inversion that comes from the instrumentalization of performance measurement.[25] With a statistical benchmark hanging over program administrators, inevitably there is the concern that hitting the target must be given priority, even at the expense of other important programmatic considerations. If failure to hit the performance target means adverse actions will be taken against the program, including reductions in funding, or worse, termination of the program, then the performance manage-ment benchmarks not only inform the decision-making of education adminis-trators, but can become an overriding preoccupation.

Neoliberal systems of measurement are still creating measurement panic in public elementary and secondary education today and not just among competing charter schools that vie to get their contracts renewed by local school districts. Even as high-stakes testing gets thoroughly criticized, the pressure now grows to extend this logic in deciding the allocation of federal funding to colleges and universities. While tracking graduation rates is important, tying funding to them as the Obama administration has proposed might just produce more neoliberal failure of the performance measurement kind. The hydra-headed monster of performance management has nine lives and like other neoliberal zombies it can keep on keeping on, long after it should have been declared dead.

The failures of neoliberal higher education reform include growing inequities. A major debate among critics is about neoliberalism's failure in reducing the growing inequalities of recent decades. We need to consider the possibility that neoliberalism's failures could well be intentional rather than unintentional results of neoliberal policies and practices designed to redistribute resources toward the most aggressive market actors.[26] Given the role education plays in determining the economic prospects of so many, this debate undoubtedly has direct relevance for assessing education reform in the current era.

---

[23] Tamar Lewin, "Obama's Plan Aims to Lower Cost of College," *New York Times*, August 22, 2013, http://www.nytimes.com/2013/08/22/education/obamas-plan-aims-to-lower-cost-of-college.html?_r=0 > .

[24] Beryl A. Radin, "The Government and Performance Review Act (GPRA): Hydra-Headed Monster or Flexible Management Tool?" *Public Administration Review* 58:4 (1988), pp. 307–317.

[25] On administrative policy feedback, see Joe Soss and Donald P. Moynihan, "Feedback and the Politics of Administration," *Public Administration Review* 74:3 (2014), pp. 320–322.

[26] See Harvey, *A Brief History of Neoliberalism*, p. 98.

At one level, it is unremarkable that neoliberalism generates inequality. Neoliberalism is centrally about marketization, and markets have evolved to be about creating competitions with winners and losers. Under neoliberalism, each person is seen as having primary responsibility to enhance his or her own human capital. If you took on massive amounts of debt to finance your education but cannot now get a decent job to pay off your student loans, then that is also on you as a failed market actor. Neoliberal logic is unimpressed with the record amounts of student debt and campaigns for debt forgiveness continue to waver politically. Yet, it would seem that if it were not for the hegemony of the neoliberal perspective, the student debt crisis would receive more serious political discussion.

Student debt is but the tip of a very deep iceberg, as Chris Maisano has noted.[27] By 2012, student loan debt became the largest form of all debt, exceeding credit card, housing and medical debt, and totaling approximately one trillion dollars. The main reason for increased debt is the rising cost of tuition and fees that have more than doubled since 2000. The ongoing underfunding of public colleges and universities is the main cause of these increases. Between 1990 and 2010, real funding per public full-time enrolled student declined by over 26%. Over the same period, tuition and fees at four-year public colleges and universities rose by approximately 113% while the price of public two-year colleges increased by 71%. With families' incomes stagnating for over thirty years, students increasingly turned to loans to finance their education. Maisano notes: "According to the Department of Education, 45% of 1992–1993 graduates borrowed money from federal or private sources; today, at least two-thirds of graduates enter the workforce with educational debt."[28]

The problem of what Maisano and others have called "debt overhang" weighs heavily on students after their schooling ends, increasingly in recent decades.[29] One main reason is the persistence of wage stagnation. Workers with Bachelor's degrees aged twenty-five to thirty-four saw their earnings decline 15% over the last decade. At the same time, student debt on average increased by 24%. Yet unlike other forms of debt, student loans stay with you and cannot be erased by conventional bankruptcy claims. When borrowers default on student loans, they face wage garnishment, loss of tax refunds, and the withholding of future Social Security payments and other penalties.

Under these neoliberal conditions, it is not at all surprising, and in fact it is to be expected, that education will begin to resemble a rigged lottery that ends up creating what Suzanne Mettler has called "degrees of inequality."[30] While students from the wealthiest families can purchase highly marketable degrees, only the most fortunate low-income students who somehow manage to qualify for sufficient financial backing at elite schools are likely to be able to take advantage of the opportunities afforded by graduating from college. The rest, all too predictably, end up facing the possibility that their education translates into less

---

[27] The figures reported in this paragraph are from Chris Maisano, "The Soul of Student Debt," *Jacobin* 9 (2012).

[28] Ibid.

[29] The figures reported are from ibid. Also see Ross, *Creditocracy*, Chapter 3.

[30] Mettler, *Degrees of Inequality*.

than a sure road to the middle class or worse, their student loans weigh them down so much they remain mired in poverty.

Increasingly we are seeing evidence that neoliberal marketizing reforms are leading to an education system that creates pathways to economic success for some while disservicing others who are seeking to advance educationally. This is especially apparent in the post-secondary market. At one end, many of the students attending for-profit colleges end up with massive debt and no real job prospects. Students attending under-funded public colleges also are weighed down with student loans and face grim employment prospects as well. In fact, there is now growing evidence that seeking a college degree continues to be a safe financial investment but only for those students who attend the better, often exclusive private, non-profit colleges and other elite universities.[31]

The public universities are increasingly confronting budget cuts as states fail to support them at prior levels. The anti-tax movement and the hollowing out of the welfare state over time have forced state universities to seek alternative sources of funding. Among public colleges and universities, state and local funding per student decreased only 2–4% in 2011—substantially lower than the 6–15% declines observed during the Great Recession. Nonetheless, state and local support reached a decade low in 2011, averaging about six to eight thousand dollars per student at public four-year colleges and universities.[32]

As a result, students at public colleges and universities now pay 50–60% of the cost of their education—an eighteen to twenty-two percentage point increase for 2001–2011.[33] For the same period, at community colleges, student costs rose by fifteen percentage points, amounting to 38% of their total educational costs. Overall, increases in the student share of costs at public institutions grew for the decade between 54 and 62% on average. Increases in tuition have led students to borrow more money but also work more while attending school and the results indicate declining performance.[34] Neoliberalization results in more students learning less while shouldering more of the costs.

With the shift away from public support, increasingly state funding is seen as "seed money" that helps finance neoliberal efforts to attract financing from investors via bond markets (sometimes more successfully than others).[35] The degrees of inequality continue to mount under neoliberalism's marketization of education. With declines in public support, inequalities emerge not just between public and private schools but also among the public universities in the rates at which they can attract private funding.

In the face of this pell-mell rush to procure financing, inequalities mount within the ranks of the professoriate as well. Increasingly the under-funded public colleges and universities have accelerated the ongoing trend toward creating a casualized workforce of under-paid adjunct faculty to provide instruction for a

---

[31] Ibid., 30–39.

[32] Donna M. Desrochers and Steven Hurlburt, *Trends in College Spending: 2001–2011: A Delta Data Update* (Washington, DC: American Institutes for Research, 2014), p. 6.

[33] Ibid., 8.

[34] Richard Arum and Josipa Roska, *Academically Adrift: Limited Learning on College Campuses* (Chicago, IL: University of Chicago Press, 2010).

[35] Bill Graves, "The Rise and Fall of Richard Lariviere, University of Oregon President, Fired on Monday," *The Oregonian*, December 3, 2011, http://www.oregonlive.com/education/index.ssf/2011/12/the_rise_and_fall_of_richard_l.html>.

growing majority of all classes being taught at these institutions. Underpaid, most often without basic health or pension benefits, many of these adjuncts are graduate students or former graduate students with no real prospects of securing a permanent faculty appointment. A class division grows among the ranks of the faculty adding to the degrees of inequality wrought by the neoliberalization of higher education. A recent report from Democrats in the US House of Representatives in 2014 noted:

> The post-secondary academic workforce has undergone a remarkable change over the last several decades. The tenure-track college professor with a stable salary, firmly grounded in the middle or upper-middle class, is becoming rare. Taking her place is the contingent faculty: non-tenure-track teachers, such as part-time adjuncts or graduate instructors, with no job security from one semester to the next, working at a piece rate with few or no benefits across multiple workplaces, and far too often struggling to make ends meet. In 1970, adjuncts made up 20 percent of all higher education faculty. Today, they represent half.[36]

The change is even more drastic depending on how you count. Over 70% of all faculty are non-tenure track.[37] Yet, a professoriate of temporary instructors is evidently still not enough to balance the under-funded budgets of public colleges and universities. As a result, the growing ranks of administrators who have been hired to manage the transformed faculty are increasingly pushing use of the internet to deliver instruction.[38] Online instruction and other innovations are being developed, often relying on private corporate providers for content.[39] The result is yet another neoliberal market-based practice to introduce other forms of inequality between students in terms of how they take courses, and between instructors in terms of whether they are a featured lecturer or just an under-paid teaching assistant.

These changes had been developing before the Great Recession and include private colleges and universities as well as public ones. With the tumultuous changes to higher education today, it is difficult to predict whether cherished ideals of ensuring access to a decent education for all can be sustained. Also in doubt is whether education in the future can continue to be a force that works to promote both equality and democracy. Instead, it may be moving to being an agent for generating greater inequality while ignoring its role in helping educate the next generation to be effective democratic citizens.

The concern for democracy is not new but in the age of neoliberalism is at risk of being seen as an anachronistic extravagance.[40] Education is supposed to be not

---

[36] US House of Representatives, Committee on Education and the Workforce, Democratic Staff, *The Just-in-Time Professor: A Staff Report Summarizing eForum Responses on the Working Conditions of Contingent Faculty in Higher Education* (Washington, DC: January 2014), http://democrats.edworkforce.house.gov/sites/democrats.edworkforce.house.gov/files/documents/1.24.14-AdjunctEforumReport.pdf>.

[37] Adrianna Kezar, "Changing Faculty Workload Models," *TIAA-CREF Institute*, November, 2013, https://www.tiaa-crefinstitute.org/public/pdf/changing-faculty-workforce-models.pdf> .

[38] Benjamin Ginsberg, *The Fall of the Faculty: The Rise of the All-Administrative University and Why it Matters* (New York: Oxford University Press, 2011), pp. 192–202.

[39] "Major Players in the MOOC Universe," *Chronicle of Higher Education*, April 22, 2014, http://chronicle.com/article/Major-Players-in-the-MOOC/138817/?cid=wc > .

[40] Boyte, "Higher Education and Rising Inequality."

just for us individually but also for society collectively so as to help sustain democracy. While never fully realized in practice, the post-World War II period saw great strides in moving forward toward realizing that quintessentially American ideal. But that was before neoliberalism. Now the US is the home of marketized education, turning it into a commodity that individuals consume exclusively for the enhancement of each person's human capital. Yet, even if that promise of enhanced human capital is increasingly not able to translate into decent paying jobs, the prevalence of neoliberal market logic in education it seems has as yet to peak.

In the balance hangs the relationship between higher education and democracy. If the market logic of neoliberalism continues to work its way to ascendance in higher education, increasingly a college education will only be valued strictly in terms of its commodifiability. Education will be assessed strictly in terms of its ability to enhance human capital that can be bought and sold on global labor markets. Any and all education that does not directly contribute to that process of commodification will be relegated to being seen as a luxury that cash-strapped colleges and universities can ill afford. The process of neoliberalization makes education for promoting a democratic citizenry all the more precarious, vulnerable to further diminution and marginalization if not outright total elimination. The dream of mass higher education to produce a more critically minded democratic citizenry will remain further from reach.

The consequences of this financial situation in higher education today are profoundly political. As Tayyab Mahmud has pointed out, debt imposes discipline on the debtors.[41] For instance, schools which have mortgaged their futures to bondholders will be beholden to their agendas. And students weighed down by debt are not likely to feel they have the luxury to study that which makes them a critically minded citizen if that does not also provide a path to professional employment that can pay off their loans. As Andrew Ross notes:

> [T]he larger threat is to the workings of an operational democracy. A crushing debt burden stifles our capacity to think freely, act conscientiously and fulfill our democratic responsibilities. Too many young people now feel their future has been foreclosed before they have entered full adulthood. And, given the creditors' goal of prolonging debt service to the grave, the burden of repayment is shifting disproportionately toward the elderly (many of whom now are routinely asked to cosign student loans). Democracies don't survive well without a functional middle class or a citizenry endowed with an optional political imagination, and the test of a humane one is how it treats seniors when they outlast their capacity to earn a living wage.[42]

Equally worrisome is the prospect that an increasingly causalized faculty, overwhelmingly composed of adjunct faculty, who keep their jobs based on how well student-consumers prefer their courses, is not likely to serve as a strong bulwark against the erosion of a curriculum designed to sustain the education-democracy relationship. Yet, it could be that the faculty are the last line of defense against the deleterious effects of the neoliberalization of higher education. Their

---

[41] Tayyab Mahmud, "Debt and Discipline," *American Quarterly* 64:3 (2012), pp. 469–494.
[42] Andrew Ross, "Creditocracy or Democracy?" *Aljazeera America*, May 10, 2014, http://america.aljazeera.com/opinions/2014/5/credit-card-debtclassoccupycreditocracy.html⊳.

ability to find the wherewithal to rise up and resist neoliberalization may be the most crucial piece any successful movement to get beyond neoliberalization to a better future for higher education.[43] Recent successes in organizing adjuncts offer a glimmer of hope but whether those successes can lead to more is an open question.[44]

The Articles That Follow

The articles that follow help fill out this skeletal picture of the crisis of higher education today and its implications for democracy. Several provide historical or theoretical perspectives, others more empirical detail and a few poignant case studies. Together we get a much richer portrait of what the crisis looks like today.

The first article, "*Realpolitik* in the American University: Charles A. Beard and the Problem of Academic Repression," is by Clyde W. Barrow. This article provides an important historical perspective on the current situation by reminding us about the real threats to academic freedom that come when administrators start to impose their reforms on the academy. The implications for democracy are made palpable in this stirring tale about the fight to maintain academic freedom in the corporatized academy as represented in the career of the legendary historian Charles Beard.

The second article "From *E Pluribus Unum* to *Caveat Emptor*: How Neoliberal Policies are Capturing and Dismantling the Liberal University" is by Steven Ward and takes a more theoretical approach to provide deep background on the neoliberalism behind the current wave of reforms sweeping over the academy. The third article by Tracy Lightcap, "Academic Governance and Democratic Processes: The Entrepreneurial Model and Its Discontents" builds on Ward's article to explore in-depth how neoliberalism is transforming the model of academic governance. The Lightcap article provides a richly detailed case study of the debacle at the University of Virginia in 2012 that involved the eventual reinstatement of its president over this very issue. Lightcap draws out important lessons on how the push to neoliberalize the university poses real threats to collegial decision-making and academic freedom. The fourth article is by Jacob Segal and is entitled "Ideology and the Reform of Public Higher Education." It draws on the thinking of the conservative philosopher Michael Oakeshott to offer a penetrating critique of the productivist ethic operating at the base of neoliberalism. Segal shows the affinities between Oakeshott's perspective and contemporary poststructuralists who also highlight the debilitating anti-democratic consequences of the neoliberalization of education.

In "Resisting the Exploitation of Contingent Faculty Labor in the Neoliberal University: The Challenge of Building Solidarity between Tenured and Non-Tenured Faculty," Joseph Schwartz poses the critical question about faculty resistance to neoliberalization. The article explores why most tenured faculty "naturalize" neoliberalism's deterioration of the academic labor market as inevitable and why they fail to resist it in a concerted manner. Schwartz concludes

---

[43] Ginsberg, *The Fall of the Faculty*, pp. 201–220.

[44] Tamar Lewin, "More College Adjuncts See Strength in Union Numbers," *New York Times*, December 4, 2013, < http://www.nytimes.com/2013/12/04/us/more-college-adjuncts-see-strength-in-union-numbers.html?pagewanted=all&_r; = 0> .

with an argument on why tenured faculty must make alliances with the adjuncts in the name of salvaging higher education and its relationship to democracy. Vincent Tirelli's article "Contingent Academic Labor Against Neoliberalism" suggests that the extensive use of contingent academic labor contributes to the reproduction of social class stratification, though not without contradictions. Tirelli argues that organizing by contingent academic labor activists is a vital component in the fight for higher education and democracy that is now unfolding in real time.

Seaton Patrick Tarrant and Leslie Paul Thiele in "The Web We Weave: Online Education and Democratic Prospects" discuss the pedagogical implications of online education with special attention to its implications for democracy. Drawing on the thinking of the great philosopher of democracy John Dewey, Tarrant and Thiele argue that while citizenship education may be facilitated by digital technology, it also demands pedagogy of a more traditional sort, one characterized by embodied, experiential interactions between teachers and students. They employ theories of pedagogy, democratic theory, evolutionary psychology and neuroscience to underline the crucial importance of these embodied, experiential interactions and their relationship to the challenge of sustaining democracy in our times. The threat of neoliberal reforms that rely on online instruction is effectively underscored in the process. Clyde Wilcox, JoVita Wells, Georges Haddad, and Judith K. Wilcox provide a poignant case study in that regard in "The Changing Democratic Functions of Historically Black Colleges and Universities." They show how neoliberalization is not just a threat to liberal arts education; they go further to highlight how neoliberalization will affect historically black colleges and universities in ways that will be especially detrimental in fulfilling their mission to enable African American students to join the ranks of leadership among a critically-minded democratic citizenry.

Douglas A. Medina's "Open Admission and the Imposition of Tuition at the City University of New York, 1969–1976: A Political Economic Case Study for Understanding the Current Crisis in Higher Education" provides a political-economic analysis of how the City University of New York came to lose open admissions and develop a schedule for tuition increases. Medina highlights how this shift is associated with a vocationalized curriculum that better serves corporate needs. The article "Lowering the Basement Floor: From Community Colleges to the For-Profit Revolution" by Brian Caterino follows nicely by looking critically at the underside of for-profits today. He focuses on how they have outflanked community colleges and as a result have accelerated the vocationa-lization of higher education for the low-income students who predominate in these institutions. Caterino's analysis ends with a stirring defense of liberal arts education for these students.

George Ehrhardt next addresses a neglected question in "Academic Conservatives and the Future of Higher Education" when he asks what role conservatives might play in helping us make sense of and respond to the neoliberal challenge to higher education. Rather than focus on their policy recommendations, Ehrhardt examines how academic conservatives argue for the same goals as their progressive counterparts: a strong program of liberal arts, critical thinking, and access to education for diverse student populations. The analysis is not intended to persuade readers of the conservative arguments' accuracy, rather to demonstrate points of similarity and reveal potential allies in the face of outside hostility.

Last, Romand Coles in "Transforming the Game: Democratizing the Publicness of Higher Education and Commonwealth in Neoliberal Times" suggests that neoliberalism should be understood as a game-transformative set of practices. Each move is not only to gain the upper hand in the established game, but rather to repeatedly change the basic configuration of the game itself to further enhance the power to structure future decision-making. Coles argues that progressive activists need to do more than simply resist. They need to rejuvenate the mutually supportive relationships between public higher education and democracy. This includes enacting a radically democratic pedagogy that expands the meaning of publicness and publics. The article explores Northern Arizona University's Action Research Teams initiative as a case study that prefigures this possibility.

All of these articles make important contributions to this most pressing issue. In the process they create important resources for students, faculty, citizens, and policymakers who want to find ways to address contemporary threats to the higher education-democracy connection. We should read them closely on that basis and begin to engage in concerted action. Now, before it is too late. If we allow neoliberalism to further undermine the relationship between higher education and democracy, there may well come a time when it will be too late to overturn its worst effects.

Acknowledgements

The author thanks Leonard Feldman, Nancy Love, Mark Mattern, Joe Soss, and John Wallach for helpful comments on earlier drafts of this article.

Realpolitik in the American University: Charles A. Beard and the Problem of Academic Repression

Clyde W. Barrow
University of Texas-Rio Grande Valley, USA

Abstract   *Charles A. Beard resigned from Columbia University on October 8, 1917 at a time when modern universities were emerging as significant institutions in the economic and political development of the United States. Thus, Beard's highly publicized resignation came at a time when universities were under exceptional scrutiny by economic and political elites, who increasingly viewed higher education institutions as either private corporations which they owned or as extensions of the modern state apparatus. Moreover, Beard's resignation came after a long string of dismissals, resignations, and censures at American universities that progressive historians have ironically chronicled as a history of the development of academic freedom in the United States. In fact, the early "academic freedom" cases were successful acts of academic repression and, in this context, Charles A. Beard's resignation opened a window onto the* realpolitik *of American universities, which have never been ivory towers, but have always been fundamentally political institutions, where groups and individuals engage in contests for power, authority, and resources within the framework of even larger social conflicts.*

> You need only reflect that one of the best ways to get yourself a reputation as a dangerous citizen these days is to go about repeating the very phrases which our founding fathers used in the struggle for independence. (Charles A. Beard)

Between Corporations and the State

Charles A. Beard resigned from Columbia University on October 8, 1917 at a time when modern universities were emerging as significant institutions in the economic and political development of the United States (US).[1] While many of Beard's critics dismissed his resignation as the isolated action of an impetuous professor, Beard resigned at a time when universities were under exceptional scrutiny by economic and political elites, who increasingly viewed higher education institutions as either private corporations which they "owned" by virtue of their capital investments or as extensions of the modern state apparatus that should implement the decrees of powerful state elites. Indeed, in the same year that Beard resigned, Thorstein Veblen published *The Higher Learning*

---

[1] Clyde W. Barrow, *Universities and the Capitalist State: Corporate Liberalism and the Reconstruction of American Higher Education, 1894–1928* (Madison, WI: University of Wisconsin Press, 1990).

14

in America, which wryly explored "the immediate and ubiquitous effect" on faculty of operating higher education institutions *as if* they were business enterprises.[2] Similarly, shortly after Beard's resignation, Max Weber delivered a lecture to graduate students at Munich University, where he observed that the ivory tower image of American universities was "fictitious," because colleges and universities were in reality "state capitalist enterprises, which cannot be managed without very considerable funds."[3]

In fact, Charles A. Beard's resignation from Columbia University was not an isolated event in the larger context of American higher education, and in this sense it was not him personally, nor even his scholarship on the US Constitution (1913), that was under attack by a corporate elite and its political allies, but rather an engaged vision of the political and social sciences was under siege by "external" political forces operating from locations inside the university.[4] Beard's resignation came after a long string of dismissals, resignations, and censures that began with Edward Beemis, Edward A. Ross, and Richard T. Ely—all radical political economists—at the turn of the twentieth century and culminated with the founding of the American Association of University Professors (AAUP) almost exactly one hundred years ago (1915). Ironically, mainstream progressive historians, such as Richard Hofstadter and Walter P. Metgzer have chronicled these early instances of conflict between faculty, administrators, trustees, and conservative politicians as a history of "the development of academic freedom in the United States."[5] The truth is that the early "academic freedom" cases were actually successful acts of academic repression; while in the midst of World War I patriotic hysteria, the AAUP found itself not only helpless to stem a growing tide of academic repression, but leading members of the organization often colluded with administrators in implementing repressive policies.[6] In this context, Charles A. Beard's resignation turned into a much larger event, because it opened a now well-documented window onto the *realpolitik* of American universities, which have never been ivory towers, but have always been fundamentally political institutions, where groups and individuals engage in contests for power, authority, and resources within the framework of even larger social conflicts.[7]

The Problem of Academic Repression

Charles A. Beard is best remembered for his book *An Economic Interpretation of the Constitution of the United States* (1913), which explained the writing and adoption

---

[2] Thorstein Veblen, *The Higher Learning in America: A Memorandum on the Conduct of Universities by Business Men* (New York: B.W. Huebsch, 1918), p. 98.

[3] Max Weber, "Science as a Vocation," in Hans H. Gerth and C. Wright Mills (eds), *From Max Weber: Essays in Sociology* (New York: Oxford University Press, 1946), p. 131.

[4] David N. Smith, *Who Rules the Universities? An Essay in Class Analysis* (New York: Monthly Review Press, 1974); Barbara Ann Scott, *Crisis Management in Higher Education* (New York: Praeger, 1983); Ellen Schrecker, *No Ivory Tower: McCarthyism and the Universities* (New York: Oxford University Press, 1986).

[5] Richard Hofstadter and Walter P. Metzger, *The Development of Academic Freedom in the United States* (New York: Columbia University Press, 1955).

[6] Barrow, *Universities and the Capitalist State*, Chapters 7–8.

[7] Theodore J. Lowi, *The Politics of Disorder* (New York: W.W. Norton Co., Inc., 1971); Theodore Lowi, "The Politics of Higher Education: Political Science as a Case Study," in George J. Graham, Jr. and George W. Carey (eds), *The Post-Behavioral Era: Perspectives on Political Science* (New York: David McKay Company, Inc., 1972), pp. 11–36.

of the US Constitution as the political outcome of a class struggle between capitalistic and agricultural interests in the early Republic.[8] According to Beard, capitalistic interests had dominated the constitutional convention of 1787 and, consequently, they authored a founding document that appealed "directly and unerringly to identical interests in the country at large."[9] However, it is the book's political context, as well as the growing importance of universities in economic and political development, that made the book an intellectual lightning rod. Beard's book became a powerful weapon in the hands of populists, progressives, liberals, socialists and, later, even communists, who would all cite his book as evidence that the constitution was of the capitalists, by the capitalists, and for the capitalists.[10] Thus, against the recent backdrop of the Populist Revolt, the meteoric rise of the Socialist Party in 1912, and later the Russian Revolution of 1917, Beard's book set off a political firestorm inside and outside academia that made it perhaps the most controversial scholarly work of its time.[11]

Moreover, Beard was living in a highly charged academic and political atmosphere, where academic freedom, or more properly academic repression, was rapidly becoming a major issue for the American professoriate. By the time Beard published his *Economic Interpretation of the Constitution*, the problem of academic repression had grown to such proportions that even P.P. Claxton, the US Commissioner of Education, felt compelled to state in his 1915 annual report that:

> within the past two or three years...there have been so many recurrences of disciplinary action directed by trustees and presidents of prominent institutions against professors reputed to hold unorthodox political, economic, or religious views that the question of academic freedom has become temporarily one of the foremost issues in university administration.... instructors in the field of economics and political science are at the present time especially in danger.[12]

Laurence R. Veysey, the renowned historian of higher education, observes that the early cases of academic repression in the US were "a rather accurate reflection of the degree of social alarm felt at any given hour by the more substantial elements in the American population."[13] These cases signaled "seasons of fear" among the ruling economic and political elite and typically coincided with

---

[8] The historical narrative is what policy researchers call a "focused synthesis," which synthesizes the existing academic literature—much of it published in obscure or little-known outlets, unpublished research papers, biographical and autobiographical references to Charles A. Beard, newspaper articles, and other materials to present the first truly comprehensive overview of Charles A. Beard's resignation for the purpose of identifying some of the structural mechanisms of academic repression that continue to operate in contemporary state-capitalist universities, see, Ann Majchrzak, *Methods for Policy Research* (Beverly Hills, CA: Sage, 1984).

[9] Charles A. Beard, *An Economic Interpretation of the Constitution of the United States* (New York: Free Press, 1913), p. 188.

[10] Allan L. Benson, *Our Dishonest Constitution* (New York: B. W. Huebsch, 1914), pp. 5–35.

[11] Richard Hofstadter, *The Progressive Historians: Turner, Beard, Parrington* (Chicago, IL: University of Chicago Press, 1968), p. 181.

[12] United States Bureau of Education, *Report of the Commissioner of Education, 1915* (Washington, DC: Government Printing Office, 1916).

[13] Laurence R. Veysey, *The Emergence of the American University* (Chicago, IL: University of Chicago Press, 1965), p. 410.

periods of major labor and social unrest and/or international wars. While the original targets of academic repression dating back to 1894 all had ties to Johns Hopkins University and the school of institutional economics, the battleground for academic freedom shifted to Columbia University around 1912, only a year before Beard published his infamous book on the US Constitution.

Nicholas Murray Butler, Columbia University's president, was a leading proponent of a concept of academic freedom that took hold among university administrators and trustees around the turn of the century.[14] The basic premise of this managerial concept of academic freedom was its distinction between academic freedom and academic license. Butler claimed that "the *proper* freedom of speech of university professors" depended on "habits of self-control, self-direction, and self-ordering," which was not merely a personal characteristic, but based on the "reasonable presumption" that what exists should carry greater moral and intellectual authority than "untested and untried" theories.[15]

Butler was quite specific about what he meant by untested and untried theories. Academic freedom became academic license at any one of five different points. The first transgression was "irreverence" for the religious faith or political convictions of others, which clearly excluded atheism and overtly partisan politics (notwithstanding that he had run for vice-president as a Republican). A second boundary was crossed when professors attempted to contravene "the laws of nature" by advocating "all forms of artificial equality." A third transgression occurred whenever professors took classroom time to express personal opinions on any subject, including those on which the individual was an expert. Another boundary was violated when professors abused the authority of their professional expertise by making public statements about issues of current political controversy, because professors should maintain a clear distinction between their status as experts and those of a demagogue or propagandist. Butler defined a propagandist as anyone who supported socialism, prohibition, cohabitation by unmarried couples, women's suffrage, and all things "queer, odd, unconventional" or "otherwise minded," including all ideas advocated by "freaks, oddities, revolutionaries."[16] Butler's definition of propaganda obviously excluded a wide variety of ideological and political perspectives, but his concept of disciplinary specialization and professional expertise more broadly contravened the interdisciplinary vision of political science that had been articulated at Johns Hopkins University and Columbia University for the last two decades and which Beard came to epitomize in his *Economic Interpretation of the Constitution*.

Butler claimed that professors are further restricted in their pronouncements by the disciplinary boundaries that define the limits of professional expertise. Thus, for example, an economist has no expertise to talk about *political* institutions, nor can a political scientist talk about phenomena that rightfully belong to the sociologist (that is, classes), nor can a historian (who specializes in the past) talk about its relevance to contemporary politics. Furthermore, since a professional expert is defined by his command of "facts," an expert always confines his teaching to "facts" that are generally accepted by others in the field.

---

[14] Barrow, *Universities and the Capitalist State*, pp. 190–199.

[15] Nicholas Murray Butler, *Scholarship and Service* (New York: Charles Scribner's Sons, 1921), p. 64.

[16] Ibid., 65, 89–90, 158–159, 179–180.

Thus, academic freedom also becomes academic license when professors go beyond these facts, or when they transgress the boundaries of disciplinary expertise to speculate about untested political, moral, or social arrangements.[17] Of course, Beard routinely violated most of these ideological and disciplinary strictures, including an active and open relationship with the Socialist Party until 1917.[18]

Under the leadership of President Nicholas Murray Butler, the Columbia University board of trustees became particularly aggressive at rooting out the "otherwise minded," especially on its Faculty of Political Science. It is no coincidence that many of the leading figures who founded the AAUP were members of that faculty, such as E.R.A. Seligman (economics), John Dewey (philosophy), and James McKeen Cattell (psychology). However, in 1912, three years before the AAUP was founded, Beard found himself involved in a contest with the university's board of trustees in his new role as Chair of the Department of Public Law. It was a case that seemed spurious to the faculty at the time, but as similar incidents accumulated over the years, Beard observes that in retrospect it came to be seen as the opening shot in a prolonged political conflict between faculty and trustees.

This class struggle between capitalist trustees and university intellectuals started with the retirement of John W. Burgess, who held the institution's prestigious Ruggles Professorship in the Department of Public Law. The department recommended Frank Goodnow, a founder and first president of the American Political Science Association, to replace Burgess as the Ruggles Professor. However, as a professor of administrative law, Goodnow had moved beyond Burgess' legal formalism to argue that American courts should adjust their interpretation of the constitution to take account of "existing economic conditions," rather than trying to make those conditions "conform to a conception of the organization and powers of government which we have inherited from the eighteenth century."[19] Goodnow had just published a path breaking book, entitled *Social Reform and the Constitution*, where he was particularly critical of the courts' positions on government old-age pensions (social security), workmen's compensation, urban land use regulation, the public ownership of industry, the income tax, and public assistance, which he felt were being blocked by "the attitude of either the Supreme Court or the state courts."[20] Goodnow and Beard had a friendly working relationship and it was primarily Goodnow, along with the economist E.R.A. Seligman, who inspired Beard's *Economic Interpretation of the Constitution*.[21]

Goodnow refused to back off his criticism of the judiciary simply to placate the vested interests of a board that consisted of corporate lawyers, bankers, and

---

[17] Ibid., 116.

[18] Clyde W. Barrow, *More Than a Historian: The Political and Economic Thought of Charles A. Beard* (New Brunswick, NJ: Transaction Publishers, 2000), pp. 10–13; James T. Shotwell, *Autobiography* (Indianapolis, IN: Bobbs-Merrill, 1961), p. 43.

[19] Frank J. Goodnow, *Social Reform and the Constitution* (New York: Macmillan Co., 1911), pp. 331–332.

[20] Ibid., 331.

[21] Ellen A. Nore, *Charles A. Beard: An Intellectual Biography* (Carbondale, IL: Southern Illinois University, 1983), p. 30; Samuel C. Patterson, "Remembering Frank J. Goodnow," *PS: Political Science & Politics* 34:4 (2001), pp. 875–881.

former judges, who were quite satisfied with the courts' pro-business rulings on social, economic, and labor issues. The result is that Goodnow's appointment to the Ruggles Professorship was vetoed by the trustees and it was awarded instead to W.D. Guthrie, an undistinguished corporate attorney, who was a business partner of one of the trustees. Goodnow left Columbia University in disgust less than two years later to become the president (1914–1929) of Johns Hopkins University. However, at the time, the incident was kept quiet by all concerned, and even when Beard revealed the incident five years later in the *New Republic*, he referred to Goodnow as "Professor X" to protect his identity. Beard observes that "the whole affair was settled by backstairs negotiations, and it was understood by all of us who had any part in the business that no person with progressive or liberal views would be accepted" by the trustees.[22]

President Butler and the trustees were evidently encouraged by their initial success, and later the same year, they targeted Dr. James McKeen Cattell, a pioneer in experimental psychology who had founded the university's world renowned psychology laboratory. Cattell described himself as being on the "extreme left wing" of academic politics, particularly on matters of faculty control.[23] Cattell had run afoul of Butler and the trustees by organizing a national campaign to oppose the Carnegie Foundation for the Advancement of Teaching (CFAT), which was using selective access to its university pension fund (now TIAA-CREF) as leverage to introduce corporate organization and management practices into institutions of higher education.[24] These organizational changes were undermining faculty control of educational policy and shifting power to the administration and business-oriented trustees.[25] In published articles and speeches to faculty council, Cattell criticized the growing influence of corporate executives over American higher education and predicted that "in the end the people will control monopolies and the universities [will be] supported by the profits of monopolies." As a result, Cattell looked forward to a day when professors would no longer be dependent "on the generosity or caprice of millionaires."[26]

Cattell's extensive writings on this subject violated both the ideological and disciplinary strictures of academic freedom as defined by President Butler. Thus, at Butler's behest, the trustees discussed a resolution to dismiss Cattell based in part on the fact that Columbia University had been a major recipient of Carnegie largess. A majority of the trustees considered termination too harsh a punishment in this case and voted against the resolution, but President Butler convinced them to take administrative control of the psychology laboratory and dismiss Cattell as its director. Cattell's response was to publish a highly controversial collection of essays, entitled *University Control* (1913), where he again predicted that the

---

[22] Charles A. Beard, "A Statement," *New Republic* 13, December 29, 1917, pp. 249–251.

[23] Quoted in Carol S. Gruber, "Academic Freedom at Columbia University, 1917–1918: The Case of James McKeen Cattell," *Bulletin of the AAUP* (Autumn 1972), p. 300.

[24] James McKeen Cattell, "The Carnegie Foundation for the Advancement of Teaching," *Science* 29, April 2, 1909, pp. 532–539.

[25] Barrow, *Universities and the Capitalist State*, Chapter 3; Clyde W. Barrow, "Corporate Liberalism, Finance Hegemony, and Central State Intervention in the Reconstruction of American Higher Education," *Studies in American Political Development* 6 (Spring 1992), pp. 420–44.

[26] James McKeen Cattell, "Concerning the American University," *Popular Science Monthly* (June 1902), pp. 180–182.

socialization of industry would soon make it possible to dispense with the "despotism" of corporate boards of trustees and the "dictatorial power of presidents."[27]

However, it was World War I that provided trustees with the pretext for escalating their attacks on the Faculty of Political Science. Since the war's outbreak in 1914, there had been a great deal of open debate on college and university campuses about America's neutrality in the Great War, but by 1916 most campuses were joining the national preparedness movement with large numbers of students and faculty favoring US intervention on the side of the Entente Allies.[28] Beard was an early proponent of pro-war sentiment at Columbia University and, from 1914 onward, Beard routinely denounced German militarism as a "danger to civilization." He called for a declaration of war against Germany in such strident tones at one public event that he was banned from speaking about the war at the City College of New York (CCNY).[29] Beard's commitment to the war was so intense that he even joined George Creel's Committee on Public Information; thus it would seem that Beard should have been exempt from the patriotic hysteria that emerged on American campuses during the war.

However, notwithstanding the national trend, and Beard's own position on the war, Columbia University and CCNY became hotbeds of anti-war protest after passage of the National Defense Act of 1916. Later, this turned to active draft resistance organizing after America's declaration of war. The Columbia University board of trustees responded to the burgeoning anti-war movement on the campus by charging its committee on education with responsibility for discouraging anti-war activities. Columbia University's board of trustees was a self-renewing body described by Upton Sinclair as "a bastion of plutocracy...dominated by the House of Morgan."[30] In fact, most of the trustees were middle-aged corporate attorneys or bankers, orthodox Episcopalians, and establishment Republicans, although they were joined by a few so-called "Wall Street Democrats," such as Frederick Coudert. Many belonged to genealogically restricted private clubs and all of them were active in the upper-class social clubs of New York City. This group of men (and they were all men) are what President Butler once referred to as "men of our type."[31]

The new class of business trustees that was coming to dominate the governing boards of America's higher education institutions viewed the faculty as "employees" of the university corporation, while they served as a corporate board of directors.[32] Thus, Robert A. McCaughey, a Columbia University

---

[27] James McKeen Cattell (ed.), *University Control* (New York: Science Press, 1913).

[28] Willis Rudy, *The Campus and a Nation in Crisis: From the American Revolution to Vietnam* (Cranbury, NJ: Associated University Presses, 1996), Chapter 3; Carol S. Gruber, *Mars and Minerva: World War I and the Uses of Higher Learning in America* (Baton Rouge, LA: Louisiana State University, 1975).

[29] Joseph Freeman, *An American Testament: A Narrative of Rebels and Romantics* (New York: Octagon Books, 1973), p. 107; Nore, *Charles A. Beard*, pp. 72–74.

[30] Upton Sinclair, *The Goose-Step: A Study of American Education*, revised ed. (Pasadena, CA: Privately printed, 1923).

[31] Robert A. McCaughey, "'Men of Our Type': A Social Profile of the Columbia Trustees in the Butler Era, 1902–1945," (2000), <http://beatl.barnard.columbia.edu/cuhistory/archives/TrusteesTalk.htm>.

[32] Barrow, *Universities and the Capitalist State*, Chapter 2.

historian, argues that what transpired over the next two years at Columbia University was not really about the war as such, but the occasion on both sides for a direct confrontation "over who runs/owns/speaks for Columbia?"[33] Francis S. Bangs,[34] a corporate attorney, who sat on the board declared that "The power of the Trustees to regulate the affairs of the University is absolute" and as repulsive as many faculty found his words, Bangs's legal interpretation of the university's 1810 Charter was correct.[35] At the same time, some of the trustees saw World War I as an opportunity to settle scores with faculty, who in their view, had embarrassed the institution by taking public positions against the preparedness movement or for holding politically radical views in favor of socialism, trade unionism, women's suffrage, and academic freedom. In the case of Francis S. Bangs, it is now known that he was angry at several faculty "for being tough on his kids in class."[36]

In early 1916, the trustees' committee on education, chaired by Francis S. Bangs, summoned Dr. Benjamin Kendrick, a professor of history, and Dr. Leon Fraser, an instructor in politics, to appear before the committee, where they were censured for delivering speeches at a student anti-war rally that criticized the controversial military training camp in Plattsburgh, New York. Despite the two censures, many faculty members continued to participate in student-sponsored rallies and off-campus debates about the neutrality issue.[37] Consequently, the tensions between faculty and trustees again flared up when Beard became embroiled in the infamous "flag incident" of 1916.

Several labor unions sponsored a weekly labor forum on Sunday nights in the auditorium of the Washington Irving High School in New York City. On April 9, 1916, James H. Maurer, a Socialist Party state legislator and president of the Pennsylvania Federation of Labor, delivered a speech about his experiences with the Pennsylvania state police.[38] According to Maurer, he was attempting to "illustrate how patriotism is sometimes prostituted to low ends" by citing an incident from the funeral of James Campbell, a union miner and veteran of the Spanish-American war.[39] When Campbell died, his friends arranged a soldier's funeral and a large crowd gathered to honor him. The funeral procession through

---

[33] Robert A. McCaughey, "1917: The Twilight of the Idols and Columbia's 'Jewish Problem'" (2000). Accessed at <http://beatl.barnard.columbia.edu/cuhis3057/Lecture%20Notes/LectNotes12.htm>.

[34] Francis Bangs's law partner (Francis Stetson) was selected by J.P. Morgan in 1887 to become chief counsel for his bank. His adept legal maneuvers allowed Morgan to consolidate several electrical companies into the General Electric Corporation and he also figured prominently in the creation of US Steel, International Paper, and International Telephone & Telegraph (ITT).

[35] The 1810 Charter, which governed the university's operations, stated: "That the Trustees, and their successors, shall have forever hereafter full power and authority to direct and prescribe the course of study . . . and the discipline to be observed . . . and also to select the president . . . and such officers as the Trustees shall seem meet, all of whom shall hold their offices during the pleasure of the Trustees," quoted in McCaughey, "Men of Our Type," p. 1.

[36] McCaughey "1917: The Twilight of the Idols and Columbia's 'Jewish Problem,'" p. 3.

[37] Sinclair, *The Goose-Step*, pp. 45–49.

[38] In 1905, Pennsylvania created the first state police force, which developed such a notorious reputation for violent strikebreaking that union officials often called them "the American Cossacks." In 1916, the New York State legislature was considering a controversial bill to create its own state police.

[39] James Hudson Maurer, *It Can Be Done: The Autobiography of James Hudson Maurer* (New York: Rand School Press, 1938), p. 192.

Westmoreland County, Pennsylvania was led by a man carrying an American flag, but a mounted detachment of state police ordered the marchers to disperse. When the state police were shown a county permit authorizing the funeral procession, the state police commander told the marchers: "Well, you get away with it this time, but never again! Anyway, down with the flag! Furl it!"

The speech was quoted correctly by many newspapers, including the *New York Press*, the *City News Association*, the *Jewish Daily Forward*, and the *New York Call*, but a reporter from the *New York Sun*, a Hearst newspaper, wrote that: "Maurer of Pennsylvania...in his speech last night in Washington Irving High School, shouted, 'Down with the Stars and Stripes!'" This false rendition of the story flashed across news wires and was republished in daily newspapers from coast to coast. Some newspapers reported that Maurer said "To Hell with the Flag!" and others that he yelled "Down with the Flag!"[40] The incident temporarily turned national debate away from the question of whether or not America should enter the Great War to the question of whether or not public schools and universities should be allowed to sponsor debates about the war where unpatriotic opinions might be expressed by some individuals.

Charles A. Beard joined the fray on April 21, 1916 in the context of a near hysterical atmosphere, where most people assumed that Maurer had in fact said "To Hell with the Flag!" In a speech to the National Conference of Community Centers at the Astor Hotel, Beard argued that despite his pro-war stance, he believed that public schools were legitimate forums for public debate on any issue and that anti-war speakers had the same rights of access to public facilities as those who supported the Allies. Beard stated rather casually that the world's greatest republic could certainly endure the inconsequential effects of a single "To Hell with the Flag" shouted in a crowded schoolhouse. Most newspapers accurately reported Beard's off-hand remark, but once again the *New York Sun* ran a headline claiming that the already controversial Professor Beard was now in sympathy with the statement "To Hell with the Flag!"

The misleading newspaper headline was used as a pretext to summon Beard before a closed meeting of the Columba University trustees' committee on education a week later. Beard reports that in addressing the trustees he "speedily disposed of the flag incident" as an obvious mistake on the part of a single newspaper. The trustees quickly accepted his version of the event, but he was surprised to discover that the flag incident was merely the pretext for a broader inquiry into his teaching and scholarship. Ellen Nore's research documents that the committee began baiting Beard with a discussion of whether or not the government of the US had been founded "in disrespect of existing authority." When Beard responded by proposing that the committee adjourn, because its official business was concluded, Frederick Coudert and Francis Bangs launched into a lengthy harangue against Beard's *Economic Interpretation of the Constitution*, which concluded with Coudert asking Beard if he knew that it was generally understood that his teachings were "calculated to inculcate disrespect for American institutions, particularly for the Supreme Court of the United States."[41]

Beard interpreted this incident not just as an attack on his book, but as the continuation of a broader long-term assault on progressive faculty. Beard returned

---

[40] Ibid., 192–194.
[41] Quoted in Nore, *Charles A. Beard*, p. 78.

to the faculty and gave a spirited account of the inquisition to his colleagues. He relayed the trustees' warning that they were not to "inculcate disrespect for American institutions" and the assembled faculty responded with a shout of derision. Beard urged the faculty to establish a rule that "a professor should be examined in matters of opinion only by his peers, namely men of standing in his profession." The Faculty of Political Science held several caucuses over the next few days and agreed that the trustees' proceedings were "highly reprehensible." The faculty was prepared to pass a resolution condemning "general doctrinal inquisitions," but Dean Frederick Woodbridge reassured the faculty that "the trustees had learned their lesson and that such an inquisition would never happen again."[42]

E.R.A. Seligman, who chaired the economics department in the Faculty of Political Science, and who had also been present (but silent) during the inquisition, added his personal assurance that the trustees would stop their attacks on the university's faculty.[43] In a long conversation with Beard, President Butler urged him "to drop the whole miserable business." Beard finally dropped the matter partly "for the sake of peace," but mainly was forced to retreat because he lost the support of his peers, who convinced themselves that the incident was actually a victory for academic freedom, because Beard had neither been censured by the trustees nor dismissed from the university. Beard remained convinced that "action doubtless should have been taken at the time," but his colleagues accepted the assurances of Woodbridge, Seligman, and Butler "that such an inquisition would not happen again and that the trustees 'had learned their lesson.'"[44]

Yet, despite these assurances, the trustees continued their inquisition on March 6, 1917 by creating a special investigative committee:

> to inquire and ascertain whether doctrines which are subversive of, or tend to the violation or disregard of the Constitution or laws of the United States or of the State of New York, or the principles upon which it is founded, or which tend to encourage a spirit of disloyalty are taught or disseminated by officers of the university."[45]

The trustees appointed to the investigative committee consisted of President Nicholas Murray Butler; George L. Ingraham, an attorney and former justice of the New York Supreme Court; John B. Pine, an attorney; William Parsons, a consulting civil engineer; Stephen Baker, President of the Bank of Manhattan; and Francis Bangs. The official inquisition at Columbia University was praised in the nation's press and held up as an example that all loyal and patriotic universities should emulate. The *New York Times* carried an editorial that not only praised the trustees' action, but encouraged them to rebuff any assertions by faculty of a right to academic freedom. The editorial complained that a "noisy brood of boy disloyalists, anarchists, and pacifists" were being spawned in America's universities and that:

> ... if anywhere patriotism is being poisoned in the young, if anywhere our children and youth are exposed to the inculcation of fatal doctrines by their teachers, the fact

---

[42] Quoted in Beard, "A Statement," p. 249.

[43] Gruber, "Academic Freedom at Columbia University," p. 298.

[44] Beard, "A Statement," pp. 249–250; Nore, *Charles A. Beard*, p. 79.

[45] Quoted in *New York Times*, March 6, 1917, p. 2.

cannot be faced too soon. There will be the customary patter about "academic freedom." That freedom cannot protect teachers, if such they be, who are undermining the patriotism of the next generation.[46]

When the faculty learned that a special committee of the trustees had been established to investigate teaching generally at Columbia University, this time Beard successfully mobilized the Faculty of Political Science. Under his leadership, the faculty unanimously passed a resolution, which read:

> Whereas the resolution of the trustees by its very terms implies a general doctrinal inquisition, insults the members of the Faculty by questioning their loyalty to the country, violates every principle of academic freedom, betrays a profound misconception of the true function of the university in the advancement of learning, *Be it Resolved* that we will not individually or collectively lend any countenance to such an inquiry.[47]

There were even discussions of a mass resignation if the trustees continued the inquisition, but the University Council, an assembly of senior faculty, deans, and the president, where Seligman commanded more influence, moved swiftly to mollify the growing discontent by appointing its own Special Committee of the University Council. This group, which was known as the Committee of Nine, was created to "cooperate" with the trustees' special committee and to ostensibly block it from taking repressive actions against the faculty.[48] The faculty response was sufficiently vigorous that the trustees agreed to this "compromise," but only after the Committee of Nine, which would officially represent the faculty, was reconstituted to favor the administration. The Committee of Nine was initially composed of five elected professors and four deans, but after the compromise it consisted of six deans appointed by the president and three faculty members, who had to be approved by the deans. The reconstituted committee was chaired by Seligman and included John Dewey.

While things seemed to quiet down after this confrontation, Butler and the trustees merely became more surreptitious in their efforts to root out the "otherwise minded." Within days, the trustees' committee on education turned its attention back to Leon Fraser, who had ignored their earlier censure by continuing his work for the Association of International Conciliation (AIC), although with the approval of President Butler. Fraser was working directly under the supervision of Butler and Woodbridge, who as philosophical pacifists were also members of the AIC, to organize courses at university campuses throughout the country on the principles of pacifism and international conciliation.[49] However in the spring of

---

[46] "Disloyalists at School," *New York Times*, March 9, 1917, p. 6.

[47] Quoted in Beard, "A Statement," p. 250.

[48] *New York Times*, March 24, 1917, p. 10; *New York Times*, May 1963, p. 14.

[49] Fraser had been a protégé of President Butler in the AIC, while Beard had originally resisted his appointment to the Faculty of Political Science on the grounds that Fraser was unqualified for an academic appointment. Butler forced the Department of Public Law to accept the appointment of his young protégé. However, as the pro-war sentiment increased in the country, and the trustees became concerned about faculty activism, Fraser's pacifism became an embarrassment to Butler, see, Hofstadter and Metzger, *The Development of Academic Freedom*, pp. 498–499; and Beard, "A Statement," p. 250. As Nore, *Charles A. Beard*, pp. 79–80 points out: "To Beard, Butler was practicing the worst kind of disloyalty and

1917, President Butler sent word to the Faculty of Political Science that it should not nominate Fraser for reappointment the following year, because he was "not acceptable to Mr. Bangs." The faculty defiantly nominated Fraser, which led Butler to drop him from the payroll for "financial reasons" attributed to a wartime enrollment decline. However, President Butler simultaneously informed the Faculty of Political Science that even if enrollments warranted the appointment of additional instructors the following fall "under no circumstances should Dr. Fraser be re-nominated."[50]

President Butler soon followed up with additional instructions to Beard, who chaired the committee on instruction of the Faculty of Political Science, now telling him that a "Professor Y" should not be recommended by the faculty for promotion because "certain of the trustees" would not approve his promotion. The unnamed trustees asserted that Professor Y had used "disrespectful language" in speaking of the US Supreme Court. Beard was furious when his colleagues obeyed Butler's orders, because now "the trustees could proudly say that they had not rejected a faculty recommendation!"[51] Soon thereafter, the university officially withdrew a speaking invitation to Leo Tolstoy, the internationally renowned pacifist and anarchist.

Following the US declaration of war on April 6, 1917, President Butler announced a wartime moratorium on academic freedom in his June 6, 1917 commencement day address to the university's alumni. Butler (1917) drew a hard line between pre-war and wartime conditions:

> What had been tolerated before becomes intolerable now. What had been wrongheadedness was now sedition. What had been folly was now treason...There is and will be no place in Columbia University...for any person who opposes or counsels opposition to the effective enforcement of the laws of the United States, or who acts, speaks or writes treason. The separation of any such person from Columbia University will be as speedy as the discovery of his offense.[52]

However, like many other hyper-patriots, Butler declared that silence alone was not enough to evade accusations of sedition or treason. He concluded his speech by telling alumni that "This is the University's last and only warning to any among us...who are not with whole heart and mind and strength committed to fighting with us to make the world safe for democracy."[53] Gruber's detailed account of events at Columbia during this time is particularly disconcerting, because she finds that Butler's new initiative "came in part from members of the

---

Footnote 49 continued

immorality. Having promoted the career of a younger man, he was now abandoning him when his views, formerly endorsed by Butler himself, were under attack."

[50] Beard, "A Statement," pp. 249–50; Horace Coon, *Columbia: Colossus on the Hudson* (New York: E.P. Dutton and Co., 1947), p. 126.

[51] Beard, "A Statement," p. 250.

[52] Nicholas Murray Butler, "President Butler's Speech at the Alumni Luncheon, Columbia University, June 6, 1917," <http://beatl.barnard.columbia.edu/cuhis3057/textscans/butler_speech.htm>. Also quoted in Gruber, "Academic Freedom at Columbia University," p. 302.

[53] Nicholas Murray Butler, "President Butler's Speech at the Alumni Luncheon, Columbia University, June 6, 1917," <http://beatl.barnard.columbia.edu/cuhis3057/textscans/butler_speech.htm>. Also quoted in Gruber, "Academic Freedom at Columbia University," p. 302.

faculty."[54] Butler's pronouncement was made only after receiving a unanimous recommendation from the Special Committee on the State of Teaching in the University (trustees) and the Special Committee of the University Council (Committee of Nine), which had met jointly after the arrest and indictment of three Columbia University students charged with writing and distributing a draft resistance pamphlet. The pamphlet was written after a university forum where Professor Henry Wordsworth Longfellow Dana, an assistant professor of English, had spoken against the proposed Conscription Act.

At a later date, the Committee of Nine met to investigate Dana's role at the anti-conscription meeting and issued its own warning to the faculty that "If, in the future ... [Dana] or any other colleague of ours acts in any way contrary to the letter or the spirit of the President's [commencement day] declaration, we shall be prepared to bring him before the authorities of the university for necessary discipline."[55]

Beard was again shocked by the machinations of what he called the "inner administration"—that bloc of ambitious senior faculty (such as Seligman and Dewey), duplicitous deans (such as Woodbridge), and senior administrators (such as Butler)—who collude with each other to intimidate faint-hearted or vulnerable faculty, to mislead the naïve or simple-minded ones, manipulate the machinery of shared governance to isolate dissidents, and who play off personal animosities within the faculty to generate political support for their own administrative authority. Indeed, the meticulous research by Ellen Nore and Carol Gruber in the Columbia University archives reveals that one of the unanticipated consequences of establishing the Committee of Nine was that it set off a cannibalistic feeding frenzy within the faculty as individuals sought to use it as a vehicle for settling personal vendettas through "confidential memos," to curry favor with the trustees by sharpening ideological rivalries, or to advance their own department at the expense of vulnerable colleagues or departments under siege.[56]

The most dramatic example of this internal disintegration revolved around James McKeen Cattell, whose son was among the three students arrested, indicted, and eventually convicted under the Conspiracy Act for the draft resistance pamphlet. Cattell openly challenged Seligman for leadership of the faculty by pointing out in a campus memo that the Committee of Nine was merely posturing as a "faculty" watchdog, because a majority of its active members were "deans who are nominated by the president and, according to the statutes, must 'act in subordination to the president.'"[57] Cattell even leaked a confidential memorandum from Seligman that exposed his duplicity on the Committee of Nine, but this action only further isolated Cattell from his colleagues, who could see the writing on the wall.

Cattell became so infuriated with his colleagues' unwillingness to defend the principle of academic freedom, or to stand up to the trustees and the president, that he started referring to them as "clerks of the administration." W.P. Trent,

---

[54] Gruber, "Academic Freedom at Columbia University," p. 302.

[55] E.R.A. Seligman for the Committee of Nine, quoted in ibid., 302.

[56] Nore, *Charles A. Beard*, pp. 77–82; Gruber, "Academic Freedom at Columbia University."

[57] Quoted in Gruber, "Academic Freedom at Columbia University," p. 300.

a professor of literature, joined Cattell in bemoaning the "subserviency and the sycophancy of academic life," while the anthropologist Franz Boas responded to the many faculty who openly called for Cattell's termination that they should "be glad to have him [Cattell] and be grateful for what he gives to us."[58] Nevertheless, after months of memo wars and hallway bickering, seven members of the Committee of Nine (two were not present) sent the trustees a notification (June 18, 1917) that they were "convinced that it is impossible for Professor Cattell to respect the ordinary decencies of intercourse among gentlemen" and concluded that "his usefulness in the University is ended."[59] By September, Butler had made it well known on campus that he was going to ask for the immediate dismissal of H.W.L. Dana and James McKeen Cattell at the trustees' next meeting (October 1, 1917).

As expected, on October 1, 1917, the trustees dismissed Cattell from Columbia University because he "had disseminated doctrines tending to encourage a spirit of disloyalty to the Government of the United States."[60] The trustees based their charge on several personal letters Cattell had written to congressmen about the proposed conscription bill, where he urged them to vote against sending troops to Europe against their will. Many of these letters had been forwarded to the university administration by the congressmen who received them. Henry Wordsworth Longfellow Dana, the grandson of the more famous literary Longfellow, was terminated without explanation. However, Dana was a vigorous anti-war activist, who had been active in the Anti-Militarism League when it was organizing opposition to the conscription bill (June 1917). At the time of his dismissal, Dana was prominent in the People's Council for Peace and Democracy, an umbrella anti-war organization led by the left-wing of the Socialist Party.[61] Carol S. Gruber points out that Butler and the trustees were able to use patriotism as a smokescreen for achieving their broader objectives against the faculty only "because the Columbia faculty, with few exceptions, agreed that Cattell and Dana as well, deserved to be fired because his activities were injurious to the university."[62] However, the two men's dismissal with "faculty" approval finally led John Dewey to resign from the Committee of Nine, which he now conceded was merely a tool of the trustees and the administration.

The intrigue at Columbia reached a fever pitch the following week when Charles Beard resigned (October 8, 1917) from the university in what at first appeared to be an angry and ill-tempered protest against Dana's and Cattell's dismissal. In his letter of resignation to President Butler, which was widely published in newspapers and scholarly journals, Beard wrote that he was leaving Columbia University because "the institution had fallen under the control of a small and active group of trustees with no standing in the world of education, who are reactionary and visionless in politics, narrow and medieval in religion."[63] Beard's resignation was a front page item in the next day's *New York Times*, which then followed up the story with an editorial celebrating his resignation

---

[58] Quoted in ibid., 300.

[59] Quoted in ibid., 301.

[60] Quoted in *New York Times*, October 2, 1917, p. 1.

[61] Freeman, *An American Testament*, p. 105.

[62] Gruber, *Mars and Minerva*, p. 202.

[63] Charles A. Beard, "Professor Beard's Letter of Resignation From Columbia University, October 8, 1917," *School and Society* 6:146 (October 13, 1917), pp. 446–447.

as "Columbia's Deliverance" from radicalism. The story revealed that the trustees had again been hounding Beard for his public utterances in defense of free speech during wartime.[64] Seligman, who had supported Beard's career from his first days at Columbia, accused him of "stabbing the [faculty] in the back" and he implored his colleagues to take no action on Beard's behalf.[65] Seligman attempted to quell faculty discontent yet again by convincing the Committee of Nine (now without Dewey) to endorse the creation of yet another special committee that would hear all evidence in "doctrinal controversies."[66] Seligman's proposal called for a special tribunal to be chaired by President Butler and composed of nominees from the faculty appointed by the deans! This newest maneuver by the inner administration led Thomas Reed Powell, a young political scientist, to finally castigate Seligman for "a supine 'diplomacy.'"[67]

Beard's resignation proved to be the catalyst that finally brought the simmering confrontation between faculty and trustees to an explosive conclusion. The day after his resignation one hundred students met spontaneously to request that Beard withdraw his resignation. The philosopher Will Durant stepped forward to encourage the students and to decry the termination of Fraser, Dana, and Cattell. Beard refused to withdraw his resignation and the next day five hundred students gathered to put forward the same request. This time the gathering was accompanied by a series of provocative speeches denouncing "the autocracy of the Trustees."[68] Seven hundred students met for a third time on October 12 and passed a resolution demanding that trustees rescind their prohibition on academic freedom during wartime and allow Beard to return to his professorship. Similar demonstrations continued for several days until by the end of the week sporadic fist fights and minor brawls were occurring between supporters and opponents of Beard. Finally, a quasi-organized guerrilla "war" erupted on campus between roving gangs of so-called radical and patriotic students that culminated in full-scale riots on the campus.[69]

It was in this context that the board of trustees replied to Beard's resignation in a letter to the *New York Times* proclaiming:

> By all means let us have our radical colleges, our places of learning where one knows that every social law will be demolished, where every established custom will be picked to pieces in the crude alembic of the crass youth; let us have institutions of learning where marriage is laughed at, religion ridiculed, feminism fostered, picketing apotheosized, but is it not a little too much to expect that the most conservative men and women of the nation be asked any longer to cloak these institutions with their own respectability! If the radicals demand colleges, let them have them, but stop letting them run away with our staid, established ones because trustees and parents are too white livered to demand a halt, to uncover this bogey of academic freedom.[70]

---

[64] *New York Times*, October 9, 1917, p. 1; *New York Times*, October 10, 1917, p. 10.

[65] Quoted in Nore, *Charles A. Beard*, p. 82.

[66] Freeman, *An American Testament*, pp. 107–109; Randolph Bourne, *History of a Literary Radical* (New York: B. W. Huebsch, 1920), p. 98.

[67] Quoted in Gruber, "Academic Freedom at Columbia University," p. 304.

[68] Freeman, *An American Testament*, pp. 107–109.

[69] *New York Times*, October 11, 1917, p. 24; October 13, 1917, p. 13; October 18, 1917, p. 5.

[70] Annie Nathan Meyer, "Letter to the Editor," *New York Times*, October 13, 1917, p. 10. Meyer's reference to "radical colleges" is probably an allusion to Beard's long association

The political flames were fanned higher by one of Beard's close personal friends on the faculty when Dr. Raymond H. Mussey, an assistant professor of economics at Barnard College, resigned on December 3, 1917, after seventeen years at the institution, in a show of sympathy for Beard.[71] Mussey wrote to Seligman: "I'm resigning...Columbia has tipped its hand in the Beard matter. The faculty inaction is wrong, dreadfully, clearly, fundamentally wrong."[72] It was soon discovered that the radical philosopher Will Durant had also been dropped from his position as an extension lecturer after his speech at the rally protesting Beard's resignation.

As events at Columbia University reached their climax, Beard decided to answer critics such as Seligman with "A Statement" published in the December 17, 1917 issue of the *New Republic*. For the first time, Beard outlined a long and well-considered program by the trustees to reshape the ideological complexion of the Columbia University faculty going back to the so-called "Professor X" incident. Beard unveiled all that had been negotiated behind closed doors or suffered in silence at Columbia University. He concluded:

> It was the evident purpose of a small group of the trustees (unhindered, if not aided, by Mr. Butler) to take advantage of the state of war to drive out or humiliate or terrorize every man who held progressive, liberal, or unconventional views on political matters in no way connected with the war. The institution was to be reduced below the level of a department store or factory and I therefore tendered my resignation.[73]

Beard also affirmed that in early October he had been "positively and clearly informed by two responsible officers of the University [whom he did not name] that another doctrinal inquisition was definitely scheduled for an early date" and he would be the special committee's next target.

President Butler confirmed these claims indirectly in his 1917 annual report on the university, where he observed that "Bolsheviki of the intellect" had become too prevalent in the United States. Butler warned that:

> ...economic determinism...has in recent years obtained much influence among those who for lack of a more accurate term call themselves intellectuals....The time has not yet come, however, when rational persons can contemplate with satisfaction the rule of the literary and academic Bolsheviki or permit them to seize responsibility for the intellectual life of the nation.[74]

Footnote 70 continued
with the Socialist Party's Rand School of Social Science in New York City, see, John L. Recchiuti, "The Rand School of Social Science During the Progressive Era: Will to Power of a Stratum of the American Intellectual Class," *Journal of the History of the Behavioral Sciences* (April 1995), pp. 149–161. In 1921, Beard joined with Herbert Croly, James Harvey Robinson, Thorstein Veblen, Wesley Claire Mitchell, Harold Laski, and other progressive luminaries to found the New School for Social Research, see, William B. Scott and Peter M. Rutkoff, *New School: A History of the New School for Social Research* (New York: Macmillan, 1986). Beard also remained active in the left wing of the workers' education and labor college movement until 1929, see, Barrow, *More Than a Historian*, pp. 10–12.

[71] *New York Times*, December 4, 1917, p. 22.

[72] Quoted in Nore, *Charles A. Beard*, p. 82.

[73] Beard, "A Statement," p. 250.

[74] Butler quoted in the *New York Times*, December 3, 1917, p. 11.

Subsequently, Dr. Ellery C. Stowell, a renowned professor of international law, resigned on March 1, 1918. Although he too was a staunch supporter of the war, Stowell had been a vocal critic of the trustees' special investigations committee and he had frequently criticized it in newspapers as "Prussianistic." Stowell stated in his resignation that he was being pressured by university administrators, and also by members of the faculty, to stop criticizing the university's wartime policy of academic repression. However, he explained, his departure was primarily motivated by administrative "interference with my liberty of action, especially in regard to the expression of my views on international affairs through the medium of newspapers."[75] The fallout from these events lingered well into the 1920s, with James Harvey Robinson leaving Columbia University in 1921 to join Beard in founding the New School for Social Research. John Dewey continued to be disillusioned by the Butler administration. Franz Boas, who had been accused of "German anthropology" after opposing American entry into World War I remained alienated from Butler until his retirement.

Twilight of the Idols

Charles A. Beard left academia behind in 1917, but he represented a vision of political and social science that was so powerful it took a Second World War, a Cold War, and a lot more university politics to oust "Beardianism" from the American social sciences,[76] although Theda Skocpol, a past president of the APSA, has lamented that Beardianism may be an "unquenchable proclivity in American progressive historiography."[77] Paradoxically, the strength of Beard's ideas during the inter-war years and his departure from Columbia University may well be correlated, because Beard sustained his intellectual originality by leaving the university. His opus magnum, *The Rise of American Civilization*, where he applied the method of economic interpretation to the entire course of American political development, was written on his dairy farm in Connecticut and not at Columbia University. Thus, years later, from this place of seclusion, Beard wondered whether his former colleagues actually worked "under the eye of eternity" as they tell their students "or under the eye of the trustees' committee on salaries, pensions, and promotions?" Beard's point was that the modern university organizes an institutional and class relationship between intellectuals, capitalists, and the state. For better or worse, disciplines, academic departments, and universities are *politicized institutions* with both direct and indirect links to the state and to wider political struggles.[78] Thus, as John G. Gunnell observes: "what in part was manifest in these cases [of academic repression] were the problems of

---

[75] Stowell quoted in *New York Times*, March 2, 1918, p. 11. Stowell accepted a position in international relations at American University soon after leaving Columbia University.

[76] Barrow, *More Than a Historian*, Chapter 7.

[77] Theda Skocpol, "A Reply [to G. William Domhoff]," *Politics and Society* 15:3 (1986/87), pp. 331–332.

[78] Lowi, *The Politics of Disorder*, Chapters 6–7; Theodore J. Lowi, "The State in Political Science: How We Become What We Study," *American Political Science Review* 86:1 (1992), pp. 1–7; James Farr, "Political Science and the State," in James Farr and Raymond Seidelman (eds), *Discipline and History: Political Science in the United States* (Ann Arbor, MI: University of Michigan Press, 1993), pp. 63–79.

reconciling academic and political commitment and of defining the relationship between the university and politics."[79]

However, this problem should not be understood merely as an abstract philosophical or methodological problem, but as a class struggle defined by the American university's legal status as a "corporation" and its structural location between the market and the state. Beard was convinced that the structural and bureaucratic resolution of these conflicts would eventually generate a new intellectual class of civil *servants*, partly as a result of the long-term structural effect of "trustee guardianship upon the class of men who will seek academic positions." Beard wrote that in the future:

> Men who love the smooth and easy will turn to teaching. As long as they keep silent on living issues, their salaries will be secure. It will not be important that they should arouse and inspire students in the class room. They need not be teachers. They are asked to be only purveyors of the safe and insignificant.[80]

During the escalating conflict at Columbia University (1912–1918), there were very few faculty members who were willing to take a principled stand for faculty control, academic freedom, or even for the broader constitutional right of free speech during wartime. Nearly every individual who ran against the grain of institutional power and faculty opinion—Leon Fraser, Benjamin C. Kendrick, James McKeen Cattell, Charles A. Beard, Henry R. Mussey, Will Durant, and Ellery C. Stowell—were either removed from the university or effectively driven out of the university with either the cooperation or acquiescence of their erstwhile colleagues. As one case study after another documents during the period, many university faculty were frighteningly eager to sacrifice their colleagues in exchange for small increments in their paycheck, an additional faculty line, a quasi-administrative title, or to win the favor of a key administrator. The academic dissident in political science, or any other discipline, can rarely expect most faculty colleagues to rally to their defense or, as Beard's case suggests, not even leaders of the discipline can expect much support when tenure, promotions, and merit pay are at stake.

Thus, while the Progressive Era politics of Columbia University centered on a conflict between capitalist trustees and university faculty, it cannot be emphasized too strongly that it also involved conflict and intrigue within the faculty. While the politics of the trustee/faculty dispute can be meaningfully conceptualized as a "class struggle" between capitalists and intellectuals, the internal politics of the university were more pedestrian, but perhaps more consequential. The capitalist siege of the Progressive Era university created an atmosphere inside the university that intensified personal rivalries, broke student/mentor loyalties, and allowed departments and individuals to jockey for advantage, while simultaneously sharpening the ever-present cleavage between an inner administration and a faculty periphery. The Columbia massacre is a unique window on this *realpolitik* of the American university, because it is probable that the main players in this drama are really archetypes of the academy and the same events are played out more quietly on American campuses even today on a regular basis.

---

[79] John G. Gunnell, *The Descent of Political Theory: The Genealogy of an American Vocation* (Chicago, IL: University of Chicago Press, 1993), p. 39.

[80] Charles A. Beard, "The University and Democracy," *The Dial*, April 11, 1918, p. 335–337.

The Columbia massacre also chronicles the building of a repressive ideological state apparatus (ISA) that was repeated on one campus after another during World War I, the Red Scare, the Great Depression, the Cold War, the Vietnam War, and the post-9/11 War on Terror. Anyone who reads the nearly 250 histories of American colleges and universities,[81] not to mention the *Chronicle of Higher Education*, knows that there are many Nicolas Murray Butlers, Frederick Woodbridges, and E.R.A. Seligmans colluding to advance their own interests at universities, but for that reason there are many more Professor X's and Professor Y's, but very few Charles A. Beards.

The theoretical implications of these events extend well beyond the time and circumstances of Columbia University during World War I. For example, Cattell's case exemplifies what I have elsewhere called a strategy of terror without violence.[82] By throwing a spotlight on leading dissidents in the form of newspaper stories, official investigations, un-rebutted slander, hallway innuendo, rumor mongering, and secret memoranda, the official bureaucratic apparatus—whether a state or a university—generates a political atmosphere that isolates key individuals and potential leaders from their colleagues. Attention is brought to bear on individuals who are branded as radicals, traitors, un-American, hotheads or as in Cattell's case even as "insane," and this is all merely a way of isolating individuals from their colleagues by generating distrust, fear, and disorganization within a faculty. As Beard understood, the main point is not so much to terrorize those who demonstrate courage as to terrorize those who lack it. The strategy of terror without violence is designed to make an example of those who deviate too far from what is acceptable to the state, the business elite, the university administration, or even the "inner faculty," who are generally quite conservative in their social and cultural habits (and thus more easily offended by how or where something is said instead of being concerned with the truth of what is said). The strategy of terror without violence succeeds by ensuring that no one will come to the assistance of a distressed colleague for fear of similar reprisals under similar circumstances.

A telling example of this strategy's larger structural effect was actually documented at the University of Minnesota shortly after the conclusion of World War I. In 1919, the student newspaper at the University of Minnesota claimed that academic freedom had been suppressed on campus since William A. Schaper, chairman of the political science department, had been dismissed after accusations that he a was "rapid pro-German."[83] While Schaper had opposed American entry into the war, once war was declared, he stated that "every citizen owed his support to the war effort" and he advised his own students that "now they must serve in the military if needed."[84] However, after an inquisition that bore striking parallels to the Beard case, Schaper was told by one trustee that

---

[81] For a bibliography, see, John S. Brubacher, and Willis Rudy, *Higher Education in Transition: A History of American Colleges and Universities*, 4th ed. (New Brunswick, NJ: Transaction Publishers, 1997), pp. 543–555.

[82] Barrow, *Universities and the Capitalist State*, p. 232.

[83] James Gray, *The University of Minnesota, 1851–1951* (Minneapolis, MN: University of Minnesota Press, 1951), pp. 246–247; William E. Matsen, "Professor William A. Schaper: War Hysteria and the Price of Academic Freedom," *Minnesota History* 51:4 (1988), pp. 130–137.

[84] John T. Hubell, "A Question of Academic Freedom: The William A. Schaper Case," *The Midwest Quarterly—A Journal of Contemporary Thought* 17:2 (1976), pp. 111–121.

"this was not enough" and the board later voted unanimously to declare him a "disloyal American citizen."[85]

Following the student newspaper article, the local chapter of the AAUP asked the university president to call a general meeting of the faculty to investigate the students' allegation and to explore the general problem of academic freedom. The faculty meeting appointed a committee "to investigate, hear testimony, gather and sift the evidence and sense the feeling of individual faculty members."[86] The committee could not find any specific incidents of further repression after the Schaper case, but it did find that Schaper's dismissal had generated a shock, which still lingered on the campus as a climate of fear and artificial self-restraint that was being ingrained by habit into faculty culture. A climate of academic repression had been put in place relatively quickly and then consolidated during the war with the regents' investigation of the university followed by Schaper's termination. The collective response to those events was not anger and revolt, but fear and silence. The Minnesota committee found that the problem of academic repression had become "psychological" and "was often a matter of tacit understanding, recorded ... much more clearly in a feeling of what might ... impend rather than by what had already happened."[87] In other words, individual *acts* of academic repression had generated a larger *structure and culture* of academic repression that operates on a deeper level to suppress conflict *before* it occurs. This type of repressive structure is what Steven Lukes calls the "third dimension" of power, where often as a result of past displays of overt coercion by an economic or political actor, its "'mere reputation for power, unsupported by acts of power'" becomes sufficient over time to repress unacceptable ideas or actions through individual and collective acquiescence.[88]

Under these circumstances, and contrary to the heroic myth of the autonomous intellectual, Beard found that aggressive trustees, blustering politicians, and dictatorial presidents "can silence the coward and transform the frightened professor into a master of ingenious evasiveness."[89] A dozen years after leaving Columbia University, Beard's criticism of university faculty was even more biting as he came to the conclusion that even without repressive trustees, American universities were not receptive to controversial thinking, because of the communitarian nature of faculty politics. The communitarian emphasis on collegiality and conformity make the faculty of a modern university, again despite their own self-image,[90] quite intolerant of dissent or indeed any actions that disrupt their quest for a quiet world and a modest standard of living. As Beard wrote, there are in a university:

---

[85] Ibid., 112.

[86] Quoted in Gray, *University of Minnesota*, p. 256.

[87] Quoted in ibid., 257.

[88] Steven Lukes, *Power: A Radical View* (London, UK: Macmillan Press, Ltd., 1974), pp. 42–43.

[89] Beard, "University and Democracy," p. 336.

[90] Clyde W. Barrow, "Intellectuals in Contemporary Social Theory: A Radical Critique," *Sociological Inquiry* 57:4 (1987), pp. 415–430; Clyde W. Barrow, "What is to be Undone? Academic Efficiency and the Corporate Ideal in American Higher Education," *Found Object* 10 (Spring 2001), pp. 149–180.

too many charming friends who must not be offended; too many temporal negotiations that call for discreet management; too many lectures to be delivered; too many promotions requiring emphasis on the amenities of life rather than on its thinking processes; too many alumni eager to apply in 1928 what they learned in 1888; too much routine, not enough peace; too much calm, not enough passion; above all too many sacred traditions that must be conserved; too many theories, not enough theory; too many books, not enough strife of experience; too many students and not enough seekers.[91]

Charles Beard was driven out of the university, but he was not driven out of the political science discipline. Beard's main ideas actually reached the apogee of their intellectual and political influence during the 1930s, long after he left Columbia University, and they were not officially jettisoned by most political scientists and historians until the Cold War and, even then, mainly for political and ideological reasons that had little to do with honest scholarship.[92] Quite the contrary, due to the widespread impact of his work in both academic and popular circles, he became a paradigmatic figure for a vision of political science that had rapidly gained ascendancy from the late 1880s onwards, but which rapidly vanished from the American discipline of political science during the 1950s. However, it is a vision that was constantly under siege from inside and outside academia, because it not only challenged the dominant ideology of a capitalist society, but the professional interests of the emerging academic disciplines seeking to institutionalize a cozy relationship with state and corporate power.[93]

---

[91] Charles A. Beard, "Political Science," in Wilson Gee (ed.), *Research in the Social Sciences* (New York: Macmillan Co., 1929), pp. 269–291.

[92] Barrow, *More Than a Historian*, Chapter 7. A textbook content analysis conducted by Maurice Blinkoff, *The Influence of Charles A. Beard Upon American Historiography* (Buffalo, NY: University of Buffalo Monographs in History, 1936), Vol. 12, found that Beard's economic interpretation of the US constitution had achieved "orthodox status" in American colleges, high schools, and even junior high schools by the mid-1930s. In this respect, Beard's election to the presidencies of the American Political Science Association (APSA) (1926) and the American Historical Association (AHA) (1934) suggest that not just Beard, but the method of economic interpretation and class analysis was riding a crest of academic respectability in both disciplines. John Patrick Diggins, "Power and Authority in American History: The Case of Charles A. Beard and His Critics," *American Historical Review* 86 (October 1981), pp. 701–702, observes that "in the years between the two world wars, Beard's reputation was so firmly established that the adjective 'Beardian' was not only considered a compliment but denoted a respected school of thought," which fell into disrepute only after a post-Progressive generation of historians and political scientists massed a blistering counter-offensive against Beard during the Cold War.

[93] Barrow, *Universities and the Capitalist State*, Chapters 4–6.

From *E Pluribus Unum* to *Caveat Emptor*: How Neoliberal Policies are Capturing and Dismantling the Liberal University

Steven C. Ward
Western Connecticut State University, USA

Abstract   *This article provides an account of how neoliberal policies are currently in the process of capturing and dismantling the liberal pubic university that was constructed in various places around the world in the late nineteenth and early twentieth centuries. The article examines the political and epistemic relationship between liberalism, embedded liberalism, the state, and the organizational forms that the university would take throughout most of the twentieth century. It provides an overview of some of the specific neoliberal efforts to transform universities into servants of the economy and how business interests came to capture the university over the last few decades with the help of the new "enterprising state." This article concludes by examining what these recent changes mean for the future of both the liberal university as we have known it, and the larger quest for education in a democratic society.*

Although they may lack a label to describe it, for the last few decades citizens of many nations around the world have been the target of a grand social experiment. This experiment is the result of a new configuration that seeks to realign the economic, the political, and the social in a historically novel way—a configuration known as neoliberalism in most parts of the world. This neoliberal configuration has resulted in a seemingly incongruent state of affairs, at least relative to previous governmental forms, that combines a strong, activist state with a less regulated, "free market"—or, in another framing, a highly regulated and weakened public realm coupled with a highly deregulated and expanded private realm.[1] One of the many ironies of this new form of neoliberal governance is that it often promotes a laissez faire approach to markets, at least rhetorically, alongside strict auditing and intervention by the state in order to monitor state expenditures, generate markets, and encourage market-like behavior in its citizens. The goal is to establish a market society by collapsing all distinctions between politics and market and by generating a society where market principles are used to guide all institutions.

As different societies have moved from a more embedded or socially liberal form of governance identified with the welfare state to neoliberal governance over the last few decades, the role of the state has shifted from being a facilitator and

---

[1] Andrew Gamble, *The Free Market and the Strong State* (Durham, NC: Duke University Press, 1988).

protector of various social provisions to an "enterprising state"[2] or a "managerial state"[3] or perhaps a "Schumpeterian workfare state," as Bob Jessop[4] has called it, that promotes market expansion and monitors the results of that marketization through elaborate and expansive auditing mechanisms. In the neoliberal age the practice of governing essentially switches from protecting people and social institutions from the vicissitudes of the market to dramatically extending the reach of the market and deliberately exposing people and institutions to it, including even the state itself through the quasi-markets introduced through new forms of public management. Despite the 2008 economic crisis spawned by these policies, today's "strange non-death of neoliberalism"[5] means that in our current political landscape private markets still largely go unchecked in order to induce economic growth and to stimulate the pursuit of wealth while the public domain is either privatized whenever possible or increasingly diminished and monitored in order to force a mimicking of the alleged self-regulating efficiencies of markets. Indeed, in the ultimate display of political hubris, entrenchment and perhaps long term endurance, the march of neoliberalism has, in many ways, only intensified in the years since the beginning of the "Great Recession."

From the neoliberal perspective, markets or market mechanisms of competition are so successful at creating discipline and social equilibrium that they should be used not just to guide economic matters but to completely overhaul and reinvigorate all social institutions. Markets are, in the words of one of the early neoliberal economists, Wilhelm Röpke, capable of producing an entirely new "democracy of the consumers."[6] One of the social institutions that neoliberals see as in particular need of the elixir of the market is public education at all levels. They contend that over the course of the twentieth-century education became much too public and state centered, and, as a result, inefficient, unresponsive and unproductive. In the twentieth-century education had become, as Milton Friedman and Rose Friedman referred to it, "an island of socialism in a free market sea" resulting primarily from intellectuals' "distrust of the market and of voluntary exchange."[7] To correct for this government take-over and "over socialization" of education, neoliberal policy makers and politicians began to introduce a number of reforms to transform education beginning with primary and secondary schools in England and New Zealand in the mid to late 1980s. Afterward, similar reforms began spreading globally and "up the education ladder" into higher education institutions. These university reforms, like those in primary and secondary education, were specifically designed to bring competition and the discipline of the marketplace into what neoliberals

---

[2] Mark Constadine, *Enterprising States: The Public Management of Welfare-to-Work* (Cambridge, UK: Cambridge University Press, 2001).

[3] John Clarke and Janet Newman, *The Managerial State* (London, UK: Sage, 1997).

[4] Bob Jessop, "The Transition to Post-Fordism and the Schumpeterian Workfare State," in B. Burrows and B. Loader (eds), *Toward a Post-Fordist Welfare State?* (London, UK: Routledge, 1994), pp. 13–37.

[5] Colin Crouch, *The Strange Non-Death of Neoliberalism* (Cambridge, UK: Polity, 2011).

[6] Wilhelm Röpke, *The Social Crisis of Our Time* in Annette and Peter Schiffer-Jacobsohn (trans.), (Chicago, IL: University of Chicago Press, 1950), p. 103.

[7] Milton Friedman and Rose Friedman, *Free to Choose: A Personal Statement* (New York, NY: Harcourt Brace Jovanovich, 1980), p. 154. This echoes Milton Friedman's statements on education that began in the mid-1950s.

considered to be one of the last and most socially important holdouts of state-directed socialism. In more political terms, as the infamous "Powell Memo" of the early 1970s (as named for the late Supreme Court Associate Justice Lewis Powell) attests, neoliberal reforms also provided an opportunity for universities to be purged of those fields and professors who were historical critics of the unregulated market economy.[8]

In this paper I want to provide an account of how these neoliberal policies are in the process of capturing and dismantling the liberal public university that was constructed in various places around the world in the late nineteenth and early twentieth centuries. The first part of the paper examines the political and epistemic relationship between liberalism, embedded liberalism, the state, and the organizational forms that the university would take throughout most of the twentieth century. Here, I am particularly interested in what kind of epistemic and organizational space liberalism in its various historic manifestations generated for the creation and dissemination of knowledge. The second section provides an overview of some of the neoliberal efforts to transform universities into servants of the economy and how business interests came to "capture" the university over the last couple of decades with the help of the new "enterprising state." In this section, I am interested in how neoliberalism reconfigures the relationship between politics, economy, and society and, as a result, generates a very different place for the university in society. The third section concludes with an examination of what these recent changes mean for the future of both the liberal university as we have known it and the larger quest for education in a democratic society.

The Liberal State, the Liberal University, and Liberal Knowledge

Contrary to the standard Enlightenment narrative, knowledge does not just happen or unfold due to its own inherent epistemological logic. Rather, it relies on a series of networks, organizations, and institutions to produce, disseminate and maintain it. Without these social formations knowledge remains local, subjective, and weak and appears simply as opinion rather than truth.[9] The networks, organizations, and institutions that support knowledge, in turn, rely on larger social and political configuration to create the conditions for the production and distribution and knowledge. As these configurations change so do the conditions for making and distributing particular forms of knowledge and, ultimately, what knowledge will look like, what forms will prevail, and what purpose it will serve. Each social and political form both opens up and closes off particular types of epistemic space for the construction of specific modes of knowledge and for the operations of particular types of knowledge makers. In short, these social configurations and the various mechanisms of power contribute to what Michel Foucault calls "governmentality," where the state manages populations by getting people to be compliant with understandings of how they are expected to behave.[10]

---

[8] A copy of the memo can be found at http://law.wlu.edu/deptimages/Powell%20Archives/PowellMemorandumPrinted.pdf.

[9] Bruno Latour, *Science in Action* (Cambridge, MA: Harvard University Press, 1987).

[10] Michel Foucault, *The Birth of Biopolitics: Lectures at the College de France* (New York, NY: Palgrave Macmillian, 2008).

In the process, forms of governmentality ultimately regulate what truth looks like, or in Jean Francois Lyotard's phrase they determine "the truth criterion."[11]

Liberal forms of governmentality of the last couple of centuries produced their own unique knowledge-making configurations with varying understandings of the role of the university in society and particular policies for enacting those ideals. As is the case with other political "isms," the term liberalism has over the course of time been used in very different ways and with very different political meanings and outcomes. For some, liberalism is associated primarily with economic liberalism and is linked with the doctrine of laissez faire and the anti-mercantilism of Adam Smith that emerged in the eighteenth century. This form of liberalism, in modified forms, later became a key argument of the Manchester School of liberalism and a prominent political orientation of some Western governments in the nineteenth century. For others, liberalism means primarily political liberalism and involves an emphasis on the freedom and autonomy of the individual as seen in the writings of a variety of political philosophers such as John Locke, Jeremy Bentham and J.S. Mill. At the extreme margins, this form of political liberalism produced the "Social Darwinism" of Herbert Spencer in the late nineteenth century or in our own time Libertarianism and the Tea Party Movement in the United States. In other instances, political and economic liberalism are combined into a set of ideas and practices that are often at odds with one another as the inequalities generated in the marketplace clash with the expected equalities and freedoms promised in politics or, in other terms, private profit is pitted against the public good as found historically in debates over patent and copyright laws.[12]

In the early part of the twentieth-century liberalism underwent some significant makeovers, making it somewhat unrecognizable to its eighteenth- and nineteenth-century cousins. Responding both to the economic excesses and monopolization generated by the laissez faire doctrine and the growing fear of socialist-style centralized planning and fascist forms of authoritarianism, these newer forms of liberalism sought to reinvigorate and redirect the liberal movement. In one path, exhibited in the work of L.T. Hobhouse[13] in the UK or Lester Frank Ward and, a bit later, John Dewey[14] in the United States, political liberalism and cooperative socialism are theoretically reconciled in the form of social or new liberalism, or in economic terms, Keynesianism. In this new (but not neo) liberalism "social control of economic forces is equally necessary if anything approaching economic equality and liberty is to be realized."[15] In other words, liberty is predicated upon a democratically (as opposed to a bureaucratically centralized) planned economy and mechanisms for the redistribution of wealth. This approach that John Maynard Keynes described as "semi-socialism"[16] became

---

[11] Jean-Francois Lyotard, *The Postmodern Condition: A Report on Knowledge*, in G. Bennington and B. Massumi (trans.), (Minneapolis, MN: University of Minnesota Press, 1984), p. 58.

[12] Christopher May and Susan Sell, *Intellectual Property Rights: A Critical History* (Boulder, CO: Lynne Rienners Publishers, 2006).

[13] L.T. Hobhouse, *Liberalism* (London, UK: Williams and Norgate, 1911).

[14] John Dewey, *Liberalism and Social Action* (New York, NY: G. P. Putnam's Sons, 1935).

[15] Ibid., 36–37.

[16] John Maynard Keynes, *The End of Laissez-Faire* (London, UK: Hogarth Press, 1926), p. 12.

a central part of the "embedded liberalism" that came to define welfare state policies in places like the United States, the UK and elsewhere stretching from the 1930s into the late 1970s. This social liberalism combined political liberalism with socialist style government involvement and planning to produce regulated markets. It also sought to balance the interests of unions and the working class with those of businesses and the owning classes and to create both economic growth and full employment.

In another early twentieth-century reconfiguration of liberalism, the doctrine of *laissez-faire* is to be jettisoned because it had become, in the words of Walter Lippmann, "the apologist for miseries and injustices that were intolerable to the conscience."[17] This early form of neoliberalism begins to reconfigure classic economic liberalism into what would become neoliberalism. It is evident in Lippmann's *The Good Society* and the subsequent *Colloque Walter Lippmann* in Paris in 1938 that launched both the name "neoliberalism" and the "Comite international d'etude pour le renouveau du liberalism" (CIERL) to promote neoliberal ideas.[18] This newly designed economic liberalism also becomes a dominant theme in the *Ordoliberalismus* associated with Ludwig von Mises, Friedrich Hayek and the Freiburg School of Economics, many of whom had attended the Lippmann Colloguium in Paris and who later established the Mt. Pelerin Society to promote neoliberalism. Some of these members would also influence the free-marketeering economists who came to dominate the economics department at the University of Chicago in the late 1940s and later helped establish the so-called Washington Consensus in the 1980s. Others would go on to shape the economic policies of post-World War II West Germany. For these early neoliberals society is reconceptualized as a democratic marketplace where all participants are considered to be entrepreneurs who should have equal footing and opportunity in the game of competition. Here the state should "not be identified with *laissez-faire* but rather with permanent vigilance, activity and intervention."[19] Its central duty is to generate competition, make markets, and further marketization whenever possible. In the neoliberal system, as Bruno Amble describes it, "public intervention is far from being prohibited but must be justified by reference to the promotion of individual competition, not as a way to alter the results of a supposed free and fair process."[20] In the end such practices are thought to generate a "consumer sovereignty"… in which every penny represents a ballot paper."[21]

These various liberal forms of government and governmentality each made their own contribution in producing particular types of education policies and types of universities in the late nineteenth and twentieth centuries. Indeed, what we consider to be the modern public university of the first three-fourths of the last century is an amalgamation of these liberal political configurations in practice.

---

[17] Walter Lippmann, *An Inquiry into the Principles of the Good Society* (Boston, MA: Little, Brown and Company, 1937), p. 182.

[18] Philip Mirowski and Dieter Plehwe (eds), *The Road from Mont Pelerin: The Making of the Neoliberal Thought Collective* (Cambridge, MA: Harvard University Press, 2009).

[19] Foucault, *Birth of Biopolitics*, p. 132.

[20] Bruno Amble, "Morals and Politics in the Ideology of Neo-Liberalism," *Socio-Economic Review* 9:1 (2011), pp. 3–30.

[21] Ludwig von Mises, *Socialism: An Economic and Sociological Analysis*, in J. Kahane (trans.), (Indianapolis, IN: Liberty Fund, 1981), p. 428.

Echoing liberal themes, Wilhelm von Humboldt, whose plans for the University of Berlin served as a global exemplar for the modern research university, described the modern liberal university as a place that "lives and continually renews itself on its own, with no constraint or determined goal whatsoever."[22] For such a university to operate appropriately it should "take place entirely outside the limits...within which the State must confine its own activities."[23] J.S. Mill outlined a similar liberal vision of an independent education system free from government steering. He worried that state directed education was "mere contrivance for molding people to be exactly like one another."[24] For Mill there was a direct connection between liberal governance and the liberal arts and liberal learning. In his inaugural address at St. Andrew's University in 1867, he argued that "universities are not intended to teach the knowledge required to fit men for some special mode of gaining their livelihood. Their object is not to make skillful lawyers, or physicians, or engineers, but capable and cultivated human beings."[25] In the United States, Andrew White, the first president of Cornell University, echoed a similar liberal orientation toward the university. He declared the university to be a place "where intellectual culture might restrain mercantilism and militarism."[26] Here truth should always be sought for truth's sake.

The type of knowledge that emerges from nineteenth-century liberalism reflected the relative independence of the university and independence of thought of the practitioners within it. While the concept of liberal education predates the liberal state, liberal knowledge of the type we know today was largely made possible within the political configuration produced by the early liberal state of the nineteenth century. This was, of course, never a perfect liberal system of complete freedom and autonomy. Its status was always under threat by both activist industrialists wishing to sway it in their direction, as Thorstein Veblen famously described, and the consolidating power of the increasingly powerful nation state.[27] While the nineteenth-century liberal university was undoubtedly elitist and largely reserved for members of the white, male upper classes, it, like the doctrines of liberalism itself, also contained the political seeds for the larger democratization of the university that would slowly take place in the twentieth century. It also established the ground rules for the relatively autonomous and independent university and a professoriate in possession of something that would later be referred to as "academic freedom." These liberal characteristics of relatively autonomous institutions operated by self-regulating professionals and

---

[22] Wilhelm von Humboldt in Jean Francois Lyotard, *The Postmodern Condition: A Report on Knowledge*, in G. Bennington and B. Massumi (trans.), (Minneapolis, MN: University of Minnesota Press, 1984), p. 32.

[23] Wilhelm von Humboldt in UNESCO, "Wilhelm von Humboldt, 1767–1835," *Prospects: The Quarterly Review of Comparative Education* 23:3 (1993), p. 616.

[24] J. S. Mill, *Utilitarianism, Liberty and Representative Government* (New York, NY: Dutton, 1951), p. 88.

[25] J.S. Mill, "Inaugural Address Delivered to the University of St. Andrews," in John M. Robson (ed.), *The Collected Works of John Stuart Mill, Volume XXI - Essays on Equality, Law, and Education* (London, UK: Routledge and Kegan Paul, 1984), p. 218.

[26] Andrew White in S. S. Schweber, "Big Science in Context: Cornell and MIT," in P. Galison and B. Hevly (eds), *Big Science: The Growth of Large-Scale Research* (Stanford, CA: Stanford University Press, 1992), pp. 149–183, p. 153.

[27] Thorstein Veblen, *The Higher Learning in America* (New Brunswick, NJ: Transaction Publishers, 1993 [1918]).

independent administrators would become the "ideal type" of the modern university in many Western societies in the twentieth century.

The relatively hands-off approach to higher education that came to define the liberal university began to change in the early twentieth century as the state and economic configurations that supported it changed. Fueled in part by the state-directed mobilization during the World War I, various forces within and outside of the state began to push for a closer connection between the goals of the state and those of universities, particularly in areas of science and technology. Also, some academics in the West began to look approvingly to happenings in the newly formed Soviet Union where universities were beginning to be harnessed in order to further various state initiatives. This spawned a division between those who wished to keep the university independent of state direction and those who wanted to use it to improve society through state direction. This division came to a head in the late 1930s and early forties in the UK with the debate between J.D. Bernal, author of *The Social Function of Science*[28] who advocated for a more socialist, "people-centered" or state-directed science, and Michael Polanyi, a one time member of the Mount Pelerin Society, who sought to defend what he would later call the "republic of science" through the independence of science from state direction. Bernal believed that the lack of state funding allowed knowledge to be subservient to a patchwork of philanthropists and industrialists rather than an instrument to promote the public good. Echoing Mill and Humboldt, Polanyi, on the other hand, later argued that "any attempt at guiding scientific research towards a purpose other than its own is an attempt to deflect it from the advancement of science."[29]

In the United States a similar debate ignited at the end of World War II between Vannevar Bush, director of the Office of Scientific Research and Development, and Senator Harley Kilgore of West Virginia over the direction of university science.[30] Bush argued that "freedom of inquiry must be preserved under any government support of science."[31] Kilgore, on the other hand, advocated for a more direct role for the state in steering the content of university research.[32] The eventual outcome of this debate was the establishment of the National Science Foundation which used a model rooted in the process of peer review rather than state direction. As Bush described it, this new foundation must assure "complete independence and freedom for the nature, scope, and methodology of research carried on in institutions receiving public funds."[33] This division of labor between the state and universities and the science facilitation model it developed would shape the "big science" that dominated much scientific work in universities and elsewhere throughout the Cold War. In this model a balance is reached where the grant

---

[28] J.D. Bernal, *The Social Function of Science* (London, UK: George Routledge & Sons, 1939).

[29] Michael Polanyi, "The Republic of Science," *Minerva* 1 (Autumn 1962), pp. 54–74.

[30] Daniel Kevles, "The National Science Foundation and the Debate over Post-War Research Policy, 1942–1945: A Political Interpretation of Science—The Endless Frontier," *Isis* 68:1 (1977), pp. 4–26.

[31] Vannevar Bush, *Science: The Endless Frontier, A Report to the President* (Washington, DC: US Government Printing Office, 1945), p. 12.

[32] Don Price, "Federal Money and University Research," in H. Orlans (ed.), *Science Policy and the University* (Washington, DC: Brookings Institution, 1968), pp. 23–51.

[33] Bush, *Science*, p. 33.

system would work to incentivize certain government-directed university science initiatives; however, independent "blue sky" or basic research including those in the social sciences would still be supported and funded by the state and professors would be free to pursue the projects that interested them and their professions. Likewise, industry research would largely continue in its own research labs with limited crossover with work occurring in universities. This model continued in place until it began to be dismantled by the so-called "triple helix model" that evolved under neoliberal governments beginning in the 1980s.[34]

Both liberal and social or embedded liberal forms of governance took what we might term a facilitatory role in the running of public enterprises. The social liberal university, for instance, always walked a careful line between allowing various social institutions their political autonomy, even those residing within government itself, and having these institutions serve the larger public interest which was, at this point, defined largely independently of the market but one which was nevertheless directed or protected by the state. This form of liberalism understood, at least tacitly, that a light monitoring that recognizes the autonomy of institutions and professionals working within those institutions were a more effective way of "managing" public organizations than heavy-handed monitoring. Indeed, such a heavy-handed style of management was untenable under the doctrines of both classic liberalism and social liberalism. Despite the stress social or embedded liberalism placed on state planning and regulation, it still managed to protect the relative autonomy of the university and its faculty.

Both liberalism and embedded liberalism also did something else that is rather unique amongst historical forms of governmentality: they allowed those who opposed government policies, particularly those in academia, to criticize them even from within the confines of government itself. Unlike other past forms of governance, liberalism and social liberalism provided the space for various forms of academic freedom, such as those found in the 1940 *AAUP Statement on Academic Freedom and Tenure*, to become widely accepted principles. Indeed, this was viewed as a necessity for producing valid and reliable knowledge and advancing human understanding. Of course this did not mean that the liberal university was a blissful utopia of forever-happy professionals free of all coercion by any means; but rather that liberal governmentality provided the space for the generation of a relatively uncoerced but always fragile public realm where individuals could exercise a high degree of autonomy and freedom to act. Indeed, this was the idea behind public higher education—to create a public zone that encouraged freedom of inquiry but which also enjoyed government support.

However, within the liberal and social liberal juxtapositioning of state, economy, and society ironically resided the seeds of the current neoliberal capturing of the university and its current push to dismantle the public domain. For if the state is the "caretaker" of the public domain in liberal thought, this domain can easily be taken away by the state or merged with its own interests as in authoritarian forms of socialism. Or, in another scenario, if the state is captured by particular powerful interests, the public domain risks being reconfigured to reflect the values and interests of those who captured it. Here within lies the story

---

[34] Henry Etzkowitz, *The Triple Helix: University-Industry-Government Innovation in Action* (New York, NY: Routledge, 2008).

of the birth of neoliberalism and its tenuous relationship with the public domain, democracy and the public university.

The Neoliberal State, the Neoliberal University, and Neoliberal Knowledge

While liberalism in its various guises produced particular types of spaces for the production and dissemination of knowledge that came to define the character of the twentieth-century university, the rise of neoliberalism in the late 1970s and 80s also began to produce its own unique configuration within which universities could operate. Although, as we saw earlier, the rise of neoliberalism as a social movement can be traced to the activities of Walter Lippmann, Ludwig von Mises, Frederick Hayek and others in the 1930s, as a larger political movement it largely lay dormant until its resurrection in the 1970s by a group of conservative think-tanks and politicians. When these politicians came to power in the late 1970s and early 1980s they began a push to fundamentally reform various social institutions using neoliberal principles, including the generation of an entirely new form of citizenship built around the construction of the new responsible citizen consumer as described by Röpke.

Early neoliberal governments contained two general impulses or phases that reflected the allegiance to both the classic economic liberalism of the nineteenth century and the newer neoliberalism of Hayek and Friedman. In the "roll back" phase neoliberals sought to reduce the role of the state in order to allegedly lower taxes and, following the argument of the public interest theory put forward by Buchanan and Tullock,[35] alleviate the burdens placed on the state by the escalating demands of various "special interests" (except for business ones). In practice the "roll back" idea served more as a rhetorical trope since neoliberal governments did not so much reduce state expenditures as reprioritize them using neoliberal principles. In the other, more "roll out" phase of neoliberalism the state is increasingly used as a mechanism to increase marketization and monetary monitoring throughout society.[36] Here, following Hayek, the state is used as an instrument to enable marketization to occur throughout all of society.

Key to many of the reforms launched by early neoliberal governments in the 1980s were attempts to "denationalize schooling" along the lines suggested by Milton Friedman while also increasing oversight and monitoring and realigning administrative functioning through the adoption of new public management tactics. These changes can first be seen in the education reforms launched in England by Margaret Thatcher and her compatriot Secretary of Education Keith Joseph in the early 1980s. These reforms sought to create greater consumer choice in schools while simultaneously weakening the Local Education Authorities (LEAs) and increasing centralized control by the state in the name of accountability and auditing. In New Zealand a similar strategy was utilized in the "Tomorrow Schools" reforms put forward under the Labour government of David Lange in the late 1980s. In the United States with its more federated system of education already in place—one that some neoliberal reformers sought to

---

[35] James Buchanan and Gordon Tulloch, *The Calculus of Consent* (Ann Arbor, MI: University of Michigan Press, 1962).

[36] The phrases "roll back" and "roll out" neoliberalism are taken from J. Peck and A. Tickell, "Neoliberalizing Space," *Antipode* 34:3(2002), pp. 380–404.

mimic—reforms were a bit slower in taking off. The rhetoric of neoliberal change began with the release of the report *A Nation at Risk* in 1984 under the Reagan Administration but did not get fully underway until the Clinton and George W. Bush Administrations in the 1990s and early 2000s. Like neoliberal reforms in the UK and New Zealand, reforms in the United States sought to provide greater choice through the expansion of charter schools, vouchers and the right to leave schools that were deemed failing, as in the "Adequate Yearly Progress" (AYP) provision found in the No Child Left Behind Act of 2001. These reforms also sought to strengthen "quality control" through intensified teacher monitoring, the standardization of the curriculum, and increased reliance on high-stakes standardized testing to punish and reward schools and teachers. Later, under the Obama Administration, these standards became further nationalized and more punitive through the funding pressures and "value added measures" used in the "Race to the Top" and "Common Core" policies.

For universities in the US neoliberal reforms have unfolded in different areas at different speeds. University researchers began to feel the effects of neoliberal style reforms with the passage of the Bayh-Dole Act in 1980. The coordinated linking of universities, businesses and financiers had been around for a while but in a rather patchwork form. Under the Bayh-Dole Act the intellectual property generated by federal research grants could now be owned by the inventors and universities through "exclusive licenses" and sold directly to private companies. Prior to the Act the ownership of this intellectual property from government sponsored research was considered a public good and was retained by the government and available only through "non-exclusive licenses." Today the legacy left by the Act can be seen in places such as the technology transfer offices of universities, the growth of science parks around many major universities, the importance placed on patenting and intellectual property rights by universities, the rhetoric of various knowledge economy reports coming from the OECD and World Bank and in various knowledge society policies constructed from these reports.[37]

Another round of neoliberal reforms got underway with the release of the report of *A Test of Leadership* by the Spellings Commission under the G. W. Bush Administration in 2006.[38] This report borrowed heavily from reforms already occurring in the UK as outlined in the 1997 *Dearing Report* and advocated globally by groups such as the World Bank and OECD.[39] The Spellings Commission Report called for reforms to "make sure our higher education system continues to spur innovation and economic growth and gives more Americans the chance to succeed in the knowledge economy."[40] The Report maintained that "the continued ability of American postsecondary institutions to produce informed and skilled citizens who are able to lead and compete in the 21st-century global

---

[37] In one version of this in the spring of 2014 Penn State University auctioned off its intellectual property at a public auction with limited success. See http://www.pennlive.com/midstate/index.ssf/2014/03/penn_state_to_be_first_univers.html

[38] US Department of Education, *A Test of Leadership: Charting the Direction of U.S. Higher Education, A Report of the Commission Appointed by Secretary of Education Margaret Spellings* (Washington, DC: US Department of Education, 2006).

[39] National Committee on the Inquiry into Higher Education, *Higher Education in a Learning Society* (Retrieved from: bei.leeds.ac.uk/Partners/NCIHE/, 1997).

[40] US Department of Education, *A Test of Leadership*, p. 13.

marketplace may soon be in question."[41] The Commission further argued that "higher education must change from a system primarily based on reputation to one based on performance."[42] Although the Spellings report had less of an effect at the national level and generally failed to make a significant impact on its intended target, the Higher Education Reauthorization Act of 2008, it did help generate a series of changes to higher education at the state level. *A Test of Leadership* became the seminal document that groups such as the National Council of State Legislatures and the National Governors Association could use to push for the reform of higher education. One of the siren calls of the Spellings Commission and subsequent state reforms was to align the university's curriculum with the skills and "competency" needs of companies. Today this linkage can be readily seen in discussions of the so-called skills gap, the resurrection of the once discredited competency-based education model and the "college completion agenda" being pushed by various online universities, such as Western Governors University and Southern New Hampshire University, as well as neoliberal think-tanks, such as the American Enterprise Institute and the Heritage Foundation and philanthropic groups such as the Lumina Foundation and the Bill and Melinda Gates Foundations.

Reforms of university research and teaching initiated by Bayh-Dole and the aftershocks of the Spellings Commission have been directed and held in place by two other neoliberal directed reforms—the rationalization of university managerial practices brought about by the importation of New Public Management into the administration of universities and the creation of schemes that generate student choice, consumerism, and responsiblization. In the former set of reforms, universities have moved from operating on a combination of bureaucratic-administrative and shared governance models of management to a corporate style of management replete with top down and stream-lined decision making, strategic planning, and slick-branding techniques.[43] Here, the older and slower forms of shared governance are replaced with a line-chain authority strategy to increase organizational control and allow the institution to become more "flexible" and responsive to changing workforce needs.[44] Part of this formula involves employing more contingent workers throughout all areas of the university, including teaching and research, in order to lower labor costs. For instance, in 1969 non-tenure track faculty comprised 21.7% of the total teaching force in higher education; however, today non-tenure track faculty make up almost 70% of the instructional faculty.[45]

In the latter set of reforms, neoliberal tactics are used to create "demand pressure" on educational institutions and individual departments and professors through various mechanisms designed to generate "consumer choice," such as forcing increased reliance on student loans and creating various league tables or world rankings of universities and departments, Research Assessment Exercises,

---

[41] Ibid.

[42] Ibid., 21.

[43] Steven Ward, "The Machinations of Managerialism: New Public Management and the Diminishing Power of Professionals," *Journal of Cultural Economy* 4:2 (2011), pp. 205–215.

[44] See Leslie Barry, "Faculty Governance in the New University," *Academe* 99:5 (2013), pp. 17–22.

[45] Adrianna Kezar and Daniel Maxey, "The Changing Academic Workforce," *Trusteeship* 3:21 (2013), at http://agb.org/trusteeship/2013/5/changing-academic-workforce.

devolved budgeting and user pays systems, sophisticated marketing techniques, and measures of customer satisfaction to encourage "shopping around" and "good customer service."[46] Here university students are required to move from being "welfare recipients" to wise and responsible consumers, investors, and risk managers who must be in charge of their debt load and career choice. This has been driven, in part, by a steep decline in state support for higher education institutions, which dropped from an average of 60.4% of university budgets in 1975 to 34.1% by 2010 with some states, such as Colorado, projected to reach zero percent by 2017.[47]

The university that is now emerging in the wake of these neoliberal reforms looks and feels quite different from the liberal university that preceded it. Unlike the liberal university, the neoliberal university is reconfigured to both act like a competitive enterprise in the marketplace and to serve the always shifting interests of those in the market. In the first configuration universities are considered a business like any other enterprise and need to start acting like one.[48] In the second they are now required to serve business interests through research that is innovation- and product-focused and teaching that is centered on creating the "soft" and "hard" skills needed in business and the new enterprising society.

Conclusion: Illiberal Liberalism and the New Enterprising University

How is it that a movement with its roots in the liberal rejection of centralized control came to embrace centralization when put into practice? How did an approach to education that initially promised "autonomy for accountability," as found in the UK's 1988 Education Reform Act or George H.W. Bush's reform efforts, actually end up in many instances decreasing autonomy and magnifying accountability? The answer to these questions resides in the complex and conflicting governmentality that neoliberalism produced as it moved from the university lecture hall to think-tanks into political parties and became government policy. In the realm of practice neoliberalism's ideal type was mingled with and evolved from other political practices and ideologies. This "actually existing neoliberalism"[49] combined the vitalistic market enthusiasm of classic economic liberalism and laissez fairism with the activist, progressive state of embedded liberalism or socialism. As neoliberalism came to be practiced in the 1980s and onward it became not a pure form of political economy but an amalgamation of the systems that had gone before it.

---

[46] It is worth noting that the Apollo Group, parent company of the University of Phoenix, spends twice as much on marketing as on teaching. Also, at for profit colleges 17.4% of annual revenue was spent on teaching while almost 20 percent was distributed as profit. In Stefan Collini, "Sold Out," *London Review of Books*, October 24 (2013), pp. 2–3.

[47] American Council on Education, "State Funding: A Race to the Bottom," 2012, available at http://www.acenet.edu/the-presidency/columns-and-features/Pages/state-funding-a-race-to-the-bottom.aspx

[48] Stefan Collini has described the situation in UK as one where the "coalition government took the decisive steps in helping to turn some first-rate universities into third-rate companies." Collini, "Sold Out," p. 14.

[49] This phrase "actually existing neoliberalism" contrasts the more ideal typical neoliberalism with the modifications it underwent in the actual realm of politics. It is taken from N. Brenner and N. Theodore, "Cities and the Geographies of 'Actually Existing Liberalism,'" *Antipode* 34:3 (2002), p. 351.

On the one hand, neoliberalism's activist, strong state came to resemble the demand management of the welfare state, not in its redistributional or "slice of the pie" politics or support for an independent public realm which it desperately wishes to privatize, but in the level of zeal directed toward generating "growth" and "improvement" through continued economic expansion. Indeed, this is what made neoliberalism so appealing not only to traditional political parties filled with market enthusiasts but also to so –called Third Way politicians in Center-Left, Democrat, and Labor parties globally. This zeal generated a state that continually looks to direct policy not toward society-making, the preservation of the public realm, or full employment policies as social liberalism did but toward market-making and imposing market discipline on people wherever and whenever possible. Following the *Ordoliberalens* market-making is seen today by neoliberals as the only way that society is made and the public good is produced. The greater social good is produced only thought the creative destruction and incentives that the unequal provisions of the market bring to all realms of life. Here, it is actually the privatization of the public realm that brings about the greater good, not economic equalization or the further socialization of society by the state. So, for example, when a company obtains exclusive patenting rights for something produced from the public monies provided by the National Science Foundation or Google or Disney turn works that are in the public domain into private, for profit products they are actually performing a public good. They are protecting things from becoming "wasted" and "falling into the public domain" by bringing them to the marketplace and putting them to use. Such market enthusiasm creates a loose regulation of private enterprise and valorization of the markets where business interests largely go unchecked and a general demonization of the public realm and social welfare exists. The end result in terms of practical politics is that business interests are able to engage in "nation capture" and seize society's central institutions such as education and medicine. This is not necessarily what early neoliberals like Lippman, Röpke, and Hayek had in mind when they formulated the neoliberal agenda with its forever churning market and spontaneous and non-directional social ordering in the 1930s. For them the economy was a reality *sui generius* that was much too important to be captured, monopolized, and manipulated by one particular set of interests, even those of business and corporations. Indeed, in their view, that was the very disaster that doomed nineteenth-century laissez faire liberalism.

Neoliberals' push to generate markets in education and elsewhere seems to come from ignoring their political counterpart and the balance it historically exerted. There is little doubt that markets generate lots of choice so that consumers, in the words of Anthony Giddens, "have no choice but to choose."[50] However, in generating all this consumer choice markets also differentiate and create a hierarchy. Markets are not democracies nor are democracies reducible to consumer choice. Markets are not based on each person's equal participation and voice but on his or her ability to pay. They are, by their very social form, places of differentiated product and price—a place of Walmarts and Neiman Marcus. In the current zeal of neoliberals to diminish the public sphere or "privatize the commons" in order to produce public goods through private profit-seeking, they

---

[50] Anthony Giddens, *Modernity and Self-Identity: Self and Society in the Late Modern Age* (Stanford, CA: Stanford University Press, 1991), p. 75.

have conflated economic liberalism with political liberalism and have largely collapsed the latter into the former. In doing so they have generated a public realm in danger of complete privatization, dismantling, and collapse. Indeed, that is the explicit goal of neoliberals. They have transformed the market economy with its political and moral systems of support and counterbalances into the market society where the state eagerly serves as the grand auctioneer at the great public realm thrift sale. Yet, in this accomplishment they, as early institutional economists argued, risk undermining the very institutional and societal supports and political balances that make markets possible in the first place.

The end result of "actually existing neoliberalism" is a "worst of all worlds" situation where a market authoritarianism or illiberal liberalism prevails. Here all previous social and political checks and balances on markets are essentially released. Embedded liberalism recognized the importance of various public and political checks on the vicissitudes of market swings and the importance of creating and maintaining a robust public realm outside of the market and free from state interference. It was, as I have argued throughout, within this space where both social democracy and the liberal university came of age, as imperfect as they undoubtedly were. As this public commons is increasingly enclosed the public university (and public education generally) is being captured and "sold off" and "sold out." The model that has emerged deliberately underfunds and cheapens public education in order to move it toward product differentiation and ultimately privatization where its true value can be priced by the ever wise market. It then responds to the inevitable decline in educational institutions or "race to the bottom" created by this policy-driven funding neglect and marketization to increase auditing and surveillance in the name of enhancing "quality control" and "accountability." As this process begins to create deskilling and deprofessionalization in the ranks of the professionals working in these organizations, neoliberal policy responds with calls for even more monitoring and surveillance or by creating the opportunity for even more privatization to happen.

If successful, the public university experience that will be left in the wake of these various neoliberal reforms currently being pushed at the state and national levels will be radically different than that experienced in the past, although elite, private institutions will probably go on doing what they have always done. There will be manager-full and professor-less campuses with materials designed by "edu-metricians" at "edu-companies" and provided by Massive Open Online Courses (MOOCs). These materials will be administered to students by "education specialists" using standardized rubrics and "competency mapping." These cut rate education retailers will be used to service mostly middle- and lower-income students at community colleges or at mid-level, "directional" state universities. There will be "scared responsible" students who are required under neoliberal policies, ironically, to become both market aware rational knowledge consumers who must be ever resourceful and responsible in the choice of university, debt load, and major but who are also treated as objects of surveillance in order to make sure they spend their time and money prudently as they go about checking off the student learning outcomes at their discount competency-based education superstore. There will be universities whose budgets increasingly rely on patents and the "good will" of philanthropists, or when provided by the state or via federal student aid budgets, will depend solely on how well they show "value added" through the performance measures provided by competency-based education. And, there will be an increasing number of "knowledge managers" (formerly known as administrators) who will spend most of their day in a "data death spiral" gazing at spread sheets and managing and mining the "big data" generated by all this monitoring. In the end, neoliberal policies undoubtedly will produce market variation but they will do so with increased stratification, surveillance and auditing—killing, ironically, the very liberalism that gave both neoliberalism and the modern university as we have known them their birth. The only means for stopping this may be an unlikely alliance between those who fear the increased intrusion and monitoring of the state and those who wish to maintain a robust, well-supported, independent and trust-worthy public domain. However, such a style of social or embedded liberalism, written about and advocated by John Dewey and L.T. Hobhouse in the early part of the twentieth century, seems nowhere to be found today.

Academic Governance and Democratic Processes: The Entrepreneurial Model and Its Discontents

Tracy L.R. Lightcap
LaGrange College, USA

Abstract *Institutional power over the decision-making process in post-secondary institutions has traditionally been concentrated in the academy itself and, to a lesser extent, in state regulatory offices. Recently, however, this type of governance has been challenged and, in many places, replaced by a new, entrepreneurial model emphasizing more control by college administrations, increased involvement by outside "stakeholders," and the use of competition among and within schools for students and resources as the main criterion for determining investment and curricular priorities. This article describes the entrepreneurial model of academic governance, then shows it in action through a detailed examination of the presidential succession crisis at the University of Virginia. This case study reveals many aspects of the discourse of entrepreneurial governance and illustrates the utilitarian nature of the model. The article proceeds to consider the reasons why such a discourse developed, tying the entrepreneurial model to the promulgation of neoliberal ideologies that are remaking social institutions more generally. The effects on the role of education in democratic politics in the United States are then analyzed. The conclusion of the article speaks to the difficulties of addressing these effects and recommends ways of analyzing responses to the model by the institutions and individuals involved.*

In 1982, Clark Kerr pointed out that,

> About eighty-five institutions in the Western world established before 1520 still exist in recognizable forms, with similar functions and unbroken histories, including ... seventy universities. Kings that rule, feudal lords with vassals, guilds with monopolies are gone. These seventy universities, however, are still in the same locations with some of the same buildings, with professors and students doing much the same things, and with governance carried on in much the same ways.[1]

To a very large extent, what Kerr said then is true today, but the whole question of collegiate governance has reached new levels of salience, both within and without the academy. What happened to change what has been a remarkably stable and sustained institutional history?

This question raises issues of governance. I define governance as a process for making decisions about the direction and goals of organizations. Organizations will differ according to their organizational fields and core technologies and this

---

[1] Clark Kerr, *The Uses of the University* (Cambridge, MA: Harvard University Press, 1982), p. 152.

will color any discussion of their governance.[2] Today, what is not in question, however, is the context of the emergence of discussions about governance across the organizational spectrum: it is the widespread adoption of neoliberal ideas concerning the state. In contemporary discussions, governance is the product of the de-centralization of state regulatory functions, the adoption of market mechanisms and "self-management" as a substitute for regulation, and calls for further accountability and transparency of organizational decision-making. As these pressures have extended to higher education, serious problems arise that pose challenges not only for the future of higher education, but also for its relationship to democracy.

In this article I will attempt to describe the features of the new, entrepreneurial model of academic governance that has begun to proliferate in higher education in the United States (US) and around the world. After a preliminary look at academic governance in general, I will describe how the entrepreneurial model precipitated the most public meltdown in academic governance in the US in the last century, the presidential succession crisis at the University of Virginia. Drawing on that experience, I will discuss the emergence of entrepreneurial academic governance, tying it closely to neoliberal ideas of politics and exposing its character as a discourse adapting to these trends. I then discuss how the discourse of entrepreneurial academic governance has affected both processes in academic institutions and the depoliticization of higher education in the US. I end with a discussion of some of the effects of the discourse of entrepreneurial academic governance on democratic processes in American higher education and some speculations concerning how they can be countered.

Higher Education and Governance

To see why governance matters in academic institutions, we have to look at the kind of organization found in higher education. The core technology of post-secondary education is based on a series of specialized areas of study—the disciplines. The reason for this is two-fold. First, specialization of fields of knowledge has greatly decreased the problems of identifying and examining states of affairs. Indeed, the advent of the university is tied directly to the need to segregate areas of study and bore in on formulating questions and developing ways to acquire the knowledge to answer them. As in other areas of modern societies, this differentiation has continued as the overall level of social complexity has increased. Second, there is the inherent need for disciplines to develop gatekeeping mechanisms to ensure that knowledge is accumulated correctly and that the methods for doing so are continued and improved. This is what leads to the hierarchy of mastery built into every academic field and institutionalized, all the way down to the ceremonial level, in colleges and universities the world over.[3]

---

[2] Paul J. Demaggio and Walter W. Powell, "The Iron Cage Revisited: Institutional Isomorphism and Collective Rationality in Organizational Fields," *American Journal of Sociology* 48 (1983), pp. 147–160. They define an organizational field as "...sets of organizations that, in the aggregate, constitute a recognized area of institutional life; key suppliers, resource and product consumers, regulatory agencies, and other organizations that produce similar services or products (p. 148)."

[3] For an overview, see Franz van Vught, *Patterns of Governance in Higher Education: Concepts and Trends* (Paris, France: UNESCO, 1993).

Neither of these imperatives is particularly well-suited for developing the centrally directed organizational strategies associated with business management. However, as Kerr points out above, for most of the history of universities, this was of little import. Originally, universities were for a selected few who needed esoteric knowledge to fulfill their functions in life (clergymen and lawyers). Most people could find their way in the world quite well without higher education, and could care less what the universities were doing and how they did it. The advent of modern science changed this picture abruptly by (a) instituting constant changes in knowledge and, consequently, increasing flexibility into the disciplines, (b) proliferating specialization of knowledge far beyond the original Great Professions, and (c) making discoveries of immense practical value that led to the invention of entirely new fields of scientific engineering (aeronautical, electrical, industrial, and computer engineering are good examples) and to the transformation of classic applied studies (architecture, construction, and civil engineering) beyond all recognition.

However, these changes were not reflected at once in the way institutions of higher education were run. That came with the expansion of collegiate education to much wider swaths of the population. The state had always had some interest in the conduct of education in colleges and universities, of course, but the commitments of vast public monies to post-secondary education changed both the scope and intensity of that interest. Indeed, the very idea of governance in post-secondary education dates from this expansion. To see the scope of the changes involved more clearly, refer to Figure 1.

This is the "governance equalizer" Jochen Fried developed to give a clearer view of how governance has changed in modern higher education.[4] Instead of trying to define the concept generally—that has proven exceedingly difficult for reasons examined below—he looks at five dimensions of governance:

1. State regulation: governing higher education by " . . . a formalized set of legal rules and specific regulations."[5]
2. Academic self-governance: governing higher education using collegiate processes and academic merit as general principles.
3. Stakeholder guidance: governing higher education by goal setting from external representatives. The increasing influence of Boards of Trustees drawn from non-academic professions and private business is indicative of this.
4. Managerial self-governance: governing higher education through goal setting and administrative decision-making by senior leadership (presidents and deans, for example).
5. Competition: governing higher education through competition for students and resources. Decisions would be made on the basis of allocating resources to those areas most likely to convey a competitive advantage to the institution.

---

[4] Jochen Fried, "Higher Education Governance in Europe: Autonomy, Ownership, and Accountability—A Review of the Literature," in Jurgen Kohler and Josef Huber (eds), *Higher Education and Governance: Between Democratic Culture, Academic Aspirations, and Market Forces* (Strasbourg, France: Council of Europe, 2006), p. 87. Fried's figure is based on work by Harry de Boer, Jurgen Enders, and Uwe Schimank, "Orchestrating Creative Minds. The Governance of Higher Education and Research in Four Countries Compared" (Unpublished paper, University of Twente, 2005).
[5] Fried, "Higher Education Governance in Europe," p. 85.

Traditional governance | Entrepreneurial governance

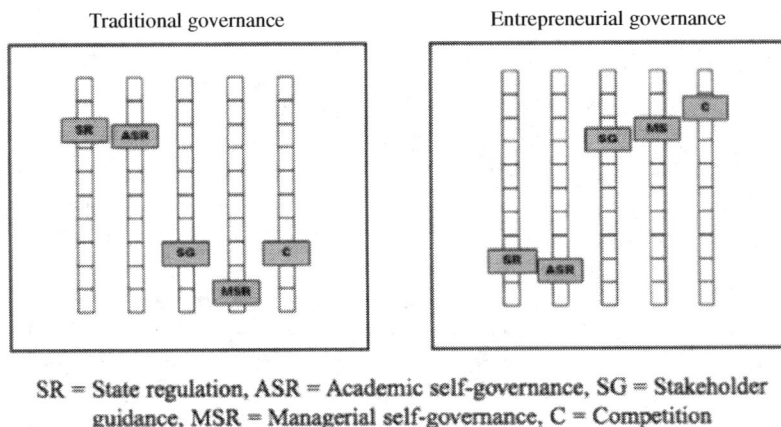

SR = State regulation, ASR = Academic self-governance, SG = Stakeholder guidance, MSR = Managerial self-governance, C = Competition

Figure 1. Fried's Academic Governance Equalizer

As Fried says, each of these aspects of higher education governance has been around for some time. Yet, in recent years there has been a shift with state regulation and academic self-governance (the "traditional" model of governance in panel one of Figure 1) decreasing while stakeholder guidance, managerial self-governance and competition (the "entrepreneurial" model in the second panel of the figure) is increasing. What has caused the shift from the traditional model that had adapted quite well to the new environment of expanded post-secondary education to the entrepreneurial model that weighs stakeholder guidance, managerial self-governance, and competition so much more heavily?[6] And why the controversy involved in adopting new ways of doing things? To begin to understand these changes and the conflicts they have engendered, let us examine a case study of the entrepreneurial model being applied.

The Entrepreneurial Model in Action: The Presidential Succession Crisis at the University of Virginia

On June 10, 2012, the Rector of the University of Virginia's Board of Visitors (BOV), Helen Dragas, announced suddenly to the deans and vice presidents of the university that Teresa Sullivan, brought in to become the university's president in March 2010, had agreed to resign her office on August 15. In remarks to the middle administrators after the announcement, Dragas asserted that the BOV felt

> . . . the need for a bold leader who can help develop, articulate, and implement a concrete and achievable strategic plan to re-elevate (sic) the University to its highest potential. We need a leader with a great willingness to adapt the way we deliver our

---

[6] It is worth remembering that the vast expansion of both public and private education in the US was supervised largely by a combination of faculty members working as administrators and state regulators. California's experience in building what is still generally considered the best public university system in the world is illustrative. See Aron Bady and Mike Konczal, "From Master Plan to No Plan: The Slow Death of Public Education," *Dissent* (Fall 2012), pp. 10–16, for an excellent short history.

teaching, research, and patient care (the University has a nationally recognized medical school) to the realities of the external environment.[7]

Sullivan's resignation shocked the university's entire community. The university's first female president, she had been a successful provost at the University of Michigan before she was hired and was quite popular with faculty and students at the university and with its alumni. Reaction from the faculty was swift, calling the next day for an explanation of the BOV's decision. The faculty senate's resolution immediately pinpointed the main problem for Dragas and her main supporter, Vice Rector Mark Kingdon: Sullivan's resignation was accepted at an emergency meeting of the BOV's executive committee and, as soon became apparent, without due consideration by a full meeting of the BOV. Despite initial support from the university's provost and chief operating officer, the uproar increased, especially on social media sites created virtually overnight and overrun with traffic soon afterward. At a subsequent emergency meeting of the faculty senate on June 17, a resolution of no confidence in the BOV passed virtually without dissent and the provost, John Simon, abandoned his position supporting the board's decision.[8]

Despite (or maybe because of) a defiant but evasive reply to the faculty resolution on June 17—Dragas refused to reveal any details of Sullivan's firing since this was a personnel question and thus "confidential"—the drumbeat of criticism continued. By now, one of the university's "star" faculty, William Wulf, former President of the National Academy of Engineering, had resigned, there were rumors of several other prominent faculty planning to join him, and at least two new faculty hires had suspended further negotiations.[9] The faculty responded the next day by calling on both Dragas and Kingdon to resign. By now it was becoming clear that the situation had gone further, faster then Dragas and her allies had anticipated. The BOV, after a twelve-hour meeting ending on June 19, tried to continue the process of selecting new leadership, picking Carl Zeithami, Dean of the McIntire School of Commerce (the university's business school), as interim president and appealing for calm. Perhaps as a gesture to the board's opponents, Kingdon submitted his resignation from the BOV at the same meeting that selected Zeithami.[10]

On June 21, Dragas attempted to retrieve the situation by issuing a long justification of the decision to fire Sullivan, citing ten major challenges that the university faced and asserting that Sullivan had not performed effectively in meeting them. By that date, however, the *Cavalier Daily*, the student newspaper, had filed Freedom of Information Act (FOIA) requests for Dragas's emails. These revealed that the real basis for moving against Sullivan had been a few op-eds in prominent newspapers predicting that the swift onset of online learning would

---

[7] Carol S. Wood, "Remarks of Rector Helen Dragas, Meeting With Vice Presidents and Deans, June 10, 2012," *UVA Today*, June 10, 2012, < http://news.virginia.edu/node/18791? id=18791 > .

[8] An exceptionally complete record of the entire affair with appropriate comments from principals and interested parties can be found in the Fall 2012 issue of the *University of Virginia Magazine*, "17 Days in June: From Resignation to Reinstatement" (Charlottesville, VA: University of Virginia Alumni Association, 2012).

[9] William Wulf, "Message From Bill Wulf," < http://sullivan.lib.virginia.edu/items/ show/148>.

[10] *University of Virginia Magazine*, "17 Days in June," pp. 12–13.

undermine traditional university education. Further, the emails made it apparent that Dragas and Kingdon had essentially bluffed other members of the BOV into accepting their decision that Sullivan had to go.[11] Finally, to the delight of her opponents, it was revealed that Dragas had hired a prominent New York public relations firm for, "...burnishing her image."[12]

In light of these revelations and the swiftly deteriorating public image of the university, Dean Zeithami suspended further negotiations with the BOV the next day and the state's Governor, Robert McDonnell, demanded an end to the controversy, one way or another. On June 26, the BOV met again and voted unanimously to reinstate Sullivan. She addressed an overflow crowd gathered in her support on "The Grounds," the university's traditional quadrangle. Dragas was subsequently reappointed rector of the BOV by Governor McDonnell and the situation appeared to return to normal.

Why is this complicated story an example of the entrepreneurial model? Recall the three aspects of university governance given more prominence in this new scheme: stakeholder guidance, managerial self-governance, and competition. An examination of Dragas's justification for dismissing Sullivan issued on June 21 reveals a remarkably complete listing of the causes for alarm about academic governance among those who embrace the entrepreneurial model.[13] The university had no new strategic plan in place to address vital concerns and was in danger of losing ground to its competitors. It needed to adopt more stringent ways to assess its academic output, preferably with objective measures of how well different programs prepared students for "...the increasingly complex, international world in which they will live and compete."[14] It needed to institute online learning at once before its competitors stole the march. It needed better "PR" more attuned to attracting donors and increasing the use of social media. It needed more research funding as soon as possible. Above all, it needed a leadership that would put incremental change aside and use a "...deliberate and strategic approach" to push the university forward to engage its competitors.[15] It had become evident that, while Sullivan recognized these problems, she did not share the BOV's assessment of the urgency of addressing them through top-down management initiatives. She had to go.

Interestingly, as Sullivan said in her response to the BOV, many of these concerns were already in the process of being addressed, albeit in an incremental manner. The online controversy was one of these; the university had been a leader

---

[11] Hawes Spencer, "Dragas to Kingdon: 'Why We Can't Afford to Wait,'" *The Hook*, June 20, 2012, <http://www.readthe hook.com/104310/dragas-kingdon-why-we-cant-afford-wait>.

[12] Countney Stuart, "Dragas Shrugged: Defiant Rector Hires PR Firm," *The Hook*, June 18, 2012, <https://www.readthehook.com/104274/dragas-shrugged-who-rector >.

[13] It is possible that Dragas did not write this document. It has been reported that it was written by her recently hired public relations firm (Stuart, "Dragas Shrugged"). For a blistering analysis of the basic incoherence of the BOV's explanations of Sullivan's dismissal, see Siva Vaidhyanathan, "Strategic Mumblespeak: Er, UVA's Teresa Sullivan Was Fired For What?" *Slate*, June 15, 2012, <http://www.slate.com/articles/news_and_politics/hey_wait_a_minute/2012/06/teresa_sullivan_fired_from_uva_what_happens_when_universities_are_run_by_robber_barons_.single.html>.

[14] Helen Dragas, "Statement of Helen E. Dragas, Rector, University of Virginia," June 21, 2012, <http://www.virginia.edu/presidentialtransition/120621dragas.html>.

[15] Dragas, "Statement."

in digital education for decades and had joined Coursera, the online consortium of elite institutions, just weeks before. Further, the university had been a leader in establishing a new consortium, 4VA, using advanced technology to share courses in cooperation with other Virginia universities. She had put into place a new financial system with strong incentives for the deans of different schools at the university to prioritize resources and assess programs. The university had seen a rebound of donor commitments. Finally, Sullivan pointed out that she had been told *to not initiate any new strategic planning when she had been hired*. But, she also said that a top-down management style would not work in a research university setting and that incremental change based on buy-in by the faculty was necessary for the University to work effectively.[16] In short, she repudiated the very essence of the entrepreneurial model: the need for administrative preponderance in academic governance to ensure "flexibility" in the face of competitive challenges.

The Discourse of Entrepreneurial Academic Governance

> Have you ever read any criminological texts? They are staggering. And I say this out of astonishment, not aggressiveness, because I cannot comprehend how the discourse of criminology has been able to go on at this level. One has the impression that it is of such utility, is needed so urgently and rendered so vital for the working of the system, that it does not even need to seek a theoretical justification for itself, or even simply a coherent framework. It is entirely utilitarian.[17]

This often-quoted passage from Michel Foucault could as easily apply to the entrepreneurial model of academic governance. For what we are facing here is a discourse, a set of practices that create "...the mechanisms and instances which enable one to distinguish true and false statements, the means by which each is sanctioned, the techniques and procedures accorded value in the acquisition of truth, the status of those who are charged with saying what counts as true."[18] In other words, to analyze what was going on at the University of Virginia we have to go into why Dragas and the BOV felt that they had no choice but to dismiss President Sullivan and that the grounds for doing so were so obvious that there was little need to explain what they were doing or why.

The usual administrative visions of collegiate decision-making reveal the principles at work in the entrepreneurial discourse. College administrators and their supporters often decry what they see as a glacial pace of decisions and policy change in colleges and universities when academics are put in charge of major initiatives. This is contrasted with a world that is changing at a rapid pace and that presents challenges to colleges that must be addressed *now* or dire circumstances will ensue. Further, evaluation of academic efforts and how they fit with the role of post-secondary institutions in providing an educated workforce should not be left to the academic community itself. The possibility of self-interested avoidance of necessary changes is too great. The answer to both conundrums is to centralize authority over collegiate affairs in administrative hands, empowering them to

---

[16] Teresa Sullivan, "Message From President Sullivan to the Board of Visitors," June 18, 2012, <http://www.virginia.edu/president/speeches/12/message120618.html>.

[17] Michel Foucault, *Power/Knowledge: Selected Interviews and Other Writings*, ed. Colin Gordon (New York: Pantheon, 1980), p. 37.

[18] *Power/Knowledge*, p. 131.

make the kinds of rapid changes needed and involving a wide range of "stakeholders" in those decisions to ensure the support decisive action will require. I am sure most readers of this article have run across these kinds of statements before.[19]

The academic community is well aware of the increasing pace of social change; indeed, it is largely responsible for it. Far from being inflexible, disciplines change their object of inquiry regularly, creating entirely new subjects and techniques and crossing the "knowledge silos" wherever gains in understanding present themselves. Further, as President Sullivan pointed out in her response to Dragas, colleges and universities are alive with innovations in both teaching and research that administrators often know nothing about (and, revealingly, seldom show interest in) and that usually arise as a result of responses to changing environments like those that so concern the epigones of entrepreneurial governance. The "glacial pace" often referred to is on wider policy matters. This is usually driven by the need for research before taking action and is part of the consensus-building characteristic of collegial decision-making in professional organizations. It is interesting that the real concern appears to be the inability of administrators to control and direct the pace of the change going on about them, not so much the change itself.

Second, the need for evaluation of academic programs is nothing new and has been embraced by academics for eons. Here again the real concern appears to be the lack of control of those evaluations. Academic evaluations are usually cast in terms of the credentialing process at the center of university and college education. This, by its very nature, must be insulated from market pressures. Indeed, credentialing that is divorced from professional standards—standards that are largely set by disciplines themselves and are in the hands of evaluators outside the schools and departments being evaluated—would be counter-productive. Yet it is this independence of evaluation, inherently qualitative in part since it is based on generally accepted intellectual standards, that appears to be the root of the problem to proponents of entrepreneurial governance. Those who follow this model call for standardized quantitative indicators that can be produced to compare outcomes for courses of study to those demanded, not by professional organizations, but by "stakeholders" (that is, businesses that will hire the graduates of academic programs), Boards of Trustees now often representing political interests, and the students (and their parents) themselves. This is accompanied by a push for outcomes that will satisfy donors, increase funding, and enhance the "accountability" of post-secondary education to market forces.

By now this whole strategy should be recognizable: it is quite close to the de-skilling of artisan work described by Braverman many years ago.[20] By more closely controlling the process of generating technical innovations (or, to be more exact, by acting as a gatekeeper for innovation), by controlling the curriculum to more closely meet business needs, by ensuring that there is quick reaction,

---

[19] For a widely influential exposition, see Chapter 12 in Derek Bok, *Our Underachieving Colleges: A Candid Look at How Much Students Learn and Why They Should Be Learning More* (Princeton, NJ: Princeton University, 2008). Bok's title makes the utilitarian emphasis that Foucault describes as self-evident.

[20] Harry Braverman, *Labor and Monopoly Capital: The Degradation of Work in the Twentieth Century* (New York: Monthly Review Press, 1974).

controlled within university administrations, to "competitive" pressures, and by close monitoring of measurable outcomes, collegiate administrations can ensure more interchangeable and compartmentalized skills. That in turn will mean that the manipulation of academic programs will be easier, that academic personnel will be more adaptable to administratively determined institutional needs and less capable of exerting market pressure, that universities and colleges will be better able to meet market (read employers') demands, and that both community norms within colleges and universities and the ability of professional standards to dictate institutional strategies will be undermined.[21]

As is always the case, the real object of an analysis of a discourse should not be to determine whether the structure of the discourse is a representation of actual reality, but rather what kinds of configurations of power make the discourse necessary for the people and organizations that promulgate it.[22] Here the answer is straightforward: the shift in assumptions concerning education brought on by the widespread acceptance of neoliberal political ideologies. University administrators must deal with the world as they find it. That world has increasingly turned to corporate models of the educational process.

The neoliberal governments that came to power in the later part of the twentieth century had a variety of immediate goals, but their most important one was to decrease taxation levels and, consequently, the size and regulatory power of government. When applied to higher education this could only be accomplished by depoliticizing three aspects of academic governance. As Bady and Konczal point out, the first administration of Ronald Reagan as Governor of California showed the way. Reagan combined an assault on the University of California's (UC) tradition of student protest with a shift of perspective on the role of post-secondary education. Until his administration, UC's place as a driver of growth in the state through creating a highly educated workforce that could exploit California's position as the leading technological and scientific state economy in the US was a bipartisan given in California politics. Reagan cleverly used popular resentment of the student protest movement as a tool to subvert this vision of the UC's function and change perceptions in California of post-secondary education as a public good. His major initiative was to change the state's commitment from supporting tuition for the UC system to one of requiring students to pay for their own education through fees. At roughly the same time, he stopped the massive building program for UC that had been part of the original commitment to provide a college education for the state's youth. The result was lower expenses for the university system, lower tax burdens, a substitution of

---

[21] The explosion of the use of adjunct faculty, easily replaced and largely interchangeable, is the obvious result of this process. See Nicolaus Mills, "The Corporatization of Higher Education," *Dissent* (Fall 2012), pp. 6–9. For an overview of the effects of these changes on academic governance itself, see Adrianna Kazar, Jamie Lester, and Gregory Anderson, "Challenging Stereotypes That Interfere With Effective Governance," *Thought and Action* (Fall 2006), pp. 121–134.

[22] Perhaps the best indicator of why this strategy is necessary here is the difficulty in finding a coherent definition of the concept of academic governance. See Jurgen Kohler, "Higher Education Governance—Background, Significance, Purpose," in Kohler and Huber, *Higher Education Governance*, pp. 17–32, for an overview of the many ways governance has been conceived for higher education. Like many analysts faced with this problem, I have opted for a description of the features of the discourse rather then trying to give any general conceptual overview.

market control for state involvement and regulation, and the displacement of higher education from its formerly central place in California politics. This example has been closely followed elsewhere.[23]

The second facet of depoliticization involved governance of colleges and universities. If market forces are allowed to dictate the form of curricula, if tenure (and hence academic freedom) is allowed to lapse, if norms of shared governance are marginalized or abolished and university faculty treated as individual employees, and if students and parents are seen and treated as consumers of post-secondary education, then the position of post-secondary education as one of the main non-market institutions in society could be destabilized as well.[24] The result is described by Bostock in his discussion of similar trends in Australia: "Corporatized universities simply cannot afford to experiment, maintain uneconomic courses, or allow their employees to act as social critics."[25]

The last aspect of depoliticization impinges directly on the curtailment of what Horace Mann called "political education"; that is, education about the powers and functions of government and how to use basic democratic processes to change laws and officers.[26] Recall that the public target of the first campaign to institute entrepreneurial governance was the student demonstrations at various campuses of UC, especially at the flagship campus at Berkeley.[27] The methods used were straightforward enough; the demonstrations were met with force and further curbed by making students—and their parents—more responsible for the costs of collegiate education. This would increase pressure to attend class, do well, and avoid possible administrative penalties, thus justifying the family investment required. Also, it would remove students from confrontational political activity at the very time when they first gained the franchise and began the process of partisan affiliation. This worked to some extent; the level of student activism never returned to the quietism of the 1950s, but the overall level of engagement has greatly decreased and participation in protests is largely confined to the generation of the 1960s.[28] A public much less likely to confront authority and much more likely to funnel its increasing frustrations into avenues easily handled through political manipulation has resulted.

---

[23] Bady and Konczal, "From Master Plan to No Plan."

[24] William Bostock, "To the Limits of Acceptability: Political Control of Higher Education," in John Biggs and Richard Davis (eds), *The Subversion of Australian Universities* (Wollongong, NSW: Fund For Intellectual Dissent, 2002), pp. 19–40. http://www.bmartin.cc/dissent/documents/sau/index.html.

[25] Bostock, "To the Limits of Acceptability." See also Bob Bessant, "A Climate of Fear: From Collegiality to Corporatization," in Biggs and Davis, *The Subversion of Australian Universities*, pp. 51–84.

[26] Horace Mann, *Report Number 12 of the Massachusetts Board of Education (1848)*, <http://usa.usembassy.de/etexts/democrac/16.htm>. Indeed, the very idea of a responsibility for political education has largely disappeared in post-secondary educational institutions in the US. See Barry Checkoway, "Renewing the Civic Mission of the American Research University," *The Journal of Higher Education* 72:2 (2001), pp. 125–147.

[27] Bady and Konczal, "From Master Plan to No Plan."

[28] See Neal Caren, Raj Andrew Ghoshal, and Venesa Ribas, "A Social Movement Generation: Cohort and Period Trends in Protest Attendance and Petition Signing," *American Sociological Review* 76:1 (2011), pp. 125–151. Their findings indicate that the majority of Americans who have either attended a protest or even signed a petition is very low overall and dominated by the cohort that came of age in the 1960s.

As these perspectives spread with the hegemony of neoliberal ideas from the 1980s onward, the discourse of entrepreneurial academic governance evolved to accommodate them. With state legislatures and the federal government increasingly demanding better results (however defined) for less money, public and private university administrations found themselves faced with a conundrum. Either they could try to restructure the institutions they led to meet the new demands of now more active boards of trustees and the boards' political allies, to attract private donors and federal grants to supplement dwindling state resources, and to centralize control over both faculties and curriculum to meet "competitive pressures" or they could attempt to preserve the basic collegial structure of their universities in the face of continuing demands for introducing corporate control to contain costs and increase "accountability." The debacle at the University of Virginia shows the struggle in bold relief: the BOV's insistence on more emphasis on corporate command structures and "flexibility" to meet the "challenges" of funding in a more "competitive" environment versus the insistence of President Sullivan and the university's faculty, students, and alumni that collegiality and the tradition of research-driven decision-making by consensus be respected. It should go without saying that similar strains of conflict driven by similar differences in perspective can be found in private institutions. It should also go without saying that the present world economic crisis has exacerbated these struggles as neoliberal governments attempt to address depressed economic activity with austerity measures.[29]

Discussion

The depoliticizations associated with the entrepreneurial model have had serious consequences. Stagnant commitments for government funding have meant that, while the US still spends the highest overall amount on higher education among Organisation for Economic Co-operation and Development (OECD) countries, there has been virtually no recent change in spending per student. One result has been in the proportion of young adults with collegiate education which has been stagnant as well; in 2011 the US ranked eleventh among OECD countries.[30] As might be expected, these trends have led to considerable disquiet concerning future competitiveness of the American economy. The assault on shared governance, academic freedom and tenure, and the increasing use of internal evaluation of academic programs based on managerial and "market-based" criteria is an even more serious problem. These initiatives pose grave danger to the central mission of post-secondary education—providing a system of independent credentialing for the acquisition and mastery of skills for general purposes. Credentialing greatly decreases information costs to all organizations by identifying levels of skill for prospective employees. More importantly, however, the credentialing system is at the center of the hierarchy of mastery that

---

[29] Kevin Kiley, "Don't Mess With Texas," *Inside Higher Education*, May 14, 2012, <http://www.insidehighered.com/news/2012/05/14/university-texas-community-rallies-behind-austin-president-dispute-politicians#sthash.8z2jxa4I.dpbs>.

[30] OECD, *Education at a Glance, 2013: OECD Indicators* (OECD Publishing, 2013), <http://dx.doi.org/10.1787/eag-2013-en>. It is revealing that the US spends twice as much on "ancillary services" (transport, room, and board) for post-secondary education than its nearest OECD competitor (the United Kingdom).

supports scientific and technological advance in modern societies. Subverting it, in other words, directly threatens the basis for the continued well-being of entire societies. Finally, difficulties caused by entrepreneurial governance for the academy are flanked by concerns about the ongoing disengagement of post-secondary students from politics and civic affairs. Here, valiant efforts have been made to initiate student interactions with their communities and interest in public affairs through service-learning courses or community research centers and the projects they sponsor. However, these efforts to provide civic involvement to already disengaged students tend to be restricted in scope—it is possible to go through an entire course of study without participating in either service-learning or community research—and, to some extent, manufactured (the projects usually are chosen by the faculty involved in consultation with communities and not by the students).[31] Since empowering the concerns of the students *themselves* is seldom the focus of these programs, there are predictable problems with motivation and student involvement.[32] As a consequence, the effort has not affected the underlying problem of lagging civic engagement appreciably.[33]

At this point, one would expect a series of solutions to this dilemma. The promulgation of a discourse, however, does not usually admit such an easy path. There are two reasons for this. First, the discourse of entrepreneurial academic governance is, as I have already pointed out, an adaptation of an existing policy environment. Due to the changes wrought in elite perceptions of post-secondary education and the close interweaving of those perceptions to neoliberal ideas, there is considerable support for the discourse among the political and educational elites involved.[34] Even those most critical of neoliberal nostrums are affected by them; academics themselves often become tied up in the individual competition fostered by the discourse.[35] Further, some aspects of the discourse have merit. Putting the interests of students in getting a good education first

---

[31] It is interesting to see how often these programs are justified as a tool for positively affecting "success" in meeting quantitative learning outcomes. Promoting civic engagement itself is seen as secondary, not as a goal in itself. See the symposium in *Diversity and Democracy* 15:3 (2012), <http://www.diversityweb.org/DiversityDemocracy/vol15no3/vol15no3.pdf>, for examples of this kind of thinking. The influence of the entrepreneurial model is plainly evident.

[32] When students do get a voice in planning and carrying out service learning projects, the results are more encouraging. See William Morgan and Matthew Streb, "Building Citizenship: How Student Voice in Service Learning Develops Civic Values," *Social Science Quarterly* 82:1 (2001), pp. 154–169.

[33] It is not that such initiatives do not have desirable effects; there is considerable evidence that community research and service learning do increase volunteerism and the desire to work within communities. However, the level of *civic* engagement reported, even after educational interventions, remains depressingly low. See the figures reported in The National Task Force on Civic Learning and Democratic Engagement, *A Crucible Moment: College Learning and Democracy's Future* (Washington, DC: Association of American Colleges and Universities, 2012), pp. 5–7.

[34] See the contrast of views on p. 6 of Jean Johnson and Christopher Di Stasi, *Divided We Fail: Why It's Time for a Broader, More Inclusive Conversation on the Future of Higher Education,* (The Kettering Foundation, 2014), <http://kettering.org/wp-content/uploads/PA-KF-Divided-We-Fail-Final.pdf>. As can be seen, there is little support for many of the entrepreneurial model's ideas in the general public.

[35] Bronyn Davies and Eva Bendix Petersen, "Neo-Liberal Discourse in the Academy: The Forestalling of (Collective) Resistance," *Learning and Teaching in the Social Sciences* 2:2 (2005), pp. 77–98.

should be (and usually is) a universally accepted goal in post-secondary institutions. Further, given the present funding environment, it is necessary to court both private donors and increased government aid. The problem does not arise from these necessary goals, but rather from how they are addressed.

The second aspect has to do with intentionality. As Ferguson reminds us in his classic study of "development" in Lesotho,

> The thoughts and actions of "development" bureaucrats are powerfully shaped by the world of acceptable statements and utterances within which they live; and what they do and do not do is a product not only of the interests of various nations, classes, or international agencies, but also, and at the same time, of a working out of this complex structure of knowledge . . . outcomes of planned social interventions can end up coming together into powerful constellations of control that were never intended and in some cases never even recognized, but are all the more effective for being "subjectless."[36]

As I have tried to show in this article, the changes brought about by the widespread acceptance of the entrepreneurial model of governance are quite similar. The bewilderment of Rector Dragas at the virtual explosion of opposition to the dismissal of President Sullivan at the University of Virginia is illustrative. Surely any concerned observer could see the urgency of the situation and the need for immediate action? And, after her public explanation of the BOV decision, that she was working with the interests of the university at heart? Yet every declaration of good intentions simply increased the size and level of intensity of the protests. She had followed the strictures of the discourse she was part of and the stakeholders that she thought she was representing turned on her in massive numbers, threatening the streams of donor income the board depended on, and undermining both the university's political support and its national reputation.[37] It is virtually certain that this was not what she intended. However, it was the result of her actions—actions that fit the model of governance she had come to regard as part of the accepted policy landscape. Her lack of perception ended up creating the most public meltdown in American university administration in the last one hundred years. It was also predictable, given the character of the discourse itself.[38]

By the same token, one cannot look at the opposition to Dragas's decision as a clarion call to resistance. Ferguson also has significant insights to offer about how the advent of entrepreneurial governance is normally resisted:

> It seems clear that the most important transformations, the changes that really matter, are not simply "introduced" by benevolent technocrats, but fought for and made through a complex process that involves not only states and their agents, but all those with something at stake, all the diverse categories of people who craft their

---

[36] James Ferguson, *The Anti-Politics Machine: "Development," Depoliticization, and Bureaucratic Power in Lesotho* (Minneapolis, MN: University of Minnesota, 1994), pp. 18–19.

[37] See the numerous emails to the Board of Visitors concerning the Sullivan affair included in Henry Graff, "New E-mails Give Insight Into Sullivan Ouster," *NBC29 News*, September 26, 2012, <http://www.nbc29.com/story/19530076/new-emails-give-insight-into-sullivan-ouster>.

[38] It is quite likely that the same scenario will be repeated. See Kevin Kiley, "What's Up with Boards These Days?" *Inside Higher Education*, July 2, 2012, <http://www.insidehighered.com/news/2012/07/02/trustees-are-different-they-used-be-and-uva-clashes-will-be-more-common#sthash.HkX5QBpz.UHRHiPOC.dpbs for a useful overview of the factors involved>.

everyday tactics of coping with, adapting to, and, in their various ways, resisting the established social order.[39]

Applied to the discourse of entrepreneurial academic governance, this means that what Ferguson says a bit earlier is the best advice, "Indeed, the only general answer to the question, 'What should they do?' is: 'They are doing it!'"[40] Again, the fracas at the University of Virginia is illustrative. The "forces of change" were not Dragas and the BOV. Instead, it was the action of the improbable coalition—faculty, academic administrators, students, alumni, journalists, social media participants, outside commentators—that sprang up virtually (much of the organizing was done through social media) overnight into a resistance that was never planned, seldom coordinated, and never coherent in aims that led to the collapse of support for the BOV's decision and its ultimate reversal.[41]

Conclusion

Of course, the declines of political commitment to post-secondary education and of civic engagement in the US cannot be laid completely at the door of the intentional depoliticization of American higher education.[42] However, the continuing abandonment of collegial norms of governance and the intentional depoliticization of collegiate education have had detrimental effects, as I have shown above. It is unlikely that anything short of a reversal (or, at least, a tempering) of neoliberal policy hegemony will put the entrepreneurial discourse on the shelf. That will take a long period of boring on some very hard boards. Attempts to create movements like that at Virginia to support embattled presidents have failed at the universities of North Carolina and Oregon, for a variety of largely unrelated reasons.[43] But, in my opinion, this is secondary to the usual ways that faculties, students, alumni, and others interact with the entrepreneurial juggernaut. The particular circumstances in different institutions will dictate the degree of success achieved. One thing can be predicted, however: it is unlikely that the epigones of the entrepreneurial approach will see a new way forward until outside pressure forces them to. Kiley's description of the BOV retreat after the crisis is illustrative. The main topic of interest was not, as one might expect, the basic framework that led to the BOV's disastrous decision, but

---

[39] Ferguson, *The Anti-Politics Machine*, p. 281.

[40] Ibid.

[41] Looking at the crisis at the University of Virginia, it becomes clear that the entrepreneurial model has neglected the concern that graduates of universities and colleges have for the value of their degrees, a value created by the integrity of the credentialing process mentioned earlier. Fears about the impact of Sullivan's preemptory dismissal on the university's national reputation—and, hence, the value of their degrees—was at the center of the outrage expressed by Virginia graduates as they threatened to withdraw their support from the university and castigated interference by the political appointees of the BOV. See Graff, "New E-mails Give Insight."

[42] For an overview of declining American social and political engagement that is particularly relevant to the themes in this article, see Theda Skcocpol, *Diminished Democracy: From Membership to Management in American Civic Life* (Norman, OK: University of Oklahoma Press, 2003).

[43] Kevin Kiley, "The Virginia Effect," *Inside Higher Education*, September 25, 2012, <http://www.insidehighered.com/news/2012/09/25/reaction-unc-chancellor-resignation-shows-influence- virginia-controversy>.

how the BOV should view its role with other stakeholders and how its committee structure could be improved.[44] Those imprisoned in a discourse are not the ones to look to for actual reform; their opponents are.

Ferguson is right; discourses exist because they justify the exercise of power and the predictable consequences of their actions often serve goals at odds with the intentions of the actors involved. This has and will create substantial problems for academic institutions. The academic community is the most flexible, creative, openly inquisitive, risk acceptant, and fiercely meritocratic segment of every society. That is why it so often castigated by those who find the existence of a sphere of modern life that, to this day, is largely immune to market forces both inefficient and, in many instances, a personal affront.[45] The results of these often incoherent resentments can be seen throughout the academy today. This is certainly the case at the University of Virginia; neither the tensions on "The Grounds" between Rector Dragas and President Sullivan nor the nationwide interest in the entire episode have abated. As I have tried to show here, the upcoming episodes in the struggle against entrepreneurial governance can only be worked out within academic institutions by faculty, students, alumni, and (yes) administrators themselves. Understanding the character of the framework of entrepreneurial governance, however, is a vital first step in that process, one I hope this article will help them to make.

---

[44] Kevin Kiley, "What's a Board to Do?" *Inside Higher Education*, August 17, 2012, <http://www.insidehighered.com/news/2012/08/17/uva-board-retreat-focuses-structure-and-attitudes>.

[45] An excellent example of this is former Senator Rick Santorum's tirade against expansions of collegiate education during the 2012 presidential campaign. See Scott Jaschik, "Santorum's Attacks on Higher Ed," *Inside Higher Education*, February 27, 2012, <http://www.insidehighered.com/news/2012/02/27/santorums- views-higher-education-and-satan>.

Ideology and the Reform of Public Higher Education

Jacob Segal
Kingsborough Community College of the City University of New York, USA

Abstract   *In this article, I critically examine calls for reform of public higher education. I construct a counter-intuitive alliance between the conservatism of twentieth-century philosopher Michael Oakeshott and the more recent thinking associated with post-structuralism. It is argued that in Oakeshott and post-structuralism, we find a similar critique of the idea behind these reforms as imposing instrumental or productivist values on higher education. What is produced is a type of person organized to produce more and to demand of herself greater production. This critique is associated with a broader criticism of liberalism found both in Oakeshott and post-structuralism that the liberal order produces a normalized and docile individuality. Conversely, it is argued that theories of higher education in Oakeshott and post-structuralism inform a broader positive idea of individuality, enacted in a "style," having intrinsic worth, and never reducible to any finished form.*

Introduction

My work as a political theorist has always had an uneasy relationship with my politics. Although a committed leftist, my scholarship has focused on the British conservative Michael Oakeshott, who I discuss mostly, but not entirely, in favorable terms. While Oakeshott's correct political characterization is a matter of debate, in conventional political terms, Oakeshott had a number of conservative political views. He was a qualified supporter of the market and a relentless critic of the interventionist state. Oakeshott defends an elitism common to conservatism, namely a belief that not everyone is capable of enjoying or achieving freedom.

Despite this, I have linked Oakeshott to the more recent thinking associated with post-structuralism.[1] Post-structuralism is a radical doctrine, critical of various aspects of liberal society, such as market activities and conventional gender norms. While the positive program of post-structuralism is less clear than its critique, many post-structuralists tend to advocate a fairer distribution of wealth and greater egalitarianism in social relationships, for example involving gender. What unites the conservatism of Oakeshott with post-structuralism is a shared belief that liberalism, purportedly the political order of freedom and individuality, actually produces forms of normalized and docile individualism. Conversely, I argue that theories of education and higher education in Oakeshott

---

[1] See Jacob Segal, "Freedom and Normalization: Poststructuralism and the Liberalism of Michael Oakeshott," *American Political Science Review* 97:3 (2003), pp. 447–458.

and post-structuralism inform a broader positive idea of individuality which is enacted in a "style," having intrinsic worth and never reducible to any finished form.

The peculiar status of Oakeshott was disclosed to me at a recent conference on his work where I was in the somewhat unusual situation of being surrounded by academics who were chiefly conservative. I intervened in the proceedings, with mixed results, through progressive comments regarding, for example, a defense of equality against Oakeshottian criticisms. I did, however, find myself in agreement with fellow conferees on the issue of reforms of higher education. Various conferees argued, in line with Oakeshott's theory of education, that these reforms reduce education to the merely useful, whereas for Oakeshott, education and the life of the university integrates the individual into the meanings of the culture she inhabits.

In this article, I develop this potential alliance between the conservatism of Michael Oakeshott and prominent strands of post-structuralism. I use this alliance to deepen the critiques of contemporary reforms in higher education. Oakeshott identified changes in education in the 1960s and 1970s that are very similar to current reforms certain post-structuralists criticize. In both, changes in higher education are criticized for imposing educational instrumental or productivist values on higher education. A productivist view of education means it is valued as a process for producing external outcomes, such as greater wealth. Reforms are productive in the additional sense of the production of a type of student who attains certain skills and capacities and is fitted for the global and regional job market.

This critique fits the broader positions of many post-structuralists and Oakeshott. The radical critique of post-structuralists is that agency does not simply develop freely when governmental obstacles to choice are removed, as argued by classical liberals, or when agents are provided substantial economic benefits by the state, as argued by social democrats. Post-structuralists call into question the freedom of choice of liberal capitalism (although they do not completely dismiss or reject it) because of how agents are constructed and constrained by the norms of liberal processes and practices (the market, gender relationships) and liberal institutions (hospitals and prisons).

Michel Foucault and others associated with post-structural thinking have traced how the agent is "normalized" in the liberal order; that is, comes to organize itself to be "normal" and avoid the "abnormal." The agent is its own trainer. It demands that its own conduct conform to a myriad of standards of normality. Freedom is the emblem of the subordination of the self if freedom means acting in a certain way. Higher education reform is an example of the transformation of the individual to be "normal" and more useful.

Second, and less well developed, is Foucault's later work on the "aesthetic of the self," wherein agents disclose themselves in a style. Foucault imagined freedom as an "ethical practice" in which one is concerned with one's own conduct (as honorable or moderate) and in doing so constrains oneself as regards to others (a person with moderate temperament is moderate in action with others).[2] For Foucault, this agency is constantly engaged with its own

---

[2] Michael Foucault, *The Care of the Self: Volume 3 of the History of Sexuality* (New York: Vintage Books, 1988), p. 284.

construction. Foucault writes: "Maybe the target nowadays is not to discover what we are but to refuse what we are."[3]

Oakeshott also traces in modern liberal order the imposition of the normal both by the state and by sub-political organizations. Although a defender of the market, Oakeshott does see in the bourgeois norms of market society the production of a certain type of agent, who works hard, cares about her reputation, and so forth. Oakeshott writes of an agency that is understood as a "style" or a performance of intrinsic worth. I develop this argument more fully through Oakeshott's work than in post-structuralism because his writings are particularly focused on activities and experiences (aesthetics, love, morality) that have "intrinsic" worth; that is, value for themselves not their outcome. For Oakeshott, agency displays itself as a "style" in which activity is an end in itself.

Oakeshott's writing on education points to a broader, radical position. Nicolas Rose, writing in the post-structuralist perspective, proposes a political program that opposes "all that which stands in the way of life being its own telos."[4] For Rose, this entails opposition to anything that subordinates the value of life to something else: an "external code, truth, authority or goal." This sentiment reflects an Oakeshottian view of the importance of experience as valued for itself, as well as the problem of an agent constructed in higher education to serve the end of production.

In the following section, I examine how higher education reform redefines the educational project in economic and productivist terms. I then provide a brief background to Foucault's thought and his relationship to liberalism and look at some specific critiques of higher education reform that flow from his work. In my section on Oakeshott, I provide a background to his thought, a discussion of the debate regarding his ideological standing and then his positive understanding of higher education, and an examination of his critique of changes in higher education during his time.

Reforms of Public Higher Education

Reforms of higher education, public and private, come in waves over time and are international in scope. In the current moment, reforms have a variety of sources. State governors, through the National Governors Association (NGA) argue, based on the skill mismatch theory of economics, that the global economy requires new skills, skills that public universities do not, but must, produce.[5] These reforms also partake of the "accountability" revolution of all levels of public schooling in general, namely that publicly funded schools must be accountable to the public about results. Support for reform cuts across ideological leanings. Some liberals support educational reform while mainstream conservatives support most market oriented reforms and also seem to enjoy attacking the hated "liberal academy."

---

[3] Michel Foucault, "The Subject and Power," in James D. Faubion (ed.), *The Essential Works of Foucault, 1954–1984, vol. 3, Power* (New York: The New Press, 2000), p. 336.

[4] Nikolas Rose, *Powers of Freedom: Reframing Political Thought* (Cambridge, UK: Cambridge University Press, 1999), p. 282.

[5] Travis Reindi and Ryan Reyna, "Complete to Compete: From Information to Action: Revamping Higher Education Accountability Systems," *NGA Center for Best Practices*, July 2011, < http://www.nga.org/files/live/sites/NGA/files/pdf/1007 COMMONCOLLEGEMETRICS.PDF > .

Left-oriented writers have developed a number of criticisms of these reforms. They argue that these reforms push disadvantaged students into low-wage labor. They justify reductions in public funding. Michael Apple makes the central argument that the reforms obscure the fundamental inequalities of class, race, and gender. Apple writes that the reforms create new identities that "are centered around enhanced technical proficiency and a set of assumptions that solutions to deep-seated problems in education and the entire social sphere can be provided by enhancing efficiency and holding people more rigorously accountable for their action."[6]

"Performance standards" are central to these reforms. The standards refer to achievement metrics developed by state governments, which public higher education institutions must work to meet. Some state governments have legislated "performance funding" in two ways. First, some states offer additional funding when public colleges and universities attain the standards. Second, other states reduce base funding when institutions fail to attain the metrics.[7]

For reformers, public universities and colleges are inefficient. Too much emphasis is placed on the inputs of public funds or tuition, and not the outputs of credits earned, diplomas gained, and skills learned. The public university system must change in order to achieve the performance standards; hence it must do more with the same, or even do more with less.

The performance standards have been grouped into three categories. First, colleges must more effectively move students through the stages of education. They must be retained in greater number, earn credits quickly, and graduate in a timely fashion. Second, universities must produce students ready for high wage jobs needed in their region, and in the national and global economy. Third, students should achieve "learning outcomes" that are common among all classes. Central to these outcomes are the learning of skills, both specified in terms of skills for particular jobs, but also more general capacities that all employers desire: skills in writing, critical thinking, and public speaking, among others. In more conservative states, there is a movement to decrease tuition for majors linked with skills for particular jobs and even to increase tuition or eliminate "unproductive" majors.

A report from the NGA, "Complete to Compete," defines reforms in strictly economic and productive terms.[8] The report identifies four efficiency and effectiveness performance metrics. Efficiency pertains to internal workings such as degree completed, while effectiveness concerns external success such as job placement. First, universities must "meet workforce needs" defined as the ratio between graduates and employed adults. Universities should produce graduates whose skills match the needs of regional employers. Second, universities should increase student outputs relative to inputs, which refers to the ratio of certificates and diplomas per enrolled student. Third, the report demands greater return on public and private investment, defined as the ratio between diplomas earned and

---

[6] Michael W. Apple, "Education, Markets, and an Audit Culture," *Critical Quarterly* 47:1–2 (2013), p. 20.

[7] For a skeptical account of performance standards see Jeff E. Hoyt, "Performance Funding in Higher Education: The Effect of Student Motivation on the Use of Outcomes Tests to Measure Institutional Effectiveness," *Research of Higher Education* 42:1 (2001), pp. 71–85.

[8] Reindl and Reyna, "Complete to Compete."

spending per student. Finally, quality must be assured; that is, universities must show that learning is not suffering in the interests of quicker graduations, and indeed that learning outcomes are increasing. The report identifies a variety of measures to assess learning, both direct (assessments of knowledge), and indirect (job placements) as well as judgment of "learning environments" (academic audits).

The authors of the report admit that systems of performance standards themselves require a system of data accumulation that is monitored. Performance metrics need metrics themselves. Performance standards should match with different types of institutions based on mission (for example, the missions of community colleges versus four-year colleges), assessment should be based on trends over time, not snapshots, universities must have adequate staff and viable work plans for annualizing data and the metrics themselves must be adoptable over time.

Proponents of reform reduce education to economic concepts. The conservative think tank, the Texas Public Policy Foundation, argues for a learning contract between college, student, and professor so the students can have clear expectations of learning outcomes.[9] A contractual relationship is not, however, an educational relationship. The obligations of a contract transform the student-teacher form.

In her infamous article in *Inside Higher Education*, "Time, Space and Learning," Alexandra Logue, a Vice-Chancellor of the City University of New York, displays how reform entails a transformation of the whole structure of higher education. Logue stresses "learning outcomes" as the true measure of learning in higher education insofar as these outcomes can be assessed and verified as learned.[10] Logue's argument is flawed in its own terms because she admits that currently there is no true way to assess whether outcomes have been learned. But her argument points to the problem of evaluating higher education based on productivist concepts. For Logue, what matters are these outcomes, not the means. She almost entirely disregards teaching and learning as a value in itself, or as having a unique meaning. This explains her puzzling assertion that learning in the future will be liberated from "time and place," because it does not matter where and when or how one gains the outcomes, only that one does. She writes that outcomes gained through work count just as much as classroom learning. This form of college learning can occur in multiple locations and use various tools. Outcomes can be gained through massive online courses or computer based courses and the various "learning tools" allow for the flexibility of timeless and placeless learning. For Logue, learning occurs in a classroom the same as on a beach through a smartphone. Logue also writes that the substance of education must also change. She writes, "Lessons may need to be broken into smaller units with the material presented in a variety of ways, accompanied by optional multiple examples, and with continuous opportunities for learning assessment

---

[9] Texas Public Policy Foundation, <http://7solutionsresponse.org/index.php?unit=s5>.

[10] Alexandra Logue, "Time, Space and Learning," *Inside Higher Education*, November 18, 2013, <http://www.insidehighered.com/views/2013/11/18/essay-changing-ideas-time-space-and-learning-higher-edu>.

and feedback."[11] Logue admits that labor relations might be changed given the impact of her proposals on academic labor.

The Post-structuralist Critique

Post-structuralism offers a critical perspective on reform in higher education today. A key dimension of this critique flows from Foucault's argument that "power" is not simply a form of command or authority but "productive" in creating types of agencies. While Foucault's work has notoriously taken different turns, a central term is "normalization," wherein individuals are trained to be "normal" and avoid abnormality in different "disciplines" or institutions. For Foucault, this power has no single source or general purpose, but has emerged in great detail in the modern era. Doctors train individuals to live in a healthy manner. This diagnosis may in fact help individuals and be meant sincerely by doctors. However, healthy living creates standards of normal functioning that require sets of care and activities, exercise, diet, and medications, that must be followed or the individual is abnormal or wrong. And individuals are well known to police their own health habits.

Foucault's ideological position and relationship to liberalism has been subject to debate. Jürgen Habermas famously called him "conservative" because Foucault obliterated any "rational standard" that might be used for social critique because any such standard itself is infected by power.[12] But in *Discipline and Punish*, Foucault relates the proliferation of the disciplines of power to the development of liberal capitalism. These disciplines underlie the "freedom" of liberal society. Foucault describes the liberal order in clear terms: "Historically, the process by which the bourgeoisie became in the course of the eighteenth century the politically dominant class was masked by the establishment of an explicitly coded and formally egalitarian juridical framework, made possible by the organization of a parliamentary, representative regime." However, "the dark side" of this system of "egalitarian...rights" was the development of the disciplinary "systems of micro-power that are non-egalitarian and asymmetrical."[13] For Foucault, the disciplines are the "foundation of the formal, juridical liberties" and the formation of "sovereignty" through the "will of all" because they constitute a "submission of forces and bodies." For Foucault the freedom and equal rights require a docile and normalized agency: "The 'Enlightenment,' which discovered the liberties, also invented the disciplines."[14]

In his later work, Foucault shifted his focus to biopower, understood not as the training of individual acts, but a focus on the manipulation of life processes and capacities of the population. Foucault writes of biopower as that which "brought life and its mechanisms into the realm of explicit calculations and made knowledge-power an agent of transformation of human life."[15] Biopower represents the overriding concern of governments, and not just governments,

---

[11] Ibid.

[12] Jürgen Habermas, *The Philosophical Discourse of Modernity* (Boston, MA: The MIT Press, 1990).

[13] Michael Foucault, *Discipline and Punish* (New York: Vintage Press, 1977), p. 222.

[14] Ibid.

[15] Michael Foucault, *History of Sexuality: An Introduction* (New York: Vintage Books, 1990), p. 143.

of "statistics" of all kinds, in overall social trends that must be increased, such as "propagation, births and mortality, the levels of health, life expectancy and longevity."[16]

Jean-Francois Lyotard in 1979, in his seminal work *The Postmodern Condition: A Report on Knowledge*, explores the negative consequences of the equation of higher education, which he understands as a result of the transformation of knowledge itself.[17] Postmodern theory is a broad concept that includes post-structuralism. And while Lyotard is not a post-structuralist, strictly speaking, he shares with a thinker like Foucault an interest in analyzing the consequences of the historical structure of knowledge.

In *The Postmodern Condition*, Lyotard argues that in postmodernity knowledge is reduced to efficiency.[18] He links this to his more general argument that postmodernity signifies the death of grand "metanarrative" of modernity. These narratives described historical processes that led to the "emancipation" of human beings from social restraints and promised unending progress. For Lyotard, postmodernity is characterized by a diversity of incommensurable "language games" that have no relationship to any logic of progress. The end of the metanarrative also brings an end to the belief that knowledge is progressive, leading to human emancipation.

For Lyotard, this transforms the very concept of knowledge, which is no longer verified through the "humanist" narrative of emancipation. What counts as truth is that which can be proved and so knowledge becomes "the production of proofs." This standard of productivity submitted to a master language game of "performativity, that is, the best possible input/output equation."[19] Lyotard argues that performativity seems to detach knowledge from the former categories of correctness: what is true or false or what is just or unjust. However, he argues that performativity actually produces the criteria for what statements are correct or not. This means that truth and justice refers not to eternal truth or truth generated out of consensus. Rather, truth and justice are subsumed into performativity; that is, all truths refer to production. The Western concept of truth is replaced by "legitimation by power."

Lyotard argues in postmodernity that no longer is the university supposed to generate knowledge connected to emancipation. He argues that performativity means that knowledge serves the social system and so must the university. On the one hand, this means that the university must produce skills that are needed for the "world market." Knowledge in this postmodern condition still exists, but its criteria are usefulness, salability, and efficiency. What matters is the transmission of information, not the method. Teaching is irrelevant and so the postmodern condition signifies the "knell of the age of the Professor." The professor is no more efficient than a data bank or interdisciplinary teams.[20]

---

[16] Ibid., 139.

[17] Jean-Francois Lyotard, *The Postmodern Condition: A Report on Knowledge* (Minneapolis, MN: University of Minnesota Press, 1984).

[18] See also, Jean-Francois Lyotard, "Performativity, Post-Modernity and the University," *Comparative Education* 32:2 (1996), pp. 245–258.

[19] Ibid., 46.

[20] Ibid., 53.

Cris Shore and Susan Wright explore how "normalization" works in the "audit culture" introduced in the 1990s in the English higher educational system.[21] Here the imperative of production of students leads to a culture wherein professors are trained to be productive in their organization of department and agency. English universities were seen as "failing" society in terms of the production of students with needed skills. Various quality assurance programs were put into place, verified by means of academic audits. At first, departments were to diagnose themselves against certain standards. Unsatisfactory results would lead to reduced funding. Later, professors had to gain accreditation through a teaching and learning institute, and "academic reviewers" examined quality departmental assurance programs for efficiency.[22]

For Shore and Wright, through academic audits, agents are trained to act in appropriate normal forms, and to be the agents of their own control as they internalize these norms. Audit culture creates a system of control, seemingly non-governmental, through which agents mold themselves, becoming accountable and auditable. Of audit culture, they write, "what we are witnessing here is the imposition of a new disciplinary grid which, by inculcating new norms, 'empower' us to observe and improve ourselves according to new neo-liberal norms of the performing professional."[23] Beyond the normalizing content, the authors claim it replaced "trust and autonomy" with "visibility and coercive accountability."[24] The program also encouraged bad faith, as academic reviewers were presented with staged presentations.

Maarten Simons links reforms in European educational systems to Foucault's concept of biopower.[25] Simons describes in general how contemporary individuals are trained to be "entrepreneurial" to develop their capacities and overall well-being in relation to health, family, diet and so forth.[26] The "entrepreneurial self' must continually invest in itself to develop itself and gain further satisfaction. Simons argues that European university systems have been restructured to maximize the capacities of individuals:

> The European space of higher education can be regarded as a public infrastructure for entrepreneurial higher education. This infrastructure offers human capital to the entrepreneurial student in order to invest in. The student chooses training and invests in training if she expects future income.[27]

Universities seek not after truth, as such, but "will invest in the research and education for which they expect they will have customers."[28] For Simons, the

---

[21] Cris Shore and Susan Wright, "Audit Culture and Anthropology: Neo-liberalism in British Higher Education," *The Journal of the Royal Anthropological Institute* 5:4 (1989), pp. 557–575.

[22] Ibid., 556.

[23] Ibid., 566.

[24] Ibid., 567.

[25] Maarens Simons, "Learning as Investment: Notes on Governmentality and Biopolitics," *Educational Philosophy and Theory* 38:4 (2008), pp. 523–540.

[26] See also, John Morrissey, "Governing the Academic Subject: Foucault, Governmentality and the Performing University," *Oxford Review of Education* 39:6 (2013), pp. 797–810.

[27] Simons, "Learning as Investment," 536.

[28] Ibid.

entrepreneurial self must engage in life-long learning and is driven to compare her learning against others.

Is there a positive position in the post-structuralist discourse for education? In his essay, "Foucault: The Ethics of Self-Creation and the Future of Education," Kenneth Wain describes how agency is its own telos in relation to educational theory.[29] He describes a variety of concepts of agency. These ideas include *parrhesia,* or the truth- telling of democratic citizenship, the notion of aristocratic "refusal" of the constructed self, and care of the self. Wain emphasizes the importance of education in the creation of an agency that has no "nature": "Foucault declares the inevitability of enculturation, its continued, lurking influence on one's life."[30] Wain focuses on a self that "cares" for its own agency. This care is "aesthetic" in the creation of a style of being, but also involves care of others, insofar as it governs itself. My care of the self means that I moderate myself and so also moderate my behavior in regard to others.

Michael Oakeshott, Higher Education, and the Style of Being

Michael Oakeshott's writings contain a critique of the productivist intent of educational reforms, indeed criticizing earlier forms of them, in terms similar to the post-structuralist writers. British Idealism heavily influenced Oakeshott's first major work, *Experience and Its Modes.*[31] Oakeshott rejects the empiricist view of knowledge as a gathering of data from the outside world, which he likens to a wall being built brick by brick. For Oakeshott, humans always have experience within a world they already inhabit. There is never a starting point of no knowledge, but rather knowledge makes sense only as part of a world of experience already known to some degree. For Oakeshott, as humans gain knowledge they make a world of experience more "coherent."

Oakeshott also argues that experience is "arrested" which means the search for coherence stops at a limited point. These modes of experience are partial and incomplete, as opposed to the possibility of absolute coherence, which would be the province of philosophy. One such arrest or mode is "practical experience" which is the world of external ends. In practice there is a world of "what is" and "what ought to be." Coherence in practice is gained by replacing the former with the latter. This coherence is temporary, not complete, because after a new "what is" is gained, another world of "what ought to be" must emerge. Here we see that Oakeshott finds external satisfactions as fleeting, so lacking in value. This valuation is tied to how Oakeshott stresses the superiority of value found in the present of acting.

In his later work, Oakeshott became known for his "critique of rationalism" developed in an essay collected in his famous work, *Rationalism and Politics and Other Essays.*[32] Oakeshott attacks the idea that humans can empty their minds of

---

[29] Kenneth Wain, "Foucault: The Ethics of Self-Creation and the Future of Education," in Michael A. Peters and Tina (A.C.) Besley (eds), *Why Foucault? New Directions in Educational Research* (New York: Peter Lang Publishing, 2007).

[30] Ibid., 174.

[31] Michael Oakeshott, *Experience and Its Modes* (Cambridge, UK: Cambridge University Press, 1986).

[32] Michael Oakeshott, "Rationalism in Politics," in *Rationalism in Politics and Other Essays* (Indianapolis, IN: Liberty Press, 1991).

"prejudices" and discover the one, correct, and rational truth. For Oakeshott, the mind cannot be emptied of biases because it is composed of such prejudices, the history of what a person has learned and experienced.

Change, for Oakeshott, can never be a revolutionary transformation since that would consist of an incoherent imposition of an "idea" of society on the concrete manner of living that has developed. This manner of living is coincident with the way in which individuals learn "how" to live. Change consistent with the "situated mind" can only be incremental, "traditional" alterations of the present.[33] For Oakeshott, the manner of throwing a cricket ball has changed over time, with one manner emerging coherently from an earlier form. For many, this argument ties Oakeshott to conservatism because of his favorable use of "tradition," although the historically minded Oakeshott had no patience with the atemporal notion of "natural law" or "God-given values."

Oakeshott identifies himself with a "conservative disposition," although in a highly specific way. For Oakeshott, conservatism entails an "aversion" to change and an attachment to the present.[34] This present is not just the present circumstances, but also the feeling of the present itself. In another essay, "The Voice of Art in the Conversation of Mankind," Oakeshott identifies aesthetics as experience which is valued for itself, where its meaning is wholly present, as the person engaged in art cares nothing for the past or future, but the enjoyment of art fills the entire space of experience. For Oakeshott, love and friendship also partake of this quality of self-sufficiency.

In his last major work, *On Human Conduct*, Oakeshott develops his political theory in full.[35] Most central is his conception of moral rules and proper law, which he calls *lex*, and which does not concern specific individuals seeking particular goals, but are adverbial considerations on actions, such as the moral rule of neighborliness, which is a condition of action that does not command a particular act. In his concept of law, we can see why he is sometimes linked with the free market theorist, F.A. Hayek.[36] Oakeshott rejects government intervention in the economy not simply as inefficient, but beyond the scope of the properly formulated *lex*.

In my research I have focused on how for Oakeshott *lex* is non-instrumental and present oriented. Proper law is codified morality and moral practices are another moment of self-sufficiency because subscription to morality is independent of the future or past, not goal directed. The value of following moral rules, selling honestly, is "present" because my honest action is independent of whether I make the sale. Honesty may or may not be the "best policy" but my honesty is not linked to either possibility. Oakeshott argues that the moment of practical experience most independent of external circumstances and most "present" is the motive behind action: honesty (or dishonesty), a sense of honor or duty, for example.

---

[33] For the concept of the situation mind, see Leslie March, "Oakeshott and Hayek: Situation the Mind," in Paul Franco and Leslie March (eds), *A Companion to Michael Oakeshott* (University Park, PA: The Pennsylvania State University Press 2012).

[34] Michael Oakeshott, "On Being Conservative," and "Rationalism in Politics," in *Rationalism in Politics and Other Essays* (Indianapolis: Liberty Press, 1991).

[35] Michael Oakeshott, *On Human Conduct* (Oxford, UK: Oxford University Press, 1991).

[36] Although Oakeshott usually comes out better than Hayek in the comparison, see for example, John Gray, "Hayek on Liberty, Rights and Justice," *Ethics* 2:1 (1981), pp. 73–81.

For Oakeshott, morality is a structural part of a personality that finds greater meaning in the moment of acting, not the outcome. Oakeshott describes a persona of the modern era who has a

> disposition to transform this unsought "freedom" of conduct from a postulate into an experience and to make it yield a satisfaction of its own, independent of the chancy and intermittent satisfaction of chosen actions...the disposition to recognize imagining, deliberating, wanting, choosing, and acting not as costs incurred in seeking enjoyments but as themselves enjoyments, the exercise of a gratifying self-determination or personal autonomy.[37]

Sprinkled throughout Oakeshott's work are criticisms of markets and what might be called bourgeois ethics. He rejects a concern for "reputation" and for calculation about the future.[38] Market activities such as buying and selling, consuming and producing are secondary and corruptive of the higher form of individuality.[39] Wendell John Coats notes Oakeshott's "aversion" to activities, however necessary "where self-sufficient engagement is not appropriate, such as the market activity of shopping for the real deal or product."[40] The solution to the problem of the market for individuality, for Oakeshott, is not to end the market or to shield individuals from its corrupting effect, but for some individuals to rise above it, to achieve the higher individuality despite the seductions of an outcome orientation that the market promotes.

Oakeshott's political designation is a subject of continuing controversy. Before the publication of *On Human Conduct* in 1975, Oakeshott was viewed as a conservative critic of liberal rationalism and the liberal "abstract self." After the publication of *On Human Conduct*, a consensus emerged that linked Oakeshott with liberalism because Oakeshott defends individual autonomy and rejects any substantive value imposed on individuals (such as a religious good life, a common value of how to live).[41] In a recent article, Andrew Gamble argues that for Oakeshott politics is a conservative enterprise that protects the basic English traditions in which individuals pursue their own ends while subscribing to properly formulated laws. For Gamble, Oakeshott rejects a number of aspects of "doctrinal liberalism," such as the focus on "human rights," laissez-faire economics and mass democracy.[42]

These debates suggest a certain unique quality to Oakeshott's work. Theoretically, Oakeshott is not a "conservative" in the sense of Edmund Burke and would not agree with Burke's affirmation of an organic society. Although

---

[37] Oakeshott, *On Human Conduct*, p. 236.

[38] Michael Oakeshott, "Religion and the World," in *Religion, Politics and the Moral Life* (New Haven, CT: Yale University Press, 1993), p. 32.

[39] Michael Oakeshott, "The Place of Poetry in the Conversation of Mankind," in *Rationalism in Politics and Other Essays* (Indianapolis, IN: Liberty Press, 1991), pp. 500–501.

[40] Wendell John Coats, Jr, *Oakeshott and His Contemporaries: Montaigne, St. Augustine, Hegel, Et Al.* (Cranbury, NJ: Associated University Presses, 2000), p. 105.

[41] See Wendell John Jr, "Michael Oakeshott as Liberal Theorist," *Canadian Journal of Political Science* 18:4 (December 1985), pp. 773–787; and Paul Franco, "Michael Oakeshott As Liberal Theorist," *Political Theory* 18:3 (August 1990), pp. 411–436.

[42] Andrew Gamble, "Oakeshott's Ideological Politics: Conservative or Liberal," in E. Podoksik (ed.), *The Cambridge Companion to Michael Oakeshott* (Cambridge, UK: Cambridge University Press, 2011), pp. 153–177.

traditional conservatives like Burke were critics of the market, Oakeshott is critical of it not because shifts in supply and demand undermine the social order or traditional authority and morality, but because market ethics undermine that which its supporters claim it enriches, namely the spirit of individuality itself. Theoretically Oakehsott is reasonably seen as a liberal who believes in the rule of law and individuality. Again, as I stated in the introduction, he is a conservative in the contemporary political sense of opposition to the interventionist state. His elitism is conservative in his disparagement of those incapable of freedom. Oakeshott argues that some cannot appreciate the difficulty of free agency that has no meaning apart from its own enactment. Oakeshott calls these who cannot deal with freedom, "anti-individuals" and "individual-*manques*," whose needs for substantive benefits or a common good transform the state as a "purposive" or "enterprise" association in which the state provides such benefits. However, while many conservatives defend the non-interventionist state because they support an "instrumental society" orientated to economic development and the achievement of goals, Oakeshott prizes a non-instrumental self that finds value in the intrinsic worth of action, not the goals achieved.

Oakeshott also explores education as an end in itself, independent of production or outcome, in a series of essays collected in the volume *A Place of Liberal Learning*. Oakeshott argues that universities are independent from these purposeful activities because learning is liberated from the tyranny of goal pursuit. As liberal education is an end in itself, a university is "not a machine for achieving a particular purpose or producing a particular result."[43]

For Oakeshott, education concerns how students understand their "cultural inheritance." This inheritance is not a collection of facts or theories. Rather, the inheritance is the system of meaning that constitutes human understanding. Here we see the holistic understanding of knowledge, characteristic of all of Oakeshott's work. For Oakeshott, the "world" is a human achievement in the sense that its meaning emerges though human interaction. He refers to Kant's famous statement of the "awe" humans experience when they consider the "starry firmament above" and the "moral law" within. Oakeshott calls these human achievements because neither has an "inherent" meaning, but instead a human meaning that emerges out of the "whole of interlocking meanings which establish and interpret one another."[44] A "human being" understands itself in terms of this meaning.

Higher education is the process by which humans become human. Through education, a person learns how to "think" and "feel." For Oakeshott, education has no goal outside of itself. An education concerns what it means to be a person, and for Oakeshott, a person is also an end in itself, in that a human life has no aim but rather continually makes choices in the circumstances in which it finds itself.

In words that echo the notion of style found in Foucault, for Oakeshott, what is learned is how to constitute oneself as a "style." Oakeshott claims that the individual in learning learns numberless rules about the meanings of moral codes and ways of being. In internalizing these rules, agents develop a personal "style" which consists in the "negative operation of the rules." This means that rules

---

[43] Michael Oakeshott, "The Universities," in *The Voice of Liberal Learning* (New Haven, CT: Yale University Press, 1989), p. 112.

[44] Michael Oakeshott, "Learning and Teaching," in *The Voice of Liberal Learning*, p. 45.

constitute a framework of action, and we exhibit a style in our personal internalization and enactment of the rules. He writes, "we may listen to what a man has to say, but unless we overhear in it a mind at work and we can detect the idiom of thought, we have understood nothing. Art and conduct, science, philosophy and history, these are not the modes of thought defined by rules; they exist only in personal exploration of territories only the boundaries of which are subject to definition." Our learned language has a "grammar," syntax, and vocabulary but through it "we think for ourselves" and create ourselves in a style.[45]

Oakeshott sees a teacher as someone who "initiates" the learner into her cultural inheritance. The teacher must "recognize" and "study" and both teacher and student must be present to each other. The teaching material must have a "deliberate order and arrangement." Oakeshott rejects a distinction between teaching as transmission of knowledge and the "self-realization of the individual." For Oakeshott, an individual can only make the most of herself through inheriting a culture. However, this self-realization constitutes a way of life, and so is independent of "circumstances" such as the job market.[46]

Oakeshott's idea of cultural inheritance might lie in tension with the post-structuralist insistence on how "power" is embedded in social relationships. For post-structuralists, the self is "agonic" in its structure and so never settled. Still, Oakeshott agrees with post-structuralists that agency is "historic" not natural, and so never "settled" or finished, and without any future goal like salvation. Oakeshott assents to Le Bon's assertion that humans have a "'history'" but no "'nature'" and so a human being is "what in conduct he becomes."[47] Consequently, Oakeshott approves of the following description of humans: "[N]ot Adam, not Prometheus, but Proteus—a character distinguished on account of limitless powers of self-transformation without self-destruction."[48]

A more serious difference between Oakeshott and post-structuralism is the question of elitism, particularly the degree to which Oakeshott's concept of education is elitist. Whereas post-structuralism is inclusive, I would argue Oakeshott's refined concept of the meaning of higher education might suggest only a few are capable of it, and the majority of individuals ought to engage in purposeful education, such as vocational training. Paul Franco discusses the different strands of thought and finds conflicting evidence. However, ultimately, Franco argues that Oakeshott "never exhibits more than tepid enthusiasm for the expansion of educational opportunities for the less wealthy."[49] Still, I believe that there is a principle of egalitarianism embedded in his doctrine of intrinsic worth. The value of the person lies in its own activity, independent of what it achieves. Higher education is an education in that experience.

We can also see how Oakeshott's work does have what Suvi Soininen calls a "Foucauldian flavor" in the "notion of individuals as being created by power."[50]

---

[45] Ibid., 62.

[46] Ibid., 47.

[47] Oakeshott, *On Human Conduct*, p. 41.

[48] Ibid., 241.

[49] Paul Franco, "Un Debut dans la Vie Humanine: Michael Oakeshott on Education," in *A Companion to Michael Oakeshott*, p. 189.

[50] Suvi Soininen, *From a Necessary Evil to an Art of Contingency: Michael Oakeshott's Conception of Political Activity* (Exeter, UK: Academic Imprint, 2005), pp. 86–87.

She writes that for Oakeshott "the more a given activity...occupies human life, the more people internalize its rules, which then become a part of conduct as such."[51]

Higher education is an example of how activity can govern conduct through governmental and sub-political institutions. Oakeshott at times criticizes reforms in his day that apply directly to current reform movements, revealing the fad-like quality of these changes. Fundamentally, he rejects understanding higher education as a means toward an end. Writing in 1972, he describes a new definition of general education, similar to the current reform, as the learning of "aptitudes and virtues" concerning speaking, and how to think and read. For Oakeshott, these aptitudes cannot be the "subject" of learning. Capacities can be "acquired" in higher education but they are not the proper subject of education nor should education be judged in terms of them.[52]

Oakeshott criticizes education and higher education reform for imposing what he calls the "plausible ethic of productivity" on the engagement of learning. For Oakeshott, in this ethic, education is valued primarily for the "extrinsic" good of production rather than the intrinsic value of cultural inheritance. He lists what counts as an extrinsic purpose and so is beyond the scope of a university: "with training for a profession, with learning the tricks of a trade, with preparation for future particular service in society or with the acquisition of a kind of moral and intellectual outfit to see him through life." Oakeshott denies that education has value for the "power it might bring." We see that Oakeshott rejects not only universities as a vehicle for economic development, but also as a means to encourage critical thinking, "civic engagement," or the left-wing view that students must learn how to be engaged critics of the status-quo.

Oakeshott uses a very similar language found in post-structuralism, namely how a focus on skill development redefines the education as an investment, increasing the social value of the individual. Oakeshott writes of a higher education report in 1963 that it,

> assimilates them [universities] into a system of so called "higher education," understood as an investment in learning who have acquired certain qualifications, designed to equip them with specially complicated skills and versatilities increasingly required if the nation is to satisfy "the aims of economic growth" and "to compete successfully with other highly developed countries in an era of rapid technological and social advance."[53]

For Oakeshott, learning should not be understood as a "socialization" because that submits the individual to a variety of social norms, including the ethic of productivity. The ethic of productivity informs the development of what it means to be a person.

Conclusion

Coalitions between left and right are not uncommon in everyday politics. Congressional liberals and conservatives attack National Security Agency

---

[51] Ibid., 94.

[52] Michael Oakeshott, "A Place of Learning," in *The Voice of Liberal Learning*, p. 32.

[53] Michael Oakeshott, "Education: The Engagement and Its Frustration," in *The Voice of Liberal Learning*, p. 90.

intelligence gathering and drone strikes. Many pieces of legislation have been defeated by this coalition, as liberals view a bill as too much, and conservatives as not enough. Indeed, in the current education debate, conservatives and liberals oppose the Common Core requirements for public schools.

Between Oakeshott and post-structuralists we see a common enemy again in the discourse of public higher education reform: productivity. For both, productivity is a delusion, a manifestation of another idea of power. For Oakeshott and the post-structuralist left, power and productivity most be limited. Power, the pursuit of control and use, can turn against the agent. In seeking power and the productive use of things, I become an object of these processes. I subject myself to uses; I must become, without limit, productive.

Paul Franco suggests a problem for Oakeshott (and so also post-structuralism) lies in whether there is any role in higher education for "any salutary influence on the world."[54] The answer lies, I think, not in any absolute prohibition on instrumental considerations in higher education, but the framing of the meaning of public universities in terms of those ideas, which thereby adds to the construction of a self oriented to productivity and making itself productive.

Nikolas Rose sees Foucault's aesthetics of the self as an "invitation to creativity and experimentation" of a "certain 'vitalism,'" the spirit of life itself, a spirit that can never be reduced to any category of meaning or desired outcome. Life overflows every limit.[55] Reforms of higher education deaden this vitalism, reducing the abundance of higher education, something profoundly valuable in itself, to a calculation of outcomes and budgets. My analysis has aimed to illuminate two perspectives, sometimes discordant, that unite against the misevaluation of education and its distorted view of the human person.

---

[54] Franco, "Un Debut dans la Vie Humanine," p. 187.
[55] Rose, *Powers of Freedom*, pp. 282–283.

Resisting the Exploitation of Contingent Faculty Labor in the Neoliberal University: The Challenge of Building Solidarity between Tenured and Non-Tenured Faculty

Joseph M. Schwartz
Temple University, USA

Abstract *This article explores why tenured faculty, particularly at major public and private research universities, often have failed to engage in collective resistance to the rise of the neoliberal university and the exploitation of "casualized" academic labor. Thirty years of steady federal and state cuts in the funding of higher education have led to the quasi-privatization of public higher education, with both public and private universities viewing themselves as corporate entities that must maximize student tuition and corporate and philanthropic revenues while minimizing costs. This has led to a massive increase in the number of exploited contingent faculty whose precarious working conditions are akin to those of low-wage, temporary workers in the rest of the economy. This article explores various reasons behind the failure of most tenured faculty—particularly the eighty percent not in faculty unions—to engage in overt, sustained protest at the radical expansion in casualized faculty labor. The article also examines the rise of professional administrators as the new governing class of neoliberal universities which compete for "student customers" on the basis of amenities and "student life" rather than on the basis of educational quality. These administrators' drive for "measurable metrics" has contributed to an increase in self-interested behavior on the part of a tenured faculty who are increasingly rewarded on the basis of "research productivity." While in the short run such a retreat from public life by tenured faculty may be rational, in the long run such behavior threatens the future existence of tenure, except in the most prestigious and well-endowed of private and public institutions. Thus those remaining tenured faculty committed to higher education providing a quality intellectual experience for all students must work politically to ensure that all faculty have humane and secure working conditions and manageable teaching loads. In short, tenured faculty committed to a future for democratic public education must take up the challenge of building solidarity across faculty rank and status.*

Introduction: Does "Rankism" Exist Between Tenured and Non-Tenured Faculty?

This article explores possible reasons that tenured faculty who have relative job security and some political voice within institutions of higher education, particularly at the most prestigious research universities, have failed to engage in large-scale collective resistance to the rise of the neoliberal university. The neoliberal state at all levels from the late 1970s onwards systematically decreased funding for public higher education and basic scientific research and shifted student aid from grants to loans. At the same time, both public and private universities came to conceive of

80

themselves as corporate entities that aim to maximize student tuition revenue and corporate and philanthropic contributions while decreasing operating costs.

Tenured faculty—who themselves frequently feel overworked and under-valued in terms of monetary reward and social status—too often have accepted this situation as a political given and failed to engage in sustained political protest against cuts in state funding. (This is less true of union activists in mid-level state institutions. However, few "flagship" Research I public universities are union-ized.) This resignation may reflect a failure of the wider political public to challenge the neoliberal erosion of higher education as a public good. But the decline of Marxist and other forms of left-wing social science since the 1980s, combined with a greater emphasis on "discourse"-driven forms of inquiry in the humanities and social sciences, may also have contributed to the failure of many tenured faculty to comprehend fully the transformation of the political economy of higher education. This may be part of the reason why too few tenured faculty explain to the public—or even their students—the material ways in which forty years of neoliberal capitalist governance has transformed the conditions of academic labor—and debases the quality of students' educational experience.[1]

In addition, the huge gulf between the working conditions of faculty on the tenure track as compared to those of contingent faculty itself poses a barrier to constructing solidarity across faculty status. Some tenured faculty at top-tier public institutions are only now beginning to consider unionization—previously an effort confined to urban commuter universities, state colleges, and community colleges. Moreover, tenured faculty have often been ambivalent about efforts of graduate students to organize—claiming it threatens the mentoring relationship between faculty and students—and indifferent to the efforts of adjuncts and non-tenure-track faculty to unionize.[2]

A brief perusal of blogs associated with the major organizations fighting for the right of contingent faculty, such as Adjunct Action and the Coalition of Contingent Academic Labor (COCAL) provides evidence that many non-tenure-track faculty and adjuncts believe that tenured faculty show little concern for their needs. The opinions expressed in hundreds of responses to the post "Adjuncts! What Should we Talk About?" in the education blog "Pan Kisses Kafka" demonstrates fairly widespread mistrust among non-tenured faculty of their tenured colleagues:

> (How) do we appeal to those in the tenure track? Do we favor a unified approach with the tenured faculty? If so, how do we get them to help us—or even to care about us as scholars and teachers (enough, for example, so that they do not attempt to discount our point of view by sneeringly referring to us as "occasional" college professors, ahem.) OR, do we say fuck it about them lifeboaters, and assume that when their jobs all get swallowed up by Financial Exigency in a few years, they'll join us without our having to kiss their asses.[3]

---

[1] On the nature of the neoliberal university, see Henry A. Giroux, *Neoliberalism's War On Higher Education* (New York: Haymarket, 2014); Nancy Folbre, *Saving State U: Fixing Public Higher Education* (New York: New Press, 2010); and Dan Clawson and Max Page, *The Future of Higher Education* (New York: Routledge, 2011).

[2] For tenured faculty concerns that adjunct unionization might erode tenured faculty control over faculty appointments and university governance, see "Union Efforts for Adjuncts Meet Resistance in Faculty Ranks," *The Chronicle of Higher Education*, April 18, 2014, pp. A23.

[3] See <http://pankisseskafka.com/2014/06/22/adjuncts-what-should-we-talk about>.

Meanwhile, Keith Holler, the editor of the collection, *Equality for Contingent Faculty: Overcoming the Two-Tier System,* argues in a widely-shared recent *Salon* article, "The Wal-Mart-ization of Higher Education: How Young Professors are Getting Screwed," that "tenurism" is a new form of "rankism" that "insults the dignity of subordinates by treating them as invisible, as nobodies." He contends that non-tenured faculty must name the attitude of their tenured colleges as *"tenurism"*. Like racism, which categorizes people by their race, and sexism, which categories people by their sex, tenurism categorizes people by their tenure status and makes the false assumption that tenure (or the lack of it) somehow defines the quality of the professor."[4]

Certainly, many tenured professors would take issue with these descriptions and some do make concerted efforts to ameliorate the conditions of non-tenured labor. But many of the forty-seven non-tenure-track faculty and forty adjuncts whom I supervise as director of a two-term "Great Books" sequence required of all undergraduates at Temple University tell me Temple tenured faculty often express attitudes toward contingent labor that confirm Holler's and "Pam Kisses Kafka's" suspicions.

One could argue that tenured faculty have always believed in the myth of meritocracy; even Weber critiqued this attitude, emphasizing instead the role "chance" and "social connections" played in academic careers.[5] My own evidence is admittedly impressionistic, as there are few empirical studies on the relationships between tenured and contingent academic labor. (We await the definitive peer-reviewed ethnographic and survey investigation, and we may be waiting a long time. Are funding agencies interested in such research, and would tenure-track faculty believe this to be a topic that would pave the road to tenure and promotion?) Nevertheless, many adjuncts and non-tenure-track faculty express the belief that not only tenured faculty, but also administrators—the persons who control the purse strings—think that the dwindling tenure class "merit" their better working conditions.[6] This attitude serves as a barrier to building political solidarity across ranks; it also runs counter to all the sociological research that demonstrates how allegedly "meritocratic" market competition too often reproduces initial class inequalities.[7]

---

[4] See Keith Hoeller, "The Wal-Mart-ization of Higher Education: How Young Professors Are Getting Screwed," *Salon,* February 16, 2014, <http://www.salon.com/2014/02/16/the_wal_mart_ization_of_higher_education_how_young_professors_are_getting_screwed>, as excerpted from the introduction to Keither Holler (ed.), *Equality for Contingent Faculty: Overcoming the Two-Tier System* (Nashville, TN: Vanderbilt University Press, 2014).

[5] See Max Weber, "Science as a Vocation," in Hans Gerth and C. Wright Mills (eds), *From Max Weber: Essays in Sociology* (New York: Oxford University Press, 1958), pp. 129–132.

[6] For a detailed account of some administrators' attitudes toward adjuncts see Rachael Riederer, "The Teaching Class," *Guernica: A Magazine of Art and Politics,* July 16, 2014, <http://www.guernicamag.com/features/the-teaching-class>.

[7] On the reproduction of class and of parental social and educational capital within the higher education system (and K-12), see Ann L. Mullen, *Degrees of Inequality: Culture, Class and Gender in American Higher Education* (Baltimore, MD: Johns Hopkins University Press, 2011). Even left wing tenured social scientists rarely admit that their class pedigree may often have as much or more to do with their academic success than their alleged innate intelligence or work ethic. Social science studies such as the one cited above show that where one goes to graduate school strongly affects one's job market prospects. And where one goes to graduate school is heavily determined by where one went as an undergraduate. And one's undergraduate pedigree is heavily determined by one's parental class background, as eighty percent of students at highly select institutions come from the top quintile of the family income distribution. That is, the class and racial patterns of recruitment into top graduate programs are partly set (not totally, of course!) before a child is born.

Furthermore, the voices of tenured faculty who defend the concept of a democratic university and of higher education as a social right have been weakened by the structure of a neoliberal university that competes for and "serves" student "customers." This has led to an inexorable growth in university administrators and a severe weakening of faculty influence. Meanwhile, the material incentive structure in institutions of higher learning, including those trying to rise in the rankings, has so shifted toward research that many tenured faculty try to keep participation in service and university governance to a minimum. This dynamic only further empowers the professional administrators.

The privatization of the neoliberal university has also engendered increasingly self-oriented behavior by tenured faculty, as promotion and increases in salary are mostly tied to "research productivity." Such behavior may be rational in the short run, but in the long run it threatens the future existence of tenured faculty at all but the best endowed elite private and public flagship institutions. It cedes the debate about the purpose of higher education to administrators, and to politicians who abjure the humanistic and critical aspect of university culture for more instrumental concerns with enhancing students' long-run earnings potential. These same ruling forces have scant interest in fighting the exploitation of casualized faculty and graduate assistant labor that erodes the quality of undergraduate education. Finally, in terms of inter-generational justice, unless tenured faculty struggle to reverse neoliberal cuts in higher education funding, there will be few, if any, tenure-track jobs for their graduate students.

The Political Economy of Neoliberal Higher Education and the Social Construction of the Academic Labor Market

Most of the political resistance to the state's defunding of higher education has come from students resisting tuition hikes and recent graduates protesting the rising student debt burden. Indeed, both groups formed a large part of the constituency behind the Occupy Wall Street protests.[8] Contingent faculty—both adjuncts and non-tenurable lecturers—and graduate teaching assistants are increasingly involved in unionization efforts aimed at improving their oppressive work conditions. But with the exception of some tenured faculty union activists, why have tenured faculty not, even at state institutions of higher education, been at the forefront of resistance to the neoliberal defunding of state higher education?

Some might claim that tenured faculty only care about their own narrow interests. But this "I've got mine Jack, screw you," cynical interpretation ignores

---

[8] Occupy Wall Street and other "flash protests" against neoliberalism in Greece, Turkey, Spain, the Middle East, and elsewhere have drawn their participants disproportionately from under-and-unemployed recent university graduates. These protests often have not been sustainable because there does not yet exist a majoritarian Left that can govern and reverse neoliberal policies. A revived governing Left would have to build cooperation among states on at least a regional, if not international, scale. For example, unless the Left and working class of northern Europe reject the bi-partisan social democratic and conservative embrace of austerity policies, there can be little hope for reversing neoliberal austerity in southern Europe. For the nature of "flash protest" movements against neo-liberalism, see David Plotke, "Occupy Wall Street, Flash Movements and American Politics," *Dissent* (online), August 12, 2012, <http://www.dissentmagazine.org/online_articles/occupy-wall-street-flash-movements-and-american-politics>.

how the neoliberal transformation of the university has negatively affected the quality of tenured faculty life, except perhaps at the most well-endowed private institutions. For example, in the wake of state budget cuts and shifts in university expenditure from instruction to administration, departments could hire fewer tenure-track colleagues and increasingly relied upon exploiting adjuncts and non-tenure-track faculty to teach undergraduates. And faculty at all levels of the state higher education system in California and elsewhere during the first decade of the twenty-first century suffered years of forced "furloughs" and stagnant wages.

Perhaps some faculty at institutions that avoided declines in faculty incomes did not care about the quality of their department or of the intellectual experience of their undergraduates. More likely, some politically aware faculty felt resistance was relatively futile, while apolitical faculty did not comprehend the larger context of the neoliberal attack on higher education. Or if they did, these cuts seemed irreversible given bi-partisan support for tax and spending cuts. Too often faculty activists were reduced to fighting against further state cuts, rather than working to restore public education to the status of a well-funded public good.

One might also make the case that the decline in the status of left-wing political economy and Marxist-influenced scholarship from the early 1980s onwards weakened the ability of the tenured faculty, overall, to comprehend the neoliberal gutting of the university. As Terry Eagleton in *After Theory* argued, studying the politics of class and economic distribution came to be considered intellectually passé with the rise of neoliberal hegemony and the decline of the Left from Thatcher and Reagan onwards.[9] In addition, a brief sociology of knowledge may help explain why even some self-defined "radical" or "critical" academics have trouble comprehending the political economy of higher education. The economics profession is dominated by those who believe in the privatization of public goods; political science consigns most radical study of the politics of public policy and the nature of the American state to the niche specialty of American political development; and radical sociologists and anthropologists over the past thirty years are more likely to study the "micro" forms of resistance to the "norming" of race, gender, and sexuality than the nature of the neoliberal state in advanced post-industrial societies. (Scholars are now returning to such subject matter given the persistence of the Great Recession.)

Furthermore, contemporary "radical" sensibilities among scholars in the humanities and interpretive social sciences tend toward subverting ontologically "rational" enlightenment conceptions of the self and "normalcy." This has produced a healthy suspicion as to how dominant discourses and practices constitute the self in masculinist, heteronormative, and Eurocentric manners. But it also has been accompanied by a decline in the study of class and "macro" state structures, the predominant forces behind the corporate elites' assault on the social sector, including the public university system.[10] If one thinks these trends have had no influence on wider public opinion, just think of how many students have solid "liberal" attitudes against individual discrimination on the basis of

---

[9] See Terry Eagleton, *After Theory* (New York: Basic Books, 2004).

[10] For a more extensive treatment of why social class has receded as a category central to discussion among "progressives," including students, see Joseph M. Schwartz, "A Peculiar Blind Spot: Why Did Radical Political Theory Ignore the Rampant Rise in Inequality Over the Past Thirty Years," *New Political Science: A Journal of Politics and Culture* 35:3 (2013), pp. 389–402.

race, gender, and sexuality, but who cannot explain the structural nature of class domination in the United States —or for that matter how institutional racism and sexism reproduces itself.

Thus, one could well argue that many tenured faculty, even those who call themselves "progressive," could benefit from a short primer on the political and economic transformation of late capitalism that engendered the proletarianization of academic labor. The past twenty years has witnessed a twenty-six percent decline in the real per capita state funding per student who attends public higher education institutions. This decrease is the driving force behind the casualization of academic labor, the massive rise in the real cost of tuition, and the growing indebtedness of college graduates.[11]

This same period has seen the post-World War II public university transformed from an institution of social market capitalism to a neoliberal semi-privatized corporate entity. Not that the post-World War II university should be idealized. The GI Bill provided upward social mobility to the white male ethnic working class, in response to the sacrifices they had made in World War II and also due to elite fears of post-war labor militancy. People of color and women, however, did not benefit from this crucial extension of educational opportunity. Only struggles by the women's and civil rights movements would open the doors of the academy to a wider range of students beginning in the 1960s.

Nevertheless, during the exceptional period of 1947–1973, corporations and the affluent tolerated higher rates of taxation and more generous funding of higher education and basic scientific research because of Cold War scientific, military, and economic competition. And opportunities for women, people of color, and working-class individuals to attend college radically expanded during the era now known as "the great compression." A less financialized and more nationally integrated economy also meant that American ruling elites took a primary concern in the well-being of the US economy. Thus, from 1947–1973, public funding for higher education grew tremendously, and college graduation rates rose from four percent of the adult population in the pre-World War II era to over twenty-five percent in the baby boom cohort.[12]

Yet beginning in the mid-1980s, graduation rates for the cohort of twenty-five to thirty-four-year-olds began to stagnate, in part because the real cost of tuition from the late 1970s onwards rose 2.3 percent a year faster than the overall rate of inflation. Both the slowdown in college graduation rates and the rise in the real cost of college resulted from a systematic decline in the tax base for state and federal government and cuts in state funding for higher education. In addition, the upwardly redistributive Reagan and the George W. Bush tax cuts each took 2.1 percent of gross domestic product (GDP) out of the federal coffers, which meant a total of 4.2 percent GDP less was available to spend on public goods, or eight-hundred billion in today's dollars.[13]

---

[11] See Suzanne Mettler, "Equalizers No More: Politics Thwart the College's Role in Upward Mobility," *The Chronicle Review*, March 7, 2014, pp. B7–B10.

[12] On the role of the GI Bill in providing opportunities for upward mobility for the white working class (and of the role of the civil rights and women's movement in expanding those opportunities more broadly), see Ira Katznelson, *When Affirmative Action was White: An Untold History of Racial Inequality in the United States* (New York: W.W. Norton, 2006).

[13] For the effects of Reagan and George W. Bush's 2001–2006 tax cuts in reducing federal tax revenue by close to 2.1 percent of GDP each, see The Tax Policy Center, "The Tax Policy

As the federal tax structure became more regressive, so did that of the states. And with increasing state expenditure on Medicaid (rising from seven percent of state budgets in the 1970s to close to twenty percent today) and on mass incarceration, state funding for higher education flattened out, with major decreases occurring in every recession from 1981–1982 onwards. To put these changes in perspective: in 1972 federal and state expenditure on higher education (including basic research) constituted 7.2 percent of combined federal and state budgets; today federal and state funding of higher education makes up only 4.9 percent of total federal and state expenditure. State expenditure on higher education from the 1970s until today fell from nearly eight percent of state budgetary expenditure to only four percent in 2010.[14] In addition, while state funding equaled over half of public college and university operating costs in 1979, today state funding only constitutes twenty-seven percent of state higher education operating costs, with tuition revenue now providing forty-four percent of total costs for higher education.[15]

This drop in state funding was accompanied by steady cuts in the real value of Pell Grants, and a shift in federal financial aid from sixty percent grants in the 1980s to close to two-thirds loans today. In the 1970s Pell Grants covered eighty percent of the average state institution's tuition and room and board costs; today it covers only thirty percent of average total college costs per student at public institutions. This is one of the major causes of the massive rise in student indebtedness.[16]

These cuts in public funding for higher education (compounded by slashes in federal funding of basic sciences from the George W. Bush Jr. administration onwards) meant that tuition at state institutions has risen four-fold in real terms since the mid-1970s.[17] State tuition is the floor underneath private tuition.[18] And

---

Footnote 13 continued

Briefing Book," 2012, especially pp. 13–17. Also see, "The Bush Tax Cuts: How Do They Compare to the Reagan Tax Cuts?," <http://www.taxpolicycenter.org/upload/Background/I-11thru1-14TheBushTaxCuts.final.pdf>.

[14] See Robert Hiltonsmith and Tamara Draut, *Demos*, "The Great Cost Shift Continues: State Higher Education Funding After the Great Recession," March, 2014, <http://www.demos.org/publication/great-cost-shift-continues-state-higher-education-funding-after-recession>. For the most comprehensive treatment of the decline over the past thirty years of public university education as a means for social mobility, see Suzanne Mettler, *Degrees of Inequality: How the Politics of Higher Education Sabotaged the American Dream* (New York: Basic Books, 2014). On the decline in the real value of per capita state funding for higher education students, see especially Mettler, pp. 118–131.

[15] For the increase in tuition as a percentage of funding of total public higher education costs, see State Higher Education Officials, "State Higher Education Finance, FY 2012," especially p. 29, <http://www.sheeo.org/sites/default/files/publications/SHEF-FY12.pdf>.

[16] On the precipitous decline in the real value of Pell Grants compared to tuition and room and board fees see Tyler Kingkade, "Pell Grants Cover Smallest Proportion of College Costs in History," *Huffington Post*, August 29, 2012, < http://www.huffingtonpost.com/2012/08/27/pell-grants-college-costs_n_1835081.html>.

[17] See "Average Rates of Growth in College Education," *Trends in Higher Education*, The College Board, <http://trends.collegeboard.org/college-pricing/figures-tables/average-rates-growth-tuition-and-fees-over-time>.

[18] See Phil Oliff, Vincent Palacios, Ingrid Johnson, and Michael Leachman, "Recent Deep State Higher Education Cuts May Harm Students and the Economy for Years to Come," *Center for Budget and Policy Priorities*, July 2013, <http://www.cbpp.org/cms/?fa=view&id = 3927 > .

with cuts in federal grants and subsidized loans, students increasingly fund their higher education through taking on debt, with nearly forty percent of newly issued debt being unsubsidized debt at market rate interest. Sixty-seven percent of recent college graduates have student loan obligations, with the average student in the twenty-five to thirty-four age cohort owing twenty-seven thousand dollars in student debt.[19] Meanwhile, this de-socialization of the costs of higher education is a windfall for neoliberal capitalists in two ways: it lowers their tax rates, and enables the financial sector to profit from the rapid rise in student indebtedness.

Today, most academic "leaders" and even the Obama administration embrace the neoliberal ideology of the "degree as a personal investment." Higher education administrators encourage students to "invest" in a college education (often via burdensome indebtedness) in order to improve their post-graduate labor market position. But this neoliberal "invest in yourself" ideology is increasingly undercut by a decline in the rate of return for the college degree. The college degree increasingly serves as the new high school diploma, a sign that a graduate would be a reliable employee in a low-level, often dead-end management position in the retail sector or hotel and restaurant industry. As economic rewards now go disproportionately to the rentier class of CEOs, financiers, and hedge fund managers, the earnings of younger college educated adults have been largely flat since 2000. Only five percent of current jobs demand high-level STEM (science, technology, engineering, and mathematics) degrees; most middle-strata jobs are either in the underpaid state or care-giving sector, or are low-level management jobs that involve supervising underpaid non-college graduates. The "value added" of the college degree is now mostly due to the steady, secular drop in the earnings power of non-college educated adults, who even in the twenty-five to thirty-four generation still make up sixty percent of the labor force. Their life prospects, and those of their children, are not even addressed in the neoliberal model of "purchase an education and the good jobs will come."[20]

---

[19] On the student debt crisis, see Rohit Chopra, "Student Debt Swells, Federal Loans Now Top a Trillion," *Consumer Financial Protection Bureau*, July 17, 2013, <http://www.consumerfinance.gov/newsroom/student-debt-swells-federal-loans-now-top-a-trillion/>.

[20] For a study of the decline in middle-class jobs as a percentage of a labor force increasingly polarized between a growing, but small number of "good jobs" and a proliferation of "low wage" jobs, see John Schmitt and Janelle Jones, "Where Have All the Good Jobs Gone?" Center for Economic and Policy Research, June 2012, <http://www.cepr.net/documents/publications/good-jobs-2012-07.pdf>. For evidence that the decline in the growth of "good jobs" is more due to neoliberal political policies (changes in tax policy, deregulation, and anti-union government policies) rather than inexorable technological changes (known as the "Skills Based Technological Change" theory of wage polarization), see Lawrence Mishel, Heidi Shierholz, and John Schmitt, "Don't Blame the Robots," Working Paper, Economic Policy Institute and Center for Economic and Policy Research, November 19, 2013, <http://s1.epi.org/files/2013/technology-inequality-dont-blame-the-robots.pdf>. For a comprehensive summary of the research on the stagnation of incomes of recent college graduates and on the scarce nature of high-wage STEM jobs, see Colin Gordon, "The Computer Did It: Technology and Inequality," *Dissent* (Spring 2014), pp. 73–76.

The "Naturalization" of the Neoliberal Academic Labor Market as an Irreversible Trend

Despite the political causes of the deteriorating conditions facing academic labor, many tenured faculty naturalize the declining academic job market as a permanent "fact of life." That is, they do not believe that a politically caused phenomenon could be politically reversed by a shift in political power and state taxation and budgetary policies. In fact, the academic job market is not "stagnant" at all; rather, its growth is robust, but accompanied by a precipitous decline in the percentage of "good jobs" in the growing higher education teaching labor force. These trends are similar to the growth of "temporary" and "casualized" jobs in the neoliberal labor market overall. The demand for academic labor is greater than ever, as a higher percentage of high school students go on to attend institutions of higher education than ever before. Seventy percent of high school graduates will enroll at some form of higher education institution; but less than half of them, or thirty-five percent, will receive four-year degrees. The number of students in four-year institutions has risen from ten million in 1970 to over twenty-one million today.[21] Meanwhile, the size of the overall higher education faculty is nearly seventy percent larger than it was thirty years ago. At close to 1.5 million individuals, there are more university faculty today than ever before; but only thirty percent of them have tenured jobs or positions eligible for tenure, versus seventy percent in the early 1970s (although even the total number of tenured and tenure-jobs has grown twenty-three percent since 1976).[22]

In other words, despite most tenured faculty believing that the academic job market is shrinking, there has been a significant increase over the past thirty years in the number of college and university teaching jobs held by PhDs. But this trend has been accompanied by a precipitous decline in the percentage of those jobs that come with non-exploitative remuneration, good benefits, and decent working conditions. Indeed, the reluctance of second-tier research universities to cut back on the size of their PhD programs is one sure sign of the strong demand for higher education teaching labor; overworked graduate teaching assistants are a huge source of cheap labor at such institutions, often teaching courses as the instructor of record.

So what is the real story? The basic statistics reveal the stark contours of the casualization of the neoliberal academic labor market. According to a chart in the April 18, 2014 issue of *The Chronicle of Higher Education*, in 1976 there were 353,681 full-time tenured or tenure-track faculty at institutions of higher learning, including community colleges. In 2011 there were 436,293, a gain of twenty-three percent. In 1976, 160,086 graduate students served as teaching assistants or instructors of record. By 2011 that number had grown to 358,743 for a gain of one-hundred and twenty-three percent, despite the crisis in the tenure-track job market. In 1976, there were 80,883 full-time non-tenure-track faculty; in 2011: 233,368, for a gain of two-hundred and fifty-nine percent. Part-time faculty (adjuncts) grew at an even higher rate, from 199,139 in 1976 to 786,071 in 2011, an increase of two-hundred and eighty-six percent!

---

[21] For historic trends in the number of students enrolled in post-secondary institutions, see National Center for Education Statistics, "Fast Facts" (2013), <http://nces.ed.gov/FastFacts/display.asp?id=372>.

[22] See again, National Center for Education Statistics, "Employees in Post-Secondary Institutions, Fall 2011," p. 9.

At the same time that the growth of tenure-track faculty stagnated, the number of academic administrators grew astronomically, reflecting the increasing role of marketing, student services, and advising on college campuses. Full-time executives at college campuses—top-level administrators, often making more than the best-paid full professors—grew from 97,033 in 1976 to 233,638, a growth rate of one-hundred and forty-one percent. In the college and university system as a whole, there exists one-half of a full-time senior academic administrator for every full-time tenurable faculty member. The growth in full-time non-faculty professional staff has likewise been truly astronomical, growing from 150,319 in 1976 to 704,505 in 2011. No wonder full-time faculty believe they no longer govern the academy. They do not.[23]

In sum, the growth in contingent faculty is commensurate with the overall growth in "temporary" labor under conditions of "flexible" neoliberal labor markets.[24] Under this neoliberal model, corporations avoid hiring unionized, permanent workers for whom they would have to provide greater job security, better wages and benefits, and a career ladder. Under conditions of "race-to-the-bottom" neoliberal competition, corporations compete by lowering labor costs rather than by increasing productivity and quality of output. Hence, "temporary" or "contingent" faculty engage in the same exact teaching labor as tenurable faculty, but at infinitely higher rates of exploitation.

This trend is comparable to what is happening to workers in other sectors of the US economy. In 1975 "independent contractors" and "contingent" labor represented only seven percent of the workforce; today the Census Bureau categorize twenty-five percent of the workforce as either "independent contractors" or "temporary" employees. In the American auto industry today, over forty percent of the production workers are "temporary" workers who make less than seventy percent of the wages of full-time workers and receive less than two-thirds of the benefit packages of "permanent" labor, both in unionized plants in the north and in foreign-owned non-unionized southern factories. These workers do the exact same work as the "full-time" employees with whom they work side-by-side; often these "temporary" workers can be employed for over a decade or longer. But they are far easier to layoff and cheaper to employ than their (often unionized) full-time compatriots.[25]

---

[23] For an analysis of the change in the composition of university faculty and administrators from 1976 to 2011 that draws upon Institute for Post-Secondary Education Statistics from 1976 and 2011, see the work of John W. Curtis and Saranna Thorton, "Losing Focus: The Annual Report of the Economic Status of the Profession, 2013–14," *Academe* (March–April 2014), <http://www.aaup.org/file/zreport.pdf>. The chart based on this study commissioned by the American Association of University Professors (the AAUP) can be found in the "In Brief" section of *The Chronicle of Higher Education*, April 18, 2014, p. A 23.

[24] Marc Bosquet's *How the University Works: Higher Education and the Low-Wage Nation* (New York: New York University Press, 2008) offers considerable insight into the rise of contingent academic labor as part of the growing proliferation of "precarious" and low-wage employment even among college graduates. He also provides considerable evidence that there is no shortage of teaching jobs for recent PhDs. Rather, too few of these jobs provide humane and just working conditions. See especially Chapter 6, "The Rhetoric of the Job Market and Reality of the Academic Labor System," pp. 186–209.

[25] For a good primer on the rise of "contract" and "temporary" workers in the neoliberal labor force, see Sarah Jaffe, "Temporary Insanity," *In These Times* (January 2014), pp. 18–21; and Barbara Ehrenreich and John Ehrenreich, "Death of the Middle Class Dream: The Professional-Managerial Class in Crisis," *In These Times* (January 2014), pp. 22–23.

What have been the personal and institutional consequences of this "casualization" of academic labor? Rather than understanding that their non-tenure-track colleagues—many of whom work in similar sub-fields and wrote equally good dissertations at comparable institutions—confront a constricted labor market and are horrendously underpaid for comparable teaching labor, some (certainly not all) tenured or tenure-track faculty justify their superior employment conditions by claiming that "I publish more" or "I better balance my teaching and research responsibilities." This not uncommon attitude fails to recognize that despite heavier teaching loads, many contingent faculty publish quality work, but usually not at a similar rate of output as tenurable faculty with lighter teaching loads. Likewise, too few tenure-track faculty comprehend the path-dependent nature of a dual labor market: after a few years of service in the non-tenured labor market it becomes very difficult to break into the tenure-track market, particularly when competing with fresh PhDs with publications.

The willingness of even younger cohorts of tenure and tenure-track faculty to naturalize their positions as "deserved" shows the continuing power of the myth of the meritocratic market, and its ability to mask the exploitative system of production. This all-too-frequent absence of solidarity between tenured and non-tenurable faculty lends credence to the old cocktail party joke about attitudes toward "meritocracy" in the academy: academics believe that those whose status is lower than their own "merit" that status; but anyone who has higher status than them must have obtained it through connections, powerful mentors, corruption, nepotism, or luck. Yet with an increasing number of young tenured scholars having close friends among graduate cohorts who are stuck in the casualized portion of the dual labor market, the possibilities for empathy and solidarity across faculty ranks may be increasing. Certainly, all faculty have an interest in making students and parents aware of the decline in the quality of education that overworked and underpaid instructors can offer. In my own program, which aims to teach young undergraduates how to read and write critically about primary texts of lasting import, non-tenure-track faculty teach four classes each semester of twenty-seven students each. This undoubtedly means the faculty cannot mentor students as closely as they would wish in regard to developing their students' analytic reading, and in particular, writing skills.

The Rise of the Professional Administrator and the Withdrawal of Tenured Faculty from Public University Life

Most of the trends outlined above have structural, systemic causes and are not primarily a product of "bad faith" on the part of tenured academics. But promoting concerted faculty action against the neoliberalization of higher education will require greater empathy by tenured faculty concerning the debased working conditions of most graduate students, adjuncts, and non-tenure-track faculty. (Obviously some adjuncts who are professionals teaching in professional schools may not be hyper-exploited; and perhaps the most affluent of universities pay non-tenure-track labor decent wages and benefits. Nevertheless, neither condition guarantees long-term employment or a clear career path to enhanced wages and benefits.) The labor market practices outlined above, however, are primarily due to the de facto privatization of public institutions; their heavy dependence on student tuition means college and university administrators focus inordinately on student recruitment and on the financial bottom line rather than on the quality of their institution's teaching mission, let alone with how justly the institution treats their teaching staff.

These financial imperatives have given rise to a permanent administrative class (and concomitant support staff) whose primary aim is attracting and retaining student "customers." This new professional-administrative class has little interest in promoting faculty governance; nor, more often than not, in the quality of the student educational experience. They often do care about the institution's US News and World Report ranking, but that is driven primarily by student SAT scores and the size of the institution's endowment and not by the university's treatment of its teaching faculty. Administrators at research universities also obsess about the "metric" of externally funded research dollars and departmental scores in the citation indices that drive National Academy of Sciences graduate department rankings. Meanwhile, the remaining tenured faculty have little incentive to fight for a shared voice in university governance, since university service by faculty is not rewarded monetarily; nor does being a good university citizen enhance one's status within the national academic hierarchy. In the competition for scarce tenurable positions and promotion, faculty know that research is the primary—often exclusive—metric that counts, except at smaller liberal arts institutions. (Even there, the more prestigious ones increasingly count research productivity as the predominant factor in tenure and promotion decisions.) Tenured faculty certainly have no self-interested motivation to engage in militant forms of political or union activism.[26]

Thus, tenured faculty at institutions that skew rewards toward research productivity put time into teaching and service largely out of a sense of moral duty. Many tenured professors are good citizens and devoted teachers. Still, one need not be a rational choice economist to know that the structure of incentives influences human behavior. Heightened competition for scarce tenure-track jobs has turned research-active faculty's publications into their most prized form of portable capital. And with non-faculty administrators less solicitous of faculty concerns, and "outside offers" the main way of moving one's salary, tenured faculty and their own institution's governing administrators have become less loyal to one another. Why should a tenured faculty member invest in an institution that predominantly values the professor for their research productivity, a metric largely determined by a scholarly community beyond one's own institution?[27]

---

[26] Benjamin Ginsberg examines how the shift in incentives toward research facilitates a new class of non-academic professional administrators becoming the dominant voice not just in university services and finance, but also in determining curricular matters and faculty hiring and promotion-decisions traditionally controlled by the faculty. See Benjamin Ginsberg, *The Fall of the Faculty: The Rise of the All-Administrative University and Why It Matters* (New York: Oxford University Press, 2011).

[27] For an ironic, perhaps tragic, look at how these trends play themselves out at a mid-tier public research university that aspires to move into the "Top 50" in the US News and World Report, see Gaye Tuchman, *Wannabe U: Inside the Corporate University* (Chicago, IL: University of Chicago Press, 2009).

An absence of faculty investment in university governance is understandable on the part of exploited adjuncts and non-tenurable faculty. But disinvestment in the governance of the university by tenured faculty facilitates the control of the university by professional, non-academic administrators or former academics who have gone over to the side of professional administration. Without strong faculty governance, university administrators are more likely to prioritize market metrics over educational quality. Witness how "responsibility centered management" (aka, RCM or decentralized budgeting) has become the hot administrative tool for sound economic governance of the university. According to RCM, institutional dollars should follow student enrollments. If that means the growth of undergraduate business schools and the closure of foreign language, classics, art history, or philosophy departments, so be it, because the market knows best. The idea of economically subsidizing intellectually valuable parts of the university that do not bring in external research dollars or that do not put large numbers of "fannies in the seats" is a non-market value, one alien to administrators who focus on the bottom line.

Moreover, many tenured faculty simply accept or take as a given the constrained economic environment that university administrators use to justify their inhumane labor policies, not only in regard to teaching labor, but also in the outsourcing and de-unionization of university support staff. Increasingly, janitorial, building and grounds, food service, and security staff functions are outsourced to cheaper non-union vendors. Many tenured faculty, believing that resources are scarce, worry that improvement in the conditions of other campus workers, including non-tenured faculty, might mean less reward for the tenured class—or, at least, higher teaching loads. Few, if any, tenured faculty are willing to have their teaching loads raised, say by just one course a year, even if that could help lower the teaching load of non-tenured faculty and improve the latter's wages and benefits. Of course, there is every reason for tenured faculty to suspect that administrators might not redistribute the savings in instructional costs in this manner. But what if such savings could be redistributed through contractual negotiations with a faculty union? Yet solidarity across a segmented workforce is hard to build; as of now such concrete acts of solidarity between tenured and non-tenured faculty rarely occur. (Another possible action to lessen the gap in wages and benefits between tenure-track and non-tenured labor would be for faculty to fight for a "solidaristic" wage policy. Such a policy would involve part or all of salary increases consisting of an equal dollar amount of increase for each faculty member, rather than a fixed percentage increase; percentage increases serve to increase disparity in wages. Scandinavian unions for generations used just such equal dollar value wage-increases to lessen wage disparities among workers.) My own faculty union represents both tenured and non-tenure-track faculty. Those of us in the elected leadership face constant criticism that we try to do "too much" for one or the other constituency, with that critique being largely determined by the constituency to which a member belongs.

But the conditions of both tenure and non-tenure-track faculty will only significantly improve if the cuts in public funding to higher education are politically reversed, and if universities and colleges restore power to a faculty who would place instructional quality ahead of "customer" satisfaction. Again, in the age of neoliberalism, higher education institutions compete for "student customers" based on amenities such as posh dormitories, modern work-out facilities, Greek life, and the quality of weekend parties. The increasing import of "student life" on residential campuses engenders a huge cadre of mid-level student services administrators. And with too few full-time faculty engaged in advising (what incentive is there to do so?), "professional advisers" increasingly advise students—mostly on how best to fulfill requirements rather than on how to construct a rich and coherent intellectual experience while enrolled. Academic administrative and staff positions have grown two-hundred and fifty percent over the past twenty years, while the number of faculty positions increased only thirty percent (with the total number of tenure-track positions staying basically flat).[28] As a result, the percentage of university revenue going to instruction has declined from sixty percent of total higher education operating costs in 1990 to under forty-five percent today.[29] Fewer permanent faculty with moderate teaching loads means fewer who formally and informally help shape students' intellectual, social, and career horizons.

Adding insult to injury, the extraordinary growth in well-paid professional academic administrators has played a large role in cowing the tenured faculty, as administrators often control faculty hiring and faculty salaries. Universities are increasingly ruled by professional administrators who conceive of the university as a competitive economic entity that must maximize revenue from lucrative corporate patents—hence the heavy investment in biomedical research and the search for declining federal research dollars, as well as in huge bureaucracies devoted to securing corporate and alumni contributions. Only the rare well-endowed, prestigious liberal arts colleges still market themselves as institutions where students will study in small classes with full-time scholar-teachers. The vision of a high-quality university education for students of modest means, a vision that underpinned the City University of New York system from the 1930s until the 1970s fiscal crisis, and the California state college and university system through the 1970s, has since succumbed to the economic logic of neoliberal austerity.

The Cultural Norming of the Tenured Professoriat: The CV as Portable Capital

But beyond the material incentives and structural constraints promoting a retreat of tenured faculty from university governance, many tenured faculty have been "normed" since their first days in elite graduate programs to prioritize professional productivity. Here Foucauldian micro-analysis makes good sense, as do Butlerian notions of "performative iteration." Clifford Geertz said shortly before his death that, because his early research defied conventional scholarly norms, he doubted if he would have received tenure in today's academy, because

---

[28] For two excellent summaries of the Delta Cost Project report on the precipitous growth in university administrative personnel, see Scott Carlson, "Administrator Hiring Drives 28% Boom in Higher-Ed Work Force Report Says," *The Chronicle of Higher Education*, February 5, 2014, <http://chronicle.com/article/Administrator-Hiring-Drove-28-/144519/>; and Jon Marcus, "New Analysis Shows Problematic Boom in Higher Ed Administrators," New England Center for Investigative Reporting, February 6, 2014, <http://www.huffingtonpost.com/2014/02/06/higher-ed-administrators-growth_n_4738584.html>.

[29] See Benjamin Ginsberg, "Administrators Ate My Tuition," *The Washington Monthly*, September 2011, <http://www.washingtonmonthly.com/magazine/septemberoctober_2011/features/administrators_ate_my_tuition031641.php?page=all >.

he failed to join an "existing scholarly conversation."[30] The same might even be said of such groundbreaking scholars as Barrington Moore, Frances Fox Piven, bell hooks, or Michael Walzer, none of whose work as younger scholars neatly joined a conventional "scholarly debate." The current worship of "research productivity" begins with the adage that successful job candidates must have published two refereed articles by the time they go on the job market, despite their older faculty mentors having had more time as graduate students to read broadly and to write more ambitious dissertations.

An inordinate emphasis on quantity over quality of publications continues for tenure and promotion decisions—even at many state and private liberal arts colleges. With college and university-level committees (often with administrators constituting half the membership) increasingly holding sway in tenure, promotion, and salary decisions, the quantity of output and the alleged ranking or "prestige" of publication venues determines one's academic status more than does any serious close reading and intellectual evaluation of one's actual work by scholarly peers. Few faculty today (except when serving on departmental tenure and promotion committees or doing an external tenure or promotion review) read each others' work, even within their own sub-fields. If the work is not directly related to their current research, reading it only slows down one's own rate of production. Editors of scholarly journals lament that senior faculty will rarely agree to do a book review, as it does not "count" as a refereed publication on one's CV. And it is harder for department chairs to secure well-published reviewers for tenure and promotion cases, as, again, such service does not enhance the reviewer's scholarly profile. If this is not the neoliberal disciplining of the academic subject, then what is?

Neoliberal competition for scarce tenurable jobs also norms the "productive academic subject" in other ways that run against the individual's intuitive moral sensibilities. Many faculty go to graduate school because they admire their undergraduate academic mentors. But as students they admired their professors more for their teaching and mentoring than they did for their publications. This point is not meant to engage in a right-wing derision of all academic publishing as indiscernible scrivening; nor is it to say that good research cannot inform good teaching. A self-critical interrogation of our own academic practices, however, might indicate that with teaching and student advising devalued, tenure-track and tenured faculty—particularly at the leading institutions whose norms have trickled down to "aspiring" second-tier institutions—have been "disciplined" out of serving wider community purposes. Tenured and tenure-track faculty prioritize life in the narrow silos of our relevant "research community." One must impress this audience of a few dozen scholarly gatekeepers to garner tenure, promotion, and salary increases.

At the same time, faculty who write for more general political or intellectual audiences are often subject to disdain by their more "academic" colleagues; this is another way in which the neoliberal university disciplines "academic subjects." The academy today mostly produces academics, not intellectuals; it channels

---

[30] For Clifford Geertz's musings on whether he would have received tenure in today's hyper-professional environment, see Chapter 1 of Clifford Geertz, *Available Light: Anthropological Reflections on Philosophical Topics* (Princeton, NJ: Princeton University Press, 2001).

wider intellectual interests into more narrow, niche forms of "methodologically sophisticated" inquiry. This also leads to an increasing separation between the demands of research and meeting the intellectual needs of one's students, particularly undergraduates. Many tenure-track and tenured faculty teach their current research interests; not just in graduate seminars, but even in undergraduate courses. We lament the loss of public intellectuals in the academy, but should we be surprised at their near-extinction?

What is to be Done?: Tenured Faculty's Role in the Broader Struggle for Democratic Equality

Undoubtedly some progressive tenured faculty work to resist the injustices of the neoliberal university. But for many, resistance, in a neoliberal era, seems futile. This attitude may change with contingent academic labor increasingly engaging in forms of protest and collective action akin to that of other exploited, low-wage workers. Yet even if non-tenure-track faculty, adjuncts, and graduate students succeed in gaining union recognition, their just demands will only be met if the state robustly funds higher education. In turn, opposition to regressive neoliberal tax and budgetary policies can only gain traction if more of the public comprehends the political origins of these policies and their ability to be politically reversed. Faculty, regardless of their status or disciplinary outlook, should consider teaching these realities in the classroom, as the quality of our students' education suffers because of them.

However, the political muscle to overturn the neoliberalization of higher education cannot be developed simply by moral persuasion. Ultimately, a political coalition of students, parents, and faculty must fight—via the myriad tactics of protest, lobbying, and electoral work—to reverse the neoliberal gutting of a crucial public good: education. In Chicago, Seattle, Philadelphia, and New York, coalitions of parents, teachers, and students have begun to contest the defunding and privatization of public schools central to the "education reform" agenda. Similar coalitions of students, indebted recent college graduates, parents, and faculty could be built around demands for increased public funding of higher education and in favor of public policies easing the student debt burden. And such coalitions would benefit from the leadership of tenured faculty, who can take more risks to speak out than can their non-tenured colleagues.

But such solidarity would take the political engagement of a largely depoliticized tenured professoriat. Despite the overt political organizing against the inhumane labor conditions on college campuses, too many tenured faculty accept the classical liberal adage that politics should not enter the classroom. Thus, they often fail to make students aware of the appalling working conditions that most faculty face and they do not inform students that brutal working conditions for faculty lead to sub-standard learning experiences for students. Overworked graduate instructors, adjuncts, and non-tenure-track faculty grade too many students and thus cannot comment in detail upon student work. Often these instructors do not have the time to hold office hours; many lack offices in which to hold them. They may or may not be around next year—or even next term—to respond to a student request for a letter of recommendation. This is particularly the case at the egregiously underfunded urban public universities that serve many first-generation college students. Adjuncts teach well over fifty percent of the seats taught in the CUNY system overall (including community colleges), for example.[31] This situation prevents many first-generation college students from receiving the personal faculty mentoring they often need. Students at well-financed private universities are more likely to receive such faculty mentoring even though such students predominantly hail from affluent suburbs and arrive on campus with considerably more cultural capital than students at public institutions.

Resistance to neoliberal K-12 "education reform" centers on the right of all students to a high-quality public education. This type of education can only be attained if society integrates neighborhoods, or at least schools, by race and class, or, at a minimum, drastically increases funding for inner-city schools so they can serve as year-round comprehensive community centers. A fight for democratic K-12 public education could well be linked to the struggle to increase public funding for higher education, particularly for public institutions that serve a disproportionate number of first-generation college students. And tenured faculty could enhance such a public conversation by starting a national dialogue about the purposes of the university in a democratic society.

We should remember that John Dewey helped found the American Association of University Professors in 1915, during a previous Gilded Age, and explicitly called upon faculty to unionize. To reverse the neoliberal policies outlined in this article, progressive faculty must reintroduce into the academy the belief that normative and political critique cannot be separated from the academic endeavor of comprehending society. "Dispassionate" social science, in the classic Weberian sense, fails to interrogate the very social tendencies that defund the university and engender a casualized and contingent academic labor force. Only a reversal of broader neoliberal policies of regressive taxation, deregulation, and defunding of public goods can forestall the steady increase in the casualization of teaching labor in higher education.

Nearly forty years of bi-partisan neoliberal policies of deregulation, regressive tax cuts, defunding of public goods, and attacks on unions have led to a vastly inegalitarian society and labor market. Reversing these trends will not only necessitate increasing the power of working people through unionization efforts, but also through political efforts to raise the minimum wage and restore a legal right to organize. And creating a more democratic and just US will also involve the revitalization of those public goods essential to the fulfillment of each individual's human potential (that is, high-quality, publicly financed health care, childcare, education, housing, and income security). Democratic social movements, such as the immigrant rights' movement and the emerging low-wage justice movement, can reintroduce into American politics the radical democratic value of equality of standing. This democratic concept holds that regardless of one's place in the labor market (or that of one's parents), all members of society—and their dependents— should have equal access to those goods that enable individuals to enjoy a decent material existence, develop their human potential, and participate in civic life. In addition, every member of society must have democratic voice in the institutions that govern their daily lives, be they the school, the community, or the

---

[31] On the status of adjunct faculty within the CUNY system see The CUNY Adjunct Project, <http://cunyadjunctproject.org/>.

workplace. These traditional radical democratic values stand in stark contrast to the classic liberal conception of market-based equality of opportunity.[32]

The contemporary "educational reform" discourse—and its higher education version of the college degree as an instrument for upward economic mobility—illustrate how many liberals erroneously equate marketplace conceptions of equality of opportunity with a democratic conception of equality of standing. Even if we had a more "meritocratic" educational system, student outcomes would still tend to reproduce the educational and social capital of parents. Should only winners in this "meritocratic" marketplace race of life lead fulfilling lives and have decent life opportunities for their children? Even if there need be market incentives for individuals to pursue dangerous jobs or professions that demand lengthy training, all members of a democratic society should have the ability to develop the fullness of their human capabilities.[33]

For several decades now the right has taken seriously the role of higher education in generating public ideas. The corporate community and their think tanks fund and "discipline" business schools and economic departments to promote "free market" ideology. Such market fundamentalism has had disastrous effects on economic policy both before and during the Great Recession. Progressive faculty in the humanities and soft social sciences, in contrast, have done a fairly good job of popularizing among their students concepts of tolerance and diversity, and even the concept of "transgression" against repressive sexual and cultural norms. We have done a poorer job of explaining how rampant social inequality stunts the lives of millions of our fellow human beings. Despite the right's claim that Marxists abound in the academy, the concept of class is fairly alien to most college classrooms. Students know why corporate boardrooms should be more diverse; but few, however, question the concept of corporate rule itself.

An enhanced understanding of the role of class and power in American society should remind us that a simple revisiting of traditional radical democratic values will not suffice to transform the neoliberal university. Only the power of numbers can overcome the power of capital. Absent the revival of a democratic labor movement it is hard to imagine how corporate control of politics can be reversed. But a democratic labor movement can only grow in the context of broader insurgencies for democracy, such as the immigrant rights' movement. If university employees can integrate their fight for a democratic university into a broader struggle for social rights, then there may be a future for a democratic university that does not exploit its workforce. But if faculty fail to fight against neoliberal capitalism, then tenure may soon go the way of the buffalo and of unionized auto workers—once there were many, now there are few.

---

[32] For the classic exposition of the concept of "equality of standing" see R.H. Tawney, *Equality* (London, UK: G. Allen and Unwin, 1931).

[33] The concept of equality of standing or democratic equality advanced here is, in some ways, a more political and policy-oriented version of Amartya Sen's and Martha Nussbaum's human capabilities approach to theorizing about justice. See Amartya Sen, *Development as Freedom* (New York: Oxford University Press, 1999); and Martha Nussbaum, *Creating Capabilities: The Human Development Approach* (Cambridge, MA: Harvard University Press, 2011).

Contingent Academic Labor Against Neoliberalism

Vincent Tirelli
Manhattan College, USA

Abstract   *If the fulfillment of American democracy includes a system of higher education that provides equal means of access, opportunity and accommodation for all social classes in society, then we need to better understand how the vastly enlarged use of contingent academic labor plays a role in its formation. This essay argues that although the expansion of higher education has been significant over the past forty years or so, there are hidden disparities within it that hinder the development of equality. The extensive use of contingent academic labor, although allowing for more affordable growth of higher education in the short run, has contributed to a higher education system that is more highly managed via an expanded administrative apparatus and focused more toward a corporate-centered agenda. It also facilitates higher education's reproductive role with regard to social class stratification. This essay presents a brief analysis of these dynamics and offers a review of some of the significant organizing activities that have taken place to counter these trends.*

Introduction

The idea that there is a link between education and democracy has long been established in American political thought, but it is an idea that has had a turbulent history. Since the age of the land-grant colleges established in the late nineteenth century known as "democracy's colleges," capitalist elites have tried to shape the system of higher education to fit their own ends, and they have been met with resistance.[1] In the 1960s, students and faculty famously fought against injustice and for a more open and democratic system of higher education. The campus has been an important site of contention: the free speech movement at Berkeley, the activities of the Students for a Democratic Society, the anti-war movement, and the fight for open admissions at the City University of New York (CUNY) and elsewhere were among the most important efforts that took place. In the decades since, social justice movements have continued to capture the imagination of students, whether it was the anti-apartheid movement, the fight against sweatshops, or the fight against the cuts to the public university and against rising tuition. The political fervor sometimes alights, but mostly it seems that it is impatiently simmering beneath the surface.

These struggles, and the battle over higher education itself, are best understood within the context of broader social class conflicts and the changing

---

[1] Clyde W. Barrow, *Universities and the Capitalist State: Corporate Liberalism and the Reconstruction of American Higher Education, 1894–1928* (Madison, WI: University of Wisconsin Press, 1990).

structure of capitalism. The assault on the welfare state which began, more or less, with the New York City fiscal crisis in the 1970s, and intensified with the Reagan revolution, entailed cuts in government spending affecting social programs, the lowering of taxes on the wealthy and, in higher education, the transferring of costs onto the student body and the continual assault on professors' salaries, reinforced by the creation of a lower tier of academic labor. The shape of higher education that was forged in this era fit in squarely with the neoliberal regime that would soon emerge on the national and international scene. During the current period there has been a deepening of the assault on unions and public sector workers by elites, embodied by the events that erupted in Wisconsin in 2013. These events have been representative of the broader efforts to diminish the bargaining power of public sector employees, and they provide a context, in part, for understanding the struggles that are taking place in higher education today.

Higher education has been recast through various means that have affected funding, technology, and curriculum, and these changes have brought the system more into line with a corporate business model rather than with an institution that seeks to develop a critical and democratic citizenry. It has become an entity that is increasingly managed from the top, more privatized, and more stratified. Publishers seeking new profit centers have influenced it, selling pre-scripted courses with test banks that harried adjuncts are often encouraged to use. These trends promote the deskilling of academic labor and deprive students of real interactive instruction that addresses their needs. Among the less visible changes that have taken place to undermine the democratic possibilities in higher education is the transformation of the faculty itself.

The use of temporary workers with diminished rights and protections has grown in higher education, as it has in other sectors of the economy, and they are now the clear majority of college faculty—contingent academic labor. They hold different titles with different degrees of status ranging from graduate teaching assistant to part-time lecturers to full-time non-tenure track contract employees, to name a few, but they all share the condition of having precarious employment. What does this mean for American democracy and what can be done about it? In this essay I will examine some broad trends in recent decades that have had a transformative influence on higher education. This will include a brief look at the effect that funding shifts have had on higher education, and analysis of the subsequent changes in the composition of the faculty. I will then describe some of the key ways that contingent academic labor and their allies have mobilized to protect their own rights and to fight against the corporate trends in higher education.

The Changing American System of Higher Education

To make any kind of general statement about higher education in the United States today is difficult because of the many different formations of colleges across the board. However, certain trends can be discerned. In the early 1970s part-time faculty made up about 22% of the nationwide college faculty. At that time, the job market was approaching the end of a golden era for college professors when full-time tenure track faculty positions had been relatively plentiful. That era, roughly from the end of World War II to the mid-1970s, was the heyday of higher education in terms of expansion of colleges, enrollments, and the rapid growth in funding by the federal government. The growth of community colleges was explosive during this era. The Servicemen's Readjustment Act of 1944 (The GI Bill) helped to increase demand for higher education following World War II, and the expansion of federal financial aid for students in the early 1970s also drove enrollments upward.

At its top tier, the university became a partner with the government in research and development for the military-industrial complex.[2] In its middle tier, it helped in the formation and growth of new managerial and professional classes. At the lower tier, on the one hand it did serve to open the doors for the huddled masses, but on the other hand it served to tamp down students' ambitions, thereby legitimating inequality.[3] The latter role is particularly insidious given the inclusion of African Americans, Latinos, women, and the broader white working class following the open admissions struggles that marked the latter part of this era. The growth of the use of part-time faculty, which began in the mid-1970s, is reflective of both the expansion of the opportunities for higher education, as well as of the grudging concessions that were made to the demands for greater equality. This will become clearer as we consider the ways that higher education has been transformed in the ensuing decades, briefly in terms of funding and more so in terms of the changing shape and status of academic labor.

Sheila Slaughter and Larry L. Leslie argue that the emergence of global financial markets in the 1970s made possible "the financing of ever larger debts in western industrialized countries," which led to funding problems for higher education.[4]

> These moneys were used primarily for entitlement programs ... for debt service, and in the United States, for military expansion. As borrowing increased, federal shares of funding for postsecondary education programs, particularly research and development, decreased ....
> As the share of federal funds for higher education decreased, the states picked up some of the burden, but not all, because the states, too, were spending the bulk of their moneys on entitlement or mandated programs such as health care and prisons.[5]

On top of these expenditures, the trend toward decreases in state revenue was inaugurated by California's Proposition 13, which contributed to the budgetary turmoil. These changes in the global, national, and state economic infrastructure left the colleges and universities struggling to find ways to shore up their funding. The various tiers of the higher education system dealt with it differently as they had different means at their disposal. At the lower and middle tiers, historically free public institutions such as CUNY implemented tuition, increased

---

[2] Rebecca S. Lowen, *Creating the Cold War University: The Transformation of Stanford* (Berkeley, CA: University of California Press, 1997); Stuart W. Leslie, *The Cold War and American Science, The Military-Industrial-Academic Complex at MIT and Stanford* (New York, NY: Columbia University Press, 1993).

[3] Steven Brint and Jerome Karabel, *The Diverted Dream: Community Colleges and the Promise of Educational Opportunity in America, 1900–1985* (New York, NY: Oxford University Press, 1989), pp. 77–79, 225, 231.

[4] Sheila Slaughter and Larry L. Leslie, *Academic Capitalism: Politics, Policies, and the Entrepreneurial University* (Baltimore, MD: The Johns Hopkins University Press, 1997), p. 7.

[5] Ibid., 7–8.

class-size, hired increasing proportions of part-time faculty at low pay, and allowed for the ranks of the full-time faculty to shrink by attrition. The community colleges relied the most upon part-time faculty. At the upper tier universities, administrators implemented some of these measures as well, though not as severely because they had the greater potential to pursue a market-based remedy to their dilemma. They relied more on graduate teaching assistants to teach their undergraduates, and they were in a better position to secure research funds under the new regime. These funding shifts that would reshape higher education were not just the result of abstract market forces at work, but political choices as well.

In March 1972, President Nixon signaled a shift in National Science Foundation (NSF) policy that would transform higher education. As demonstrated by Jennifer Washburn, this shift created an opening for industry to gain entrée to the university through investment partnerships.[6] Later, with the passage of the Bayh-Dole Act of 1980, universities were allowed to patent and license the discoveries that were the outcome of federally funded research, leading to the growth and expansion of deals with their new corporate-partner sponsors.[7] The changes in the way the upper-tier research universities conducted business was most impactful in the areas of medicine, pharmacology, and in biotechnology, an area where genetic engineering was beginning to make its mark. The development of a knowledge-driven economy "had converged to align the interests of universities and industry as never before."[8] Though federal funding remained the largest percentage of the mix, the introduction of the profit-motive radically transformed the culture of the big research universities.[9]

The dollar amount of federal support for academic research has continued to grow, but the proportion of the federal government's share of support for academic research fell from a high of 73.5% in 1966 to about 60%, where it has remained for the past few decades.[10] However, federal support for the life sciences has risen significantly, and it makes up the bulk of the total federal budget for academic research—over 60%.[11] State and local governments' investment in large-scale research and development at universities rose from 1.6 billion dollars in 1995 to 2.4 billion dollars by 2002, and up to 3.4 billion dollars as of 2012 (5.5% of total higher education R & D).[12] During the 1990s, as the share of federal support for social sciences and physical sciences decreased, the proportion of states' budgets going to fund *general* higher education had also declined.[13] More recently, state support for general higher education has begun to recover from the 2008

---

[6] Jennifer Washburn, *University Inc.: The Corporate Corruption of Higher Education* (New York, NY: Basic Books, 2005), p. 57.

[7] Ibid., 57–72; Slaughter and Leslie, Academic Capitalism, pp. 44–48.

[8] Washburn, *University Inc.*, p. 59.

[9] Ibid., passim.

[10] National Science Foundation – National Center for Science and Engineering Statistics, "Chapter 5: Academic Research and Development," National Science Board - Science and Engineering Indicators 2014, Arlington, VA (NSB 14-01), February 2014; Washburn, *University Inc.*, p. 8.

[11] Ibid; Also see Washburn notes No. 17 and 18, p. 251, for further details.

[12] National Science Foundation (NSB 14-01); Washburn, p. 180.

[13] Washburn, *University Inc.*, p. 180; Also see Patricia J. Gumport, "Universities and Knowledge: Restructuring the City of Intellect," in Steven Brint (ed.), *The Future of the City of Intellect* (Stanford, CA: Stanford University Press, 2002), p. 49.

recession, though unevenly from state to state.[14] However, students still have to make up some of the difference themselves in many cases. Additionally, in furthering the practices that promote the precariousness of the work force, higher education institutions have coped with revenue shortfalls by outsourcing custodial and food services.[15]

Higher education leaders have perennially found themselves seeking out revenues from non-state sources such as tuition increases and alumni donations, as well as implementing cost-saving measures such as the consolidation of programs, the hiring of more low-cost part-time faculty, increasing class size, and providing incentives for early retirement for full-time faculty.[16] A further analysis of how the faculty fits into the transformation that has been taking place will help to bring the picture into greater relief.

The Changing American Faculty

As noted, the responses to these budgetary challenges have varied by the level of the university that one is observing. One of the more questionable ways that academic institutions have managed these budgetary challenges over the past forty years has been through the extensive increase in the use of contingent academic labor. Aside from the budgetary savings and flexibility that this practice brings to higher education, it also brings a false sense of legitimacy, contributing to the public display of higher education as a pillar of democracy and equality. This is due to the invisibility of the contingent academic work force to the general public, who mostly cannot tell the difference between contingent faculty and regular full-time faculty, leaving the impression of a fully stocked faculty set. This is a problem for a higher education system that is purported to be democratic and egalitarian, in that, as will be argued below, an overreliance on contingent instructional staff can diminish the integrity of an academic environment. For now, it is worth noting that the growth of precarious academic labor typically weakens the power of the faculty, insofar as having a strong voice in institutional governance and meaningful leverage in collective bargaining are indicative of that power. Higher education has become increasingly managed from above. As the authority of full-time faculty has diminished, the administrative apparatus has flourished.[17]

Richard Chait in "The 'Academic Revolution' Revisited" argues that it has become a well-established proposition that different tiers of the academy display different degrees of faculty autonomy.[18] He references Burton Clark who explains

---

[14] Ry Rivard, "A Few States are Spending More on Higher Ed than Before the Recession Hit," *Inside Higher Ed*, April 21, 2014.

[15] Joe Berry and Helena Worthen, "Higher Education as a Workplace," *Dollars & Sense: Real World Economics* (November/December 2012).

[16] Gumport, "Universities and Knowledge," p. 49.

[17] John W. Curtis and Saranna Thornton, "Losing Focus: The Annual Report on the Economic Status of the Profession, 2013–2014," *Academe* (March–April 2014). They report that from 1976 to 2011 there has been a massive increase in full-time non-faculty professionals (369%), and more than a doubling of senior administrative positions (141%). This compares to full-time tenured and tenure-track faculty, which only grew by 23% during the same period.

[18] Richard Chait, "The 'Academic Revolution' Revisited," in Steven Brint (ed.), *The Future of the City of Intellect, The Changing American University* (Stanford, CA: Stanford University Press, 2002), pp. 294–295.

that at the top of the institutional hierarchy, faculty have influence individually and in their campus faculty bodies, but "as we descend the hierarchy ... faculty authority weakens and managerialism increases."[19] At the two-year colleges, faculty "feel powerless, even severely put upon."[20] Since Clark wrote these words even those faculty members at the top of the academic hierarchy are feeling their collective power erode, relative to their previous stature, but the upshot of these shifts has been the creation of a more hierarchical system of academic labor that roughly corresponds to the unequal tiers of the system of higher education. The differentiation may not be a perfect delineation, but the parameters are clear.

A description of the development of the contingent academic labor system, along with an interpretation of its implications, will further illuminate the hierarchical nature of contemporary higher education. From a broad perspective, as a proportion of the total population of full-time and part-time instructional faculty in Title IV degree-granting institutions, the national percentage of part-time faculty jumped from 22% in 1970 to 46.2% in 2003.[21] Conversely, in 2003 full-time faculty made up 53.8% of the teaching work force, including some non-tenure track faculty. These percentages only include full-time faculty and part-time faculty. When graduate teaching assistants are included, the numbers look even starker.[22] Almost three-fourths of graduate assistantships awarded in the humanities and social sciences are for teaching.[23] With this in mind, using US Department of Education figures from 2001, Ernst Benjamin estimates that full-time faculty made up 46.6% of the instructional staff in higher education, part-time faculty 34.5%, and graduate assistants 18.9%.[24] A decade later, using figures from 2011, the trend continues with full-time faculty as a percentage of total instructional staff dropping to 39.2%, whereas part-time faculty rose to 41.5%, and graduate student employees rose slightly to 19.3%.[25] Astoundingly, when we take a closer look at the 2011 full-time faculty figures we find that only 16.6% of the total faculty are full-time tenured faculty, another 6.9% are full-time tenure-track faculty, and 15.7% are full-time non-tenure track faculty, the latter being a category that is *contingent* academic labor. Full-time non-tenure track is a category that hardly even existed in the 1960s and 1970s. Thus, the recent figures indicate that full-time tenured and tenure track faculty today make up 23.5% of the overall

---

[19] Burton Clark, "Faculty: Differentiation and Dispersion," in A. Levine (ed.), *Higher Learning in America, 1980–2000* (Baltimore, MD: Johns Hopkins University Press, 1993), p. 170. Cited by Chait, The Future of the City of Intellect, p. 295.

[20] Ibid.

[21] US Department of Education, National Center for Education Statistics, Digest of Education Statistics, 2004, Table 227: Full-time and part-time instructional faculty in degree-granting institutions, by employment status and control and type of institution: Fall 1970 to Fall 2003.

[22] Ernst Benjamin (ed.), "Editor's Notes," in *Exploring the Role of Contingent Instructional Staff in Under-graduate Learning* (San Francisco: Jossey-Bass, Number 123, Fall 2003), p. 6.

[23] Ibid.

[24] Ibid. Benjamin derives this data from the US Department of Education, Digest of Educational Statistics, 2001 (Washington DC: US Department of Education, 2002), Table 226.

[25] John W. Curtis, Director of Research and Public Policy, American Association of University Professors, "The Employment Status of Instructional Staff Members in Higher Education, Fall 2011," Washington, DC, April 2014. Table 1, "Trends in Instructional Staff Employment Status, 1975 and 1976 to 2011," p. 2. Curtis tabulated the data from the US Department of Education, IPEDS Fall Staff Survey.

instructional faculty, and contingent or precarious academic labor make up 76.5% of the overall instructional faculty. These figures leave no doubt that there has been an extraordinary change in the composition of higher education faculty in the United States since the early 1970s.

These changes have been most unmistakable at the "lower" end of higher education—the community colleges, where our most disadvantaged and least prepared students enter into the system of higher education. Judith M. Gappa and David W. Leslie wrote a pioneering demographic analysis of the "invisible faculty" in 1993 that, in some important ways, still holds up under scrutiny: "The more an institution 'looked like' a community college, the more likely it was to make extensive use of part-timers. For example, part-timers were commonly used to staff evening division and extended education programs."[26] As of 2011, part-time faculty made up 70.3% of the overall faculty in the institutional category "public associate's" otherwise known as the public community college.[27]

Understanding the distribution of part-time faculty by *type of program* is important, as well, because it is reflective not just of a "market" for academic labor, but of a set of values and priorities that are dictated more by a business-oriented outlook amongst trustees and higher education managers than by sound educational policy and good pedagogy. In community colleges part-timers are used extensively in *all* programs. However, in other types of colleges we will find that part-timers are most commonly found in the fine arts, education, business, and the humanities.[28] We are also likely to find them teaching the "basic, lower-division core courses of the undergraduate curriculum," such as introductory English and mathematics.[29] They are found in high percentages in English as a Second Language (ESL) programs and in basic composition programs, which perhaps explains why so many of the leading advocates for contingent academic labor rights have emerged from these disciplines. The Humanities, arguably, has been the area of higher learning most adversely affected by the growth in the use of part-time faculty. Given the place of the Humanities in a liberal arts education, this is unsettling.

What does this all boil down to for the part-time faculty, the full-time faculty, and the students that they serve?

As for the part-time faculty, their grievances are by now well known, so I will only summarize them here. Even if they teach the equivalent of a full-time course load they typically do not get anything close to pro-rated compensation. They normally lack job security, and a reasonable benefits package. Frequently they do not have access to an office, or if there is an "adjunct office," it is likely shared by more than a few co-workers, making office meetings with students less private, thereby contributing to an unprofessional atmosphere. They often lack an office phone, an adequate computer, a desk, or even a drawer that locks. Many part-time

---

[26] Judith M. Gappa and David W. Leslie, *The Invisible Faculty: Improving the Status of Part-Timers in Higher Education* (San Francisco, CA: Jossey-Bass, 1993), p. 113. Their analysis is based on the 1988 National Survey of Postsecondary Faculty (NSOPF:88), and supplemented with extensive interviews with part-time faculty from around the country. The data from subsequent years continues to support the general thrust of their analysis.

[27] Curtis, "Employment Status," Table 5, "Instructional Staff Employment Status, by Institutional Category, Fall 2011," p. 8.

[28] Gappa and Leslie, *Invisible Faculty*, p. 118.

[29] Ibid.

faculty teach at multiple campuses leaving them little time to engage with students after class as they dash off to their next assignment elsewhere. It is not uncommon for them to have little or no advance notice of reappointment. Mostly, they do not qualify to apply for faculty research grants, nor is it common for them to obtain funding for professional development or to attend professional conferences that allow them to keep up in their field. They are typically not included in departmental decision-making, in curricular development, and in the extra-curricular life of the campus, leaving those tasks for the already overburdened full-time faculty. This all speaks to a campus culture that is not well represented in the college brochure.

As for the full-time faculty, the changing shape of tenure must also be added to the mix. The percentage of those who are tenured has been on decline, even as the number of faculty, overall, has risen substantially.[30] From Fall 2001 to Fall 2011, as a percentage of all full-time and part-time faculty, the percentage of full-time tenured faculty has dropped from 25% to 20.6%. Moreover, the number of full-time tenure-*track* faculty has recently decreased in absolute as well as relative terms, which seems to indicate that the declining trend could continue for the immediate future because there are fewer prospects in the pipeline. These trends point to a weakening of faculty power. Consequently, the decline in tenured positions is a threat to academic freedom in that relatively few members of the instructional staff have, or hope to have, the protection that tenure affords.

As for the student, there is an ongoing discussion as to whether or not the extensive use of part-time faculty diminishes the possibilities for students. The bottom line, though, is that positive learning conditions for students depend upon having a stable, professional work force, which requires decent pay and a modicum of benefits. Karen Thompson, a leading advocate for part-time faculty rights who teaches English as a part-time lecturer at Rutgers, and who is also on the staff of the Rutgers American Association of University Professors-American Federation of Teachers (AAUP-AFT), explains that undergraduates in their first two years, whether at a two-year institution or a four-year institution, are most in need of advising and attention.[31] The contingent academic labor system, she explains, diminishes and fragments part-time faculty time, thereby undermining the learning process. The frequently short lead time for classes, due to last minute hiring, the time spent commuting between multiple institutions, due to multiple sources of employment, and the lack of support for professional development all work against the kind of academic community that could be fostered through improved employment conditions for part-time faculty.[32]

It is not difficult, therefore, to recognize that the *need* for student-teacher interactions, combined with the relative insufficiency of such interactions within the scope of the contingent academic labor system, along with all of the other relative deprivations that impair those faculty on the lower rungs of the system of higher education from practicing their profession properly, all add up to a

---

[30] Curtis, "Employment Status," Table 3, "Trends in Faculty Employment Status, 1975 and 1976 to 2011," p. 5.

[31] Karen Thompson, "Contingent Faculty and Student Learning: Welcome to the Strativersity," in Ernst Benjamin (ed.), *Exploring the Role of Contingent Instructional Staff in Undergraduate Learning* (San Francisco, CA: Jossey-Bass, 2003), pp. 41–47.

[32] Ibid.

hierarchical system that presents opportunities, with the one hand, and limits them with the other.

The contingent academic labor system, and the use of part-time faculty, especially, is at the core of the higher education system that reproduces inequality and hierarchy. It seems that the presence of graduate student employees at the upper-tier institutions does not have the same depth of effect on students as does the overuse of part-time faculty on the lower tiers; that is, primarily at the community colleges (where graduate students employees do not generally teach).[33] I am not considering here distinctions between these categories with regard to the quality of teaching. However, as graduate students, it is likely that they are more integrated into the life and community of the campus than are the part-time faculty, which is perhaps an obvious observation when we recall that the part-time faculty often come to teach their class and soon after leave for their next assignment elsewhere. When we consider the social class make-up of those who attend the lower-tier colleges as compared to those who attend the upper tier institutions, it is logical to infer that the four-year and upper-tier students get the most of both worlds (that is, prior advantage in life and the greater likelihood of interaction on campus), and, conversely, that the lower tier student get the least of both worlds. The more developed cultural capital of those at the upper-tier institutions makes them less in need of the time and attention of their teachers, and when we add to this the limited time and attention received by those on the lower tier, who need it more, together these attributes serve to reinforce class differences. A study by Pascarella and Terenzini found the following:

> [T]he frequency of informal contact with faculty to discuss intellectual issues and the perceived quality of interaction with faculty and peers had their most positive influence on persistence for students with low initial and subsequent commitment to the goal of graduation or who came from families where parents had relatively low levels of formal education. As level of family education and graduation commitment increased, interaction with faculty and peers became less important for persistence.[34]

Pascarella and Terenzini's study strongly implies that students on the lower tier would benefit significantly more from faculty and peer interaction than would those on the upper rungs. Given the configuration of the academic labor system today, it will be difficult for those on the bottom rungs to overcome social class barriers. My analysis assumes that, properly done, education is not a one-way street of the teacher/subject filling the students' minds with information, but a mutual process of engagement and growth guided by the teacher where both teacher and student are interactive subjects. If so, then how can a system of higher education be reformed so as to facilitate a more egalitarian and democratic way of learning?

---

[33] Extrapolating from John Curtis' tabulations (Table 5, "Instructional Staff Employment Status, by Institutional Category, Fall 2012," p. 8) we find that zero percent of Graduate Student Employees teach at "Public Associate's Colleges" where part-time faculty, as noted above, comprise 70.3% of the instructional staff in this category.

[34] Ernest T. Pascarella and Patrick T. Terenzini, *How College Affects Students: Findings and Insights from Twenty Years of Research* (San Francisco, CA: Jossey-Bass Publishers, 1991), p. 412.

Incipient Formations

In a discussion that took place in the 1930s regarding higher education reform at that time, John Dewey made a point that still bears resonance for us today when he said, "educational reconstruction cannot be accomplished without a social reconstruction in which higher education has a part to play."[35] Finding what that part might be, and how to play it is no simple task.

In 2001, Richard Moser wrote that "The linchpin of this process of corporatization is the overuse and abuse of adjunct faculty because it weakens the group within the university that has the most power to act as a counterweight to corporate values and as a leader in creating a new vision of the university."[36] Neoliberal ideology places the university system squarely in the heart of global corporate capitalist schemes. Knowledge production and control is at the core of its far-flung network, and the faculty present the most potential to challenge that control. And just as the goal of any factory owner is to control the work force in the industrial units that he oversees, it is also in the instrumental interest of neoliberal elites to have an academic labor force that is fragmented and in check. Divide-and-conquer is an age-old technique that is as effective today as it has been in previous epochs.

If the use of adjuncts and other contingent academic labor categories serve as the linchpin of this system, then an examination of the contingent academic laborers' struggle might help us to envision democratic alternatives. The following is a brief selective overview of efforts by contingent academic labor activists and their allies to confront the problems they face. Over the course of the past few decades, these activists have come to a better understanding of their position within the broader academic labor system, but there is much to overcome if there are to be any genuinely transformative changes.

In the 1960s, academic unionism was in its infancy, having grown from associations to bona-fide collective bargaining agents. As for contingent academic labor, the independent graduate teaching assistant unions and associations were the most prominent organizations amongst them, at this time. The first independent graduate student employee union was the Teaching Assistants Association (TAA) at the University of Wisconsin, Madison, which was formed in the spring of 1966. It won a representation election by a wide margin in May of 1969, and had the first contract in the United States between a university and its graduate student employees.[37]

The TAA's initial contract demands led to a prolonged conflict. After almost a year of "fruitless" collective bargaining, the TAA had a successful strike that lasted twenty-four days and "revealed some of the key fault lines in university life."[38]

---

[35] John Dewey cited in "John Dewey on Hutchins' Philosophy of Education, 1937," in Richard Hofstadter and Wilson Smith (eds), *American Higher Education: A Documentary History*, Volume II. (Chicago, IL: The University of Chicago Press, 1961), p. 952.

[36] Richard Moser, "The New Academic Labor System, Corporatization and the Renewal of Academic Citizenship," American Association of University Professors, June 12, 2001.

[37] Daniel Czitrom, "Reeling in the Years: Looking Back on the TAA," in Cary Nelson (ed.), *Will Teach for Food, Academic Labor in Crisis* (Minneapolis, MN: The University of Minnesota Press, 1997), p. 218; Also see "TAA History, The First Thirty Years," TAA Membership Handbook, 1996–1997, Teaching Assistants' Association, AFT/WFT Local 3220, AFL-CIO, pp. 21–23.

[38] Czitrom, p. 218.

In doing so they had the support of much of the undergraduate students as well as the Teamsters, Local 695, which disrupted deliveries and campus bus service. On April 8, 1970 the membership voted to accept a contract that made important gains regarding the establishment of an impartial grievance procedure, health insurance coverage, and class-size limits, to mention a few.[39] The TAA made their mark on history by raising questions about power in the university and inequality in society. In doing so they have pointed the way for other graduate student unions to follow. In keeping with this tradition, the Coalition of Graduate Employee Unions (CGEU) was founded in 1992. Today it brings together graduate employee union leaders and activists from over fifty labor union locals that are affiliated with a variety of national unions in the United States and Canada. They meet annually to develop strategies and skills, to build solidarity, and to provide continuity for a group that has a relatively high turnover rate.

Throughout the 1970s and 1980s there were continuous, though sporadic, local and regional efforts at labor organizing by graduate teaching assistants and part-time (adjunct) faculty, both within established labor unions and independently of them. There was also a growing body of literature about contingent academic labor as expressed in local union newsletters, articles in higher education journals, various commentaries coming from the disciplinary associations, and some notable studies and reports from the AAUP and the AFT, amongst others.

An important study of contingent faculty work is *Terminal Degrees* (1984) by Emily Abel.[40] Abel paints a dramatic picture of the dashed hopes and fragmented lives caused by the job crisis in higher education. Her insight regarding the possibilities for collective action, and the obstacles which it faces, was for many years a guiding light in a dark landscape. In her extensive interviews with part-time faculty and with temporary and untenured full-time faculty she provides a look into the underground lives that they lead. Her interviews provide knowledge of a common experience that is often hidden from view in the isolated world of the part-time teacher—the dashed expectations, instability, fragmented lives, shattered relationships, burdensome student loans, self-blame, and dislocation. She points to both an individualistic ideological orientation and the transient nature of the job that are among the factors that help to foster a sense of alienation amongst the part-time faculty. Instead, she puts forward collective action, strategic alliances, and consciousness-raising as ways of prevailing over these demoralizing feelings.

As scholars and activists were struggling intellectually to grasp the meaning of "globalization" and then, later, "neoliberalism," they also continued to struggle politically to organize contingent academic labor into unions and other associations. The Yale Graduate Employee Student Organization (GESO) campaigns of 1995–1996, especially the 1995 grade strike, electrified the world of academic labor and made national headlines. Graduate students at Yale were able to form an organization that could both mobilize the work force and develop strategic alliances that clearly helped them to have more leverage. Given that they had been in the streets getting arrested with other unionists from clerical and maintenance unions, as well as leading figures in the local community, it is not a

---

[39] Ibid., 219–220.

[40] Emily Abel, *Terminal Degrees: The Job Crisis in Higher Education* (New York, NY: Praeger, 1984).

wild assumption to say that they developed a common understanding with the New Haven community and with the other unions. However, they had less success at winning the hearts and minds of the other Yale graduate students, the undergraduates, and the full-time faculty. In late 1996, the National Labor Relations Board (NLRB) General Counsel decided that graduate students were employees and that Yale had violated federal labor law by intimidating the GESO activists and threatening reprisals. The question of graduate student status continues to be contested, but the GESO campaign inspired union organizing drives and activism among graduate student employees and part-time faculty throughout the system of higher education in the United States.

In late December 1996, in the midst of the sparks of the graduate student employee campaigns, the National Congress of Part-Time, Adjunct, Non-Tenure Track, and GTA faculty met for the first time. Graduate students and part-time faculty at George Washington University (GWU) were the hosts of this convocation. There were fewer than fifty participants at this event, but they were among the leading contingent academic labor activists. Among the attendees were Karen Thompson from Rutgers, Ernst Benjamin from the AAUP, and Vicky Smallman from McMaster University in Toronto. Marc Bousquet, who was then the President of the Modern Language Association's (MLA) Graduate Student Caucus, was also present. Jon Curtiss, who was active in the CGEU, and who at the time worked for the TAA at the University of Wisconsin at Madison, also spoke at the conference. Much of the energy and vitality of the first National Congress was due to another event taking place in DC at the same time, the MLA annual convention. Many of the National Congress attendees were active in the MLA's Graduate Student Caucus, and they were in a conflict within that organization over its response to contingent faculty interests.

Subsequently, this grouping came to be known as the Coalition of Contingent Academic Labor (COCAL) and has provided a space where activists and union leaders can meet biennially to strategize, share ideas and knowledge, develop an expanding network of activists, and build solidarity. This has not only developed nationally, but international alliances and perspectives have also begun to grow. COCAL does not try to reproduce the role of labor unions, but it complements them, in some ways allowing for greater focus and flexibility across geographic and institutional lines. This flexibility has sometimes been referred to as the "inside-outside" strategy, meaning that being able to move outside of the union's boundaries can allow for an alternative center of gravity that can give a local movement some leverage inside the union, even if it is merely a short-lived burst of alternative perspective. It encourages the building of alliances with groups that are not part of the bargaining unit, but share a common interest.

After COCAL II at CUNY in April of 1998, the email list, ADJ-L@ADJ-L.ORG was established and has become a vital instrument where contingent faculty activists and their friends can continuously discuss relevant issues, develop and coordinate plans for various campaigns, share news, learn new strategies, and sometimes just complain. There are currently over five hundred list members from all across the United States, Canada, and Mexico.[41] There are also a few list members from prominent academic journals, including the *Chronicle of Higher*

---

[41] Full Disclosure: I am the founder and co-moderator of ADJ-L, one of the founders of COCAL, and a long-time member of the COCAL International Advisory Committee.

Education and *Inside Higher Ed* who have made their presence known to the other participants and have been welcomed.

One of the accomplishments of COCAL IV in San Jose was to initiate plans for Campus Equity Week (CEW), which was carried out in Fall 2001 and then on a regular basis in subsequent years. It consists of public awareness campaigns focusing on contingent academic labor issues and has been conducted all over the United States, Canada, and more recently in Mexico. The AFT, AAUP, National Education Association (NEA), and numerous other organizations have provided support, resources, and materials for the campaigns. At CUNY, for example, during Campus Equity Week 2005 there were displays of huge "seniority" scrolls, which displayed records of individual part-time faculty members' time-on-the-job. There were also forums, poetry readings, and soapbox speeches. The events of CEW have been reported widely in the higher education union newspapers, as well as in local newspapers from coast-to-coast.

In the COCAL conferences that followed, a new emphasis emerged regarding the impact of neoliberal globalization upon higher education. The presence of a small but determined rank-and-file academic labor contingent from Mexico added an essential dimension to that dialogue. The Mexican participants made clear that the effects of neoliberal practices impacted them even more greatly and that they have fewer tools with which to remedy the problem. The growing solidarity led to COCAL X in Mexico City in 2012 at Universidad Nacional Autónoma de México (UNAM), which was the occasion for two of the large labor unions at UNAM to meet and discuss academic labor affairs for the first time in many years—Sindicato Nacional de Trabajadores de la UNAM and Asociación Autónoma del Personal Académico de la UNAM.

Many adjunct faculty members in the United States would agree that most of the major academic labor unions had taken their time in finding part-time faculty on their radar and ignored their early efforts to organize. Moreover, some contingent faculty activists blame the unions dominated by full-time faculty for standing by while the two-tier system was created, sometimes even opposing the organization of part-time faculty. It is not all buddy-buddy now, but there has been a sea change over the past fifteen years or so with regard to contingent faculty and organized labor.

Recent years have shown an uptick of activity, and this is partly due to part-time faculty pushing and labor unions responding, but it is a slow and uneven process. When full-time-tenured faculty and non-tenure track faculty come into the room to discuss the issues between them, the social-class cleavage is sometimes palpable. Primarily, a common demand by unions is for an increase in full-time faculty lines. This policy could leave many long-serving highly qualified adjuncts out of a job. Bringing up the bottom would be a more equitable solution, and it would also be one that holds out the hope of ending the two-tier system and strengthening faculty power in the long run.

In early 2014 there was a bill presented in the Colorado State Legislature, HB15-1154 that would have required equal pay for equal work for part-time faculty in the state's community college system.[42] It was inspired by the Vancouver Community College (VCC) collective agreement with the VCC Faculty

---

[42] Don Eron, "Colorado Community College Equity Act Song and Video," *The Academe Blog*, American Association of University Professors, posted Feb 14, 2014.

Association that is considered to be the gold standard by many contingent faculty activists. In the Colorado bill, part-time faculty would get prorated pay, and those who support it claim that it would not be an intolerable financial burden on the state or on students and their families. The legislation, put forward by the AAUP, was endorsed by the state chapters of the AFT, NEA, and the Service Employees International Union (SEIU), as well as by the New Faculty Majority, an advocacy organization that was founded in 2009 through discussions that had taken place at COCAL and on the ADJ-L list. In April 2014, the bill was defeated in the Colorado House Appropriations Committee by a nine-to-four vote. However, the fact that such legislation was even considered is a credit to the coalition of contingent activists who spearheaded it, and it indicates that the climate has changed.

There are numerous positive signs that the tide is changing for contingent faculty, too many to discuss here. However, one campaign that has been getting a lot of attention has been in Washington DC. Joe Berry's *Reclaiming the Ivory Tower* puts forward a "metro strategy" that has been initiated by SEIU Local 500 in the Washington DC area. Subsequently the parent organization viewed it as part of a larger strategy to be copied nationally, as it was intended.[43] Local 500 began organizing all part-time faculty in the region, that is, the majority of adjuncts in DC, and in numerous surrounding campuses in Maryland and Virginia. This has been a significant investment of resources by the Local for a longer-term objective, but in this way they are not just addressing one campus, but an entire metro labor market. This holds out some promise to be an effective means to challenge the inequities in the higher education system as a whole. This strategy is also being pursued by the United Steel Workers in Pittsburgh and by the AFT in Philadelphia. Berry's work suggests that regional organizations are needed to challenge control of the labor market, but this means that labor organizations have to think along the lines of a new model more fully.

Conclusion

Neoliberalism is an ideology that affects the political, economic, and social structures of the contemporary age. It has been influencing the system of higher education in such a way that it is limiting the democratic possibilities inherent in education, and it is doing so at a time when we are in desperate need of unleashing the human potential to affirmatively create, grow, hope, and learn. The fragmentation of the faculty and the weakening of faculty influence is part of a system that promotes increasing hierarchy and specialization that situates students as consumers and limits their chances of participating critically in an egalitarian society. C. Wright Mills said that the purpose of liberal education is to teach us how to participate in public life, how to avoid being drawn into the pitfalls of mass society, and, most of all, to keep us from being overwhelmed by the burdens of modern life.[44] These purposes can only be fulfilled in an educational system that reflects democratic values, both in its curriculum and in

---

[43] Joe Berry, *Reclaiming the Ivory Tower: Organizing Adjuncts to Change Higher Education* (New York, NY: Monthly Review Press, 2005).

[44] C. Wright Mills, "Mass Society and Liberal Education," *The Politics of Truth: Selected Writings of C. Wright Mills*, selected and introduced by John H. Summers (New York, NY: Oxford University Press, 2008).

its day-to-day operations. That leaves out the corporate neoliberal model of education.

The Web We Weave: Online Education and Democratic Prospects

Seaton Patrick Tarrant & Leslie Paul Thiele
University of Florida, USA

Abstract *Near the end of* The Public and Its Problems, *John Dewey writes that the consummation of democracy will involve the art of full communication. The internet might appear to fulfill Dewey's vision, increasing opportunities for inquiry, interaction, and renewal through the social construction of meaning. Yet certain forms of technologically mediated communication threaten the development of much needed skills for democracy. While citizenship education may be facilitated by digital technology, it also demands pedagogy of a more traditional sort, one characterized by embodied, experiential interactions between teachers and students. We employ pedagogical theory, democratic theory, evolutionary psychology, and neuroscience to underline the crucial importance of these embodied, experiential interactions and their relationship to the challenge of sustaining democracy in our times.*

> Experience is never limited, and it is never complete; it is an immense sensibility, a kind of huge spider-web of the finest silken threads suspended in the chamber of consciousness, and catching every air-borne particle in its tissue...The power to guess the unseen from the seen, to trace the implication of things, to judge the whole piece by the pattern, the condition of feeling life in general so completely that you are well on your way to knowing any particular corner of it—this cluster of gifts may almost be said to constitute experience.—Henry James[1]

The development of wholly online degree programs is one of the most significant challenges that institutions of higher education face. Their quality is hotly debated, and their financial viability is unclear. The University of Phoenix, more accurately known as the Apollo Group, Inc., claims to be the nation's largest provider of online degree programs.[2] It boasted half a million students enrolled in its programs in 2010. More recently, the Apollo Group has seen declining enrollment, and a federal investigation into the way it handles federal aid is scheduled to begin in August 2014.[3] Other online degree providers, such as

---

[1] Henry James, "The Art of Fiction," in *Partial Portraits* (Ann Arbor, MI: University of Michigan Press, 1970), pp. 388–389.

[2] University of Phoenix, "Just the Facts," <http://www.phoenix.edu/about_us/media-center/just-the-facts.html>.

[3] Rich Duprey, "Apollo Education Group in the Regulators Crosshairs," <http://www.fool.com/investing/general/2014/07/16/apollo-education-group-in-the-regulators-crosshair.aspx>.

Strayer Education, Bridgepoint Education, Kaplan University, and ITT Educational Services have all seen drops in enrollment over the past two years.[4]

Despite this downward trend, or perhaps contributing to it, traditional brick and mortar colleges and universities have vigorously entered the online education business by developing their own web-based programs. The overwhelming majority of online bachelor's programs that are listed within the top 50 by the *US News and World Report* are offered by traditional universities.[5] University administrators are enthusiastic about the market for their online degrees, and the majority believe online learning is capable of delivering programs of equal merit to traditional classroom pedagogy. The majority of university professors disagree.[6]

The growth of online degree programs, whether supplied by for-profit virtual universities or brick and mortar institutions expanding their repertoire of services, poses a threat to traditional forms of pedagogy. We argue that it also poses a threat to democracy. To the extent that online degree programs eliminate the opportunity for students to engage in embodied forms of communication and interaction, and to develop the skills that follow therefrom, they substantially undermine opportunities for civics education. We supply evidence that an online degree program, that is, a college experience without classrooms, does not and cannot offer the same quality of education as an on-campus program in facilitating the acquisition of key skills for democratic citizenship. In turn, we question whether it can develop the skills demanded by the marketplace in a quickly changing world.

Upon its inception in the United States, the field of political science assumed the task of educating citizens.[7] Colleges and universities also embraced a civic mission rooted in developing citizenship knowledge, skills, and values.[8] While this mission has in many instances been neglected,[9] civics education remains at the forefront of many political and pedagogic conversations.[10]

---

[4] Ibid. For-profit online education is not limited to degree-granting institutions. Coursera, the company that made its reputation by offering free online courses, has begun to bring in revenue with its "Signature Track" program. The company advertises the signature track certificates as a form of "professional development." These courses are offered through partnership with brick and mortar universities (Ry Rivard, "Free to Profit," *Inside Higher Ed*, April 8, 2013, <http://www.insidehighered.com/news/2013/04/08/coursera-begins-make-money>).

[5] *US News and World Report*, "Best Online Bachelor's Programs," <http://www.usnews.com/education/online-education/bachelors/rankings?int=a29209>.

[6] Elain Allen and Jeff Seaman, *Grade Change: Tracking Online Education in the United States* (Babson Park, Massachusettes: The Bason Survey Group, 2013). *Originally known as the Sloan Online Survey: Jeff Seaman, *Online Learning as a Strategic Asset: The Paradox of Faculty Voices: Views and Experiences with Online Learning* (Washington, DC: Association of Public and Land-Grant Universities, 2009). Approximately 70% of "academic leaders" approve of the claim; 70% of educators disagree.

[7] James Farr, John S. Dryzek, and Stephen T. Leonard (eds), *Political Science in History: Research Programs and Political Traditions* (New York: Cambridge University Press, 1995).

[8] John Dewey, *Democracy and Education: An Introduction to the Philosophy of Education* (New York: Macmillan, 1916); Émile Durkheim, *Education and Sociology* (New York: Free Press, 1956); Lawrence Cremin, *The Transformation of the School: Progressivism in American Education, 1876–1957* (New York: Knopf, 1961); Thomas Ehrlich, *Civic Responsibility and Higher Education* (Westport, CT: Oryx Press, 2000).

[9] William Talcott, *Modern Universities, Absent Citizenship? Historical Perspectives* (The Center for Information and Research on Civic Learning and Engagement, September 2005).

[10] Anne Colby, Elizabeth Beaumont, Thomas Ehrlich, and Josh Corngold, *Educating for Democracy: Preparing Undergraduates for Responsible Political Engagement* (Stanford, CA:

Civics education does not solely, or even primarily, involve increasing students' knowledge of governmental processes. Education for democratic citizenship entails students acknowledging their social responsibilities, identifying means of involvement for responsible agents of change, and developing values such as trust, empathy, motivation and commitment.[11] It also involves the development of a specific skill set that will allow students to understand their world, fulfill their responsibilities, and enact their values. Most basically, civics education demands the development of critical thinking skills,[12] communication skills, and collaborative problem-solving skills.

If one assumes continued improvement in public access to the internet and its enhancement of an open access culture, it is clear that the internet affords great opportunity for developing civic skills. The internet provides a vast amount of information and offers varied opportunities for interaction with a large diversity of stakeholders. As such, it can facilitate critical thinking, enhance communication, and provide opportunities for collaborative problem-solving.

In this article we critically examine this potential, and point to some of the dangers associated with online learning. We challenge reformist arguments in higher education that claim a wholly online learning environment can provide a comparable development of civic skills as a traditional brick and mortar education. We argue that American higher education must continue to cultivate

---

Footnote 10 continued

Jossey-Bass, 2007); Peter Levine, *The Future of Democracy: Developing the Next Generation of American Citizens* (Boston, MA: Tufts, 2007); Global University Network for Innovation. *Higher Education in the World 4: Higher Education's Commitment to Sustainability: From Understanding to Action* (New York: Palgrave Macmillan, 2011); Martha Nussbaum, *Not For Profit: Why Democracy Needs the Humanities* (Princeton, NJ: Princeton University Press, 2010); Andrew Delbanco, *College What It Was, Is, and Should Be* (Princeton, NJ: Princeton University Press, 2012).

[11] Ehrlich, *Civic Responsibility and Higher Education*; Lonnie Sherrod, Constance Flanagan, and James Youniss, "Dimensions of Citizenship and Opportunities for Youth Development: The What, Why, When, Where, and Who of Citizenship Development," *Applied Developmental Science* 6:4 (2002), pp. 264–272.

[12] Arguably, the least critically examined concept in common pedagogical parlance is the collection of skills or behaviors called critical thinking. Its development is universally endorsed but rarely systematically pursued Arum, Richard and Josipa Roska. *Academically Adrift.* (Chicago: University of Chicago Press, 2011). Critical thinking is a cognitive process of analysis, reflection, and evaluation "that is focused on deciding what to believe or do" (Robert Ennis, "Critical Thinking," *Teaching Philosophy* 14:1 (1991) pp. 5–24). Rather than adopting opinions, convictions, values, or goals owing to their popularity or their customary or authoritative origins, critical thinkers rigorously interrogate their foundations and assess their weaknesses, merits and implications (Alan Diduck, "Critical Education in Resource and Environmental Management: Learning and Empowerment for a Sustainable Future," *Journal of Environmental Management* 57:2 (1999), pp. 85–97; John Huckle, "Sustainable Development," in *Handbook of Education for Citizenship* (London: Sage, 2008)). Critical thinkers embody a disposition of habitual inquisitiveness and focused inquiry (Peter A. Facione, *Critical Thinking: A Statement of Expert Consensus for Purposes of Educational Assessment and Instruction. Research Findings and Recommendations* (Newark, DE: American Philosophical Association, 1990)). Such deliberate and focused inquiry creates, and is a product of, our ongoing social development, what Paulo Freire called "the unfinishedness of the human condition" (Paulo Freire, *The Politics of Education: Culture, Power and Liberation*, trans. Donaldo Macedo, 1st ed. (Westport, CT: Bergin & Garvey Publishers, 1985)). Critical thinking cuts down false assumptions, and carves away at biases, including the biases of the critical thinker.

the pedagogical practices based in inter- and intrapersonal experience if it is to fulfill its democratic mandate for civic learning. These educational experiences are essentially embodied, and best conveyed through interaction in—and beyond—brick and mortar classrooms.

Democratic Motives for Online Learning

The brevity of the article prohibits an extensive review of arguments supporting the democratic potential of online learning. Here we give a brief overview of some of the arguments we find to be indicative of the larger field of interdisciplinary literatures.

Web 2.0 entered our lexicon in 2005, referring specifically to social and participatory internet technologies.[13] Also known as new social media, Web 2.0 transformed the online environment into "a dynamic, interactive and participatory medium."[14] The social constructivist pedagogy put forward by proponents of new social media technologies claims these technologies can tap into the "new citizenship styles and strategies," of a youth culture habituated to online networked activities.[15] The web, according to such thinking, can become a platform for democratic interaction, meaning sharing, and the cooperative creation of knowledge; this is said to occur largely as a result of increased access to information, and the availability of tools for communicating and aggregating diverse opinions.

There is some empirical evidence to buttress these claims. A meta-analysis conducted by the US Department of Education indicates that blended learning classrooms that mesh online resource use with face-to-face instruction exhibit superior outcomes to traditional classrooms.[16] Notably, the greater effectiveness of blended learning environments, the study concludes, is not a product of online quizzes or other computer-aided technologies. It is largely a result of increased "time on task," that is, of the amount of time students devote to learning. In effect, blended learning brings the learning experience outside the classroom, into the student's life.

---

[13] Grainne Conole, Rebecca Galley, and Juliette Culver, "Frameworks for Understanding the Nature of Interactions, Networking, and Community in a Social Networking Site for Academic Practice," *The International Review of Research in Open and Distance Learning* 12:3 (2011), pp.1–11.

[14] Rachel Brooks, Alison Fuller, and Johanna L Waters, *Changing Spaces of Education: New Perspectives on the Nature of Learning* (New York: Routledge, 2012), p. 221.

[15] Suffice to say the findings from research in this area are not all of one thread, and much remains to be seen regarding the educational potential of these activities. For instance, one study on the relationship between user-generated content and democratic engagement finds that contrasted with informational media use, user-generated content involvement is negatively related to political knowledge, even though it is positively correlated with real-world political participation (Johan Östman, "Information, Expression, Participation: How Involvement in User-Generated Content Relates to Democratic Engagement Among Young People," *New Media & Society* 14:6 (2012), pp. 1004–1021).

[16] Barbara Means, Yukie Toyoma, Robert Murphy, Marianne Bakia, and Karla Jones, *Evaluation of Evidence-Based Practices in Online Learning: A Meta-Analysis and Review of Online Learning Studies* (US Department of Education Office of Planning, Evaluation, and Policy Development Policy and Program Studies Service, 2009).

New social media not only reaches students where they live, it also has the potential to make them more than just consumers of knowledge. Employed well within the blended learning environment, Web 2.0 can facilitate the development of critical thinking, communication and collaborative problem-solving skills. This skill development occurs primarily by engaging students in the discovery and creation of knowledge.

Wikipedia and the Linux operating system are foremost examples of powerful media within the cultural commons created from the intellectual gifts and goodwill of volunteers. Linux is a free and open-source operating system whose source code can be modified and distributed by anyone. Despite this seemingly casual and unorganized approach, a version of Linux is run on 97% of the world's fastest super computers.[17] Like the open-source development of Linux, a wiki is a web application that allows people to modify, add, or delete content. It is a collaborative intellectual venture, offering internet users the opportunity to learn by doing. Wikipedia, in effect, is a wiki-*padaeia*.

Learning by interactive, internet-based doing is the focus of Clay Shirky's *Cognitive Surplus*. Cognitive surplus is the intellectual potential that is available but remains untapped in, for example, a television audience. Conversely, in internet audiences, there is increasing potential to make good use of this cognitive surplus, a fact now readily apparent given the great success of Wikipedia. The subtitle of Shirky's book is "How Technology Makes Consumers into Collaborators." Educators employing Web 2.0 technology can help students move from being passive consumers of lectures, books, and internet data into active collaborators in the development of knowledge and skills.

Students already gain much of the information they need for class assignments from publically available online sites or from proprietary online material developed specifically for them by their instructor and by their peers. The blended learning classroom has the potential to transform students from online consumers to critical evaluators of data and co-constructors of knowledge. Here the classroom ceases to be the primary place of information acquisition (lecture/instruction). Instead, it serves as an experiential venue for the acquisition of skills required for the discovery and creation of and critical engagement with knowledge.

Many Web 2.0 platforms facilitate the collaborative learning that can develop civic skills. Socrative.com, for example, allows individual students to post their responses to questions about readings, current affairs, class discussions or class assignments and then vote as a class on the best answers. Such platforms encourage the development of critical thinking, communication and problem-solving skills through collaborative learning. Beyond the exploitation of specific platforms, new social media provide countless opportunities to facilitate civic skill acquisition through collaborative learning. A class on popular media, for instance, might have students tweet whenever they come across an example of media bias in their daily lives. Here students' experiences become primary content for the course, building a social learning environment, and more personal relevance for the subject matter. The challenge in such cases is to use the web to cultivate critical

---

[17] Top 500 Supercomputer Sites, "Operating System Family/Linux," <http://www.top500.org/statistics/details/osfam/1>; a previous version of this statistic is cited at <en.wikipedia.org/wiki/Linux#cite_note-top500-osfam-21>.

thinkers, develop effective communicators, and empower responsible citizens, rather than reinforce tendencies toward spectatorship defined by the isolated consumption of information and entertainment.

Economic Motives for Online Learning

The University of Florida's (UF) new online degree program, UF Online, in many ways exemplifies the contemporary push for online learning. In 2013, the Florida legislature passed a law that begins the process of transferring the development of online courses to private corporations. The initiative promises standards for online majors equivalent to or better than those of traditional majors on campus.[18] Critics suggest that faculty involvement will be increasingly marginalized, as businesses opt for one-size-fits-all, automated, and fully online designs.[19] According to *Inside Higher Ed*, UF has outsourced key administrative tasks for its online university, such as assessment, marketing, and retention support, to Pearson Education, the "publishing turned learning company" that less than a year ago took over its largest single competitor. Pearson's chief executive, Jon Fallon, recently received an honorary degree from the University of Hull. The single most important strategy for achieving "21st century skills," Fallon claims in his acceptance speech, is online learning. Fallon emphasizes the linkage between education and economics in a global marketplace:

> Schools, universities and companies are working together to foster the creativity and collaboration us humans will need to set us apart. We are starting to see less rote learning and more critical thinking. Many global companies, and their employees, are prospering by investing more in continuous learning. Most importantly, we can see that, as we apply technology to transform education, just as surely as in every other sphere of life, it is a race that we can most certainly win.[20]

Fallon's reference to the technological race speaks to the likelihood that many of the careers that college graduates will hold in the coming decades have yet to be created. Hence the importance of teaching adaptive learning practices, such as creativity, critical thinking, and collaboration. In support of this claim, a 2008 report from the National Academy of Sciences notes a growing workplace demand for creative problem-solving, complex communication and collaboration skills, adaptability, self-management, self-development, and systems thinking.[21]

---

[18] UF's completely online university went live in 2014. Behind the initiative is a plan to increase the affordability of a university education and to produce a talented pool of future employees for the twenty-first-century workforce. The state granted UF ten million dollars in startup funds, and promised an additional five million dollars each year thereafter. UF Online's business plan outlines student savings of thirty-seven dollars per credit hour, and the development of thirty wholly online degree programs within ten years (UF Online Comprehensive Business Plan 2013–2019, in *State University System of Florida Board of Governors Agenda and Meeting Materials* (2013), p. 12).

[19] Tom Auxter, "A Corporate Take Over of the Curriculum?" in *Higher Education* (Fall 2013), <http://www.uff-uf.org/wp-content/uploads/2013/11/Tom-Auxter-A-Corporate-Takeover-of-the-Curriculum.pdf>.

[20] John Fallon, "The Great Education and Technology Race," *Pearson*, January 31, 2013, <http://blog.pearson.com/the-great-education-and-technology-race/>.

[21] Margaret Hilton, *Research on Future Skill Demands* (Washington, DC: 2008).

These skills are required to maintain a competitive edge in a quickly changing marketplace.

Traditional universities, like UF, are jumping into online education to secure their market share. But it would be misleading to suggest that online education rises on a wave composed entirely of economic incentives. Both university administrators and educators speak to "the needed skills for 21st century learning." Both acknowledge the important role that media technology can play in the development of these skills. The question at hand is whether a wholly online learning environment can adequately cultivate the critical thinking, communication, and collaborative problem-solving skills required both for the twenty-first-century marketplace and for the maintenance and strengthening of democratic societies.

It is one thing to celebrate higher-order thinking and key skills for the workplace and civil society. It is another thing to look at scientific evidence and actual pedagogy to ascertain what is required for the achievement of these skills. We now provide an overview of the relationship between skills for contemporary democratic citizenship, and philosophically and scientifically informed pedagogy. We employ evidence from democratic theory, neuroscience, and psychology to support our claim that much that is vital to civic skill development is rooted in experiential, relational activities that require embodiment and physical interaction; the very experiences lost in a wholly online degree program.

The Roots of American Democratic Education

Proponents of online degree programs posit the need for innovative learning strategies owing to the rapid changes occurring in an increasingly globalized world. The justification is reminiscent of arguments made by John Dewey a century ago. Dewey (1859–1952) was an American philosopher, psychologist, educator, and public intellectual. He was a founding voice in pragmatism, functional psychology, and experiential learning. Much of Dewey's work addressed the relationship between education and the projects of experimental democracy and reformist activism in civil society.[22] The historical roots of contemporary skills-based pedagogy in the American context can be traced to Dewey's work on democratic education and life-long learning.

Dewey perceived that science and late industrialization had initiated and sped up a "vast extension of the field of association, produced by elimination of distance and lengthening of temporal spans." He writes, "it is obvious that social agencies, political and nonpolitical, cannot be confined to localities."[23] The global connectivity promised by contemporary online networking confirms Dewey's early insight.

As early as 1898, Dewey argued that humanity must engage in conscious, adaptive learning if it is to succeed in the face of rapid change and expansive

---

[22] See James T. Kloppenberg, *Uncertain Victory: Social Democracy and Progressivism in European and American Thought, 1870–1920* (New York: Oxford University Press, 1988); Robert B. Westbrook, *John Dewey and American Democracy* (Ithaca, NY: Cornell University Press, 1991); Louis Menand, *The Metaphysical Club: A Story of Ideas in America*, 1st ed. (New York: Farrar, Straus and Giroux, 2002).

[23] John Dewey, *Freedom and Culture* (1939), in John Dewey (ed.), *The Later Works, 1925–1953* (Carbondale, IL: Southern Illinois University Press, 2008), p. 177.

complexity. But Dewey did not respond to the heightened and increasingly global connectivity of the late nineteenth and early twentieth century by abandoning the pedagogical development of interpersonal skills. Instead, he saw this worldwide process of decentering as evidence of the need for an increased emphasis on this core skill set.[24] By employing "intelligent and controlled foresight," citizens can and should both maintain the cultural and political institutions they have inherited while adapting them to a changing world.[25] This life-long learning process is grounded in the skills of critical thinking and communication.

Dewey explicitly linked the skills for practical judgment that are cultivated by critical thinking with the sophisticated understanding of the world afforded by scientific and technological advancement. What we today identify as complex (social and/or ecological) systems are basically what Dewey called situations. He writes, "In actual experience, there is never any such isolated singular object or event; an object or event is always a special part, phase, or aspect, of an environing experienced world—a situation."[26] The adequacy of any given account of a situation, he writes, is "found in the extent to which that account is based upon taking things in the widest and most complex scale of associations open to observation."[27] Social phenomena, as well as physical objects, should be understood as dynamic relational phenomena, and so "a transaction extending beyond the spatial limits of the organism."[28] Recognizing the complexity of the modern and increasingly global situation, Dewey underlined the importance of cultivating judgment as a way of critically understanding a world that is rich with dynamic interrelated processes.[29]

Dewey rooted learning in communication, the social activity that most challenged and thus refined our understanding of the world. He believed, in keeping with the philosophical tradition beginning with Plato, that a well-educated citizenry was the key to a thriving, vibrant society. Democratic education, according to Dewey, occurred through purposeful interaction in a community of great diversity. Dewey wanted to overcome the notion that communicative interaction was a mere transaction, the notion that communication was "a practical convenience but not of fundamental intellectual significance."[30] Rather, for Dewey, conversation within diverse communities led

---

[24] Ibid. See also Dilafruz R. Williams, "Educating for Democracy: Preparing Undergraduates for Responsible Political Engagement," *Michigan Journal of Community Service Learning* 14:2 (2008), p. 92.

[25] John Dewey, *Evolution and Ethics* (1898), in John Dewey (ed.), *The Early Works, 1882–1898: 1895–1898. Early Essays* (Carbondale, IL: Southern Illinois University Press, 1972), p. 48.

[26] John Dewey, *Logic—The Theory of Inquiry* (1938), in John Dewey (ed.), *The Later Works of John Dewey, 1925–1953: 1938* (Carbondale, IL: Southern Illinois University Press, 2008), p. 71.

[27] John Dewey, *The Inclusive Philosophical Idea* (1928), in John Dewey (ed.), *The Later Works of John Dewey, Volume 3, 1925–1953: 1927–1928, Essays, Reviews, Miscellany, and Impressions of Soviet Russia* (Carbondale, IL: Southern Illinois University Press, 2008), p. 42.

[28] Dewey, *Logic—The Theory of Inquiry*, p. 32.

[29] John Dewey, *Democracy and Education* (1916), in John Dewey (ed.), *The Middle Works, 1899–1924: 1916* (Carbondale, IL: Southern Illinois University Press, 2008), p. 128.

[30] John Dewey, *Experience and Nature* (1929), in John Dewey (ed.), *The Later Works, 1925–1953* (Carbondale, IL: Southern Illinois University Press, 2008), p. 134.

to the encountering of difference, and, when learning occurred, to the refinement of meaning and understanding. Communication is a cooperative venture wherein the activity of the participants is modified and regulated by their partnership.[31] He writes: "When communication occurs, all natural events are subject to reconsideration and revision; they are re-adapted to meet the requirements of conversation..."[32] Communication, in this expansive sense, is a form of collaborative problem-solving. It promotes adaptive engagement. The achievement of these adaptations in meaning, understanding, and practice are the very basis of community, and the essential ingredient of vibrant democracies.

Like Dewey's, Cass Sunstein's (2001) consideration of deliberation in democratic societies emphasizes the importance of people encountering differences of opinion, rather than "hearing countless echoes of their own voices." Sunstein also underlines the importance of common experiences for citizens in diverse societies.[33] To be sure, the internet has vastly increased our ability to encounter difference. But this vast increase in opportunities to experience a heterogeneous world does not necessarily lead to a comparable increase in actual exposure to difference. Communication technologies allow the highly selective filtering of information. Difference is easily ignored simply by "turning the channel"—or preselecting one's websites.

Today we can read, watch, or listen to individually customized sources of information and entertainment. Increasingly, our online behavior pre-determines our future exposure as invisible algorithms tailor every web search to mesh with past preferences and practices. Sunstein calls this tailoring of media exposure to conscious or unconscious preferences and practices, "consumer sovereignty." He sees it as a perfection of markets of information but a political catastrophe. Such individualized media no longer stimulates interaction with a diverse citizenry or reinforces commonly shared bonds. Rather, it reinforces one's own idiosyncrasies and predilections.

Dewey writes, "The doings and sufferings that form experience are, in the degree in which experience is intelligent or charged with meanings, a union of the precarious, novel, irregular with the settled, assured and uniform..."[34] Dewey's emphasis on the educational value of novel experiences that challenge one's predispositions is echoed in the danger that Sunstein perceives in overly personalized online interactions.

Likewise, Robert Putnam's *Bowling Alone* makes the argument that computer-mediated communication, as a result of its lack of real-time, experience-based social cues, "inhibits interpersonal collaboration and trust...Experiments that compare face-to-face and computer-mediated communication confirm that the richer the medium of communication, the more sociable, personal, trusting, and friendly the encounter."[35] Despite advancements in screen resolution or stereo sound, computer-mediated communication fails to provide a rich enough social

---

[31] Ibid., 141.

[32] Ibid., 131.

[33] Cass R. Sunstein, "Freedom of Expression in the United States: The Future," in Thomas Hensley (ed.), *Boundaries of Freedom of Expression and Order in American Democracy* (Kent, OH: Kent State University Press, 2001), pp. 319–347.

[34] Dewey, *Experience and Nature*, p. 359.

[35] Robert D. Putnam, *Bowling Alone: The Collapse and Revival of American Community* (New York: Simon and Schuster, 2000), pp. 176–178.

medium for interpersonal communication, which is key to the development of core components of strong human relationships. Putnam lists nearly a dozen experiments confirming this fact.

Dewey writes, "The belief that a genuine education comes about through experience does not mean that all experiences are genuinely or equally educative."[36] Life online, notwithstanding the tremendous increases in breadth of exposure to people, events, and things, can be a decidedly shallow and blinkered experience. Wholly online education arguably suffers from the cultivation of equally shallow and blinkered experiences. Notwithstanding the tremendous opportunities an online education offers, both economic and pedagogic, it fails to account for some of the most important ways individuals develop and learn.

The roots of American democratic education establish key pedagogical practices for the development of democratic dispositions and skills. As we have shown, proponents of wholly online learning embrace much the same skill set as traditional advocates of civics education, but fail to confront the fact that pedagogies of civic learning most often include extensive student deliberation and interaction, engagement in communities and in community service; that is, embodied learning situations.[37] In the following section, we argue that such an education outperforms wholly online learning in the development of basic civic skills because it exploits the ways humans have evolved to learn.

Education as if Evolution Mattered

Empirical studies over the last half-century have consistently confirmed that students learn best, retain more, and enjoy more thoroughly pedagogy that is experiential, interactive, and collaborative.[38] Evolutionary science helps us understand why. We learn best when we build upon natural endowments and predispositions. Learning is a nurturing of nature, rooted in personal experiences and relationships.

Evolutionary psychologists argue that human beings are innately predisposed to learn some lessons better than others. Our species is hardwired to learn. But this hardwiring, the product of millions of years of evolution, does not leave us equally receptive to every lesson. In this respect, human beings face the same constraints as the rest of the animal kingdom. Biological anthropologist Melvin Konner illustrates this fact:

> ...it is very easy to teach a rat an association between a taste and artificially induced nausea, so that it will avoid the taste thereafter; and it is easy to teach it to associate a light or sound with an electric shock, with similar results in avoidance

---

[36] John Dewey, *Experience and Education* (1938), in John Dewey (ed.), *The Later Works of John Dewey, Volume 13, 1925–1953: 1938–1939* (Carbondale, IL: Southern Illinois University Press, 2008), p. 12.

[37] Katy J. Harriger and Jill J. McMillan, *Speaking of Politics: Preparing College Students for Democratic Citizenship through Deliberative Dialogue* (2007), cited in Civic Learning and Democratic Engagement Task Force, *A Crucible Moment: College Learning and Democracy's Future* (Washington, DC: Association of American Colleges and Universities, 2012), p. 143.

[38] David. W. Johnson, Roger T. Johnson, and Karl A. Smith, *Active Learning: Cooperation in the College Classroom* (Edina, MN: Interaction Book Company, 1998).

behavior. But it is very difficult indeed to make the rat learn the converse associations...Now while these findings may have startled learning psychologists...they came as no surprise to biologists. They are obviously adaptive in the most meaningful sense. The ancestors of rats, in the wild, must surely have gotten into situations where tastes or smells led to nausea, and where lights and sounds led to external physical pain. But natural selection very likely had no opportunity to favor rats who could associate lights and sounds with nausea...It produced, instead, genetically based tendencies to learn some lessons better than others.[39]

Konner concludes that a rat's genes do not fully determine its behavioral repertoire. Rather, its genetic constitution sets the boundaries within which the rodent may behaviorally adapt to its environment, essentially framing how it will learn from experience.

It is safe to say that human beings have a much larger behavioral repertoire than rodents, or any species. We are capable of adaptive learning orders of magnitude greater than other animals. Still, as flesh and blood creatures that are, no less than other species, products of evolution, we are neurologically hardwired to learn some lessons more easily than others.[40] We learn best, and best develop our repertoire of adaptive skills, when this knowledge and these skills are the fruits of experiences that we are "biologically primed" to harvest.[41]

For the vast share of human history, learning was always achieved in context. Real-world experience, thick with contextual detail, provided the chief means by which education took place. With this in mind it is not surprising that empirical research has demonstrated that individuals presented with a surfeit of options will often fail to make any meaningful selection, or will make poorer choices than individuals presented with relatively few options. Less is often more.[42] This finding reflects our heritage as a species. For the most part, judging and choosing was conducted in the face of relatively few options within a restricted local context. Today, however, the internet provides a staggering amount of instantly accessible information and options. This "sea of gray" becomes an increasingly difficult environment in which to make critical judgments.

When surfing the internet, students are not only presented with too much information, they are presented with information that lacks a real-world context, and so lacks that which our species has, for all of our history, utilized extensively when making critical judgments. This is a general shortcoming of digital information. In direct communication, facial expressions, hand gestures, body language, and tones of voice supply the contextual information needed for the proper interpretation of the spoken word. These contextual clues are lacking in digital communication. In order to avoid misinterpretation of our intent and meaning in digital communication, therefore, we often find it necessary to make these clues explicit. For example, we use *emoticons* when texting to provide a

---

[39] Melvin Konner, *The Tangled Wing: Biological Constraints on the Human Spirit* (New York: Holt, Rinehart and Winston, 1982), pp. 27–28.

[40] See Steven Pinker, *The Blank Slate* (New York: Viking, 2002), pp. 40–41.

[41] See Steven R. Quartz and Terrence J. Sejnowski, *Liars, Lovers, and Heroes: What the New Brain Science Reveals about How We Became Who We Are* (New York: William Morrow, 2002), p. 183.

[42] Barry Schwartz, *The Paradox of Choice: Why More Is Less* (New York: Harper, 2005).

surrogate for the contextual information that otherwise would be supplied by our bodies. In a similar vein, sociologist Jesse Daniels has studied students' ability to critically discern racist discourse online.[43] Daniels finds that the online environment lacks the social clues one might find in the real world that allow the perception and interpretation of such discourse. What social clues do exist online may easily be masked by the aesthetic presentation of the information.

Implicit Learning

The vast proportion of the contextual information that we utilize to correctly interpret each other and our world is appropriated unconsciously. It is a form of tacit learning. Our sense organs collect between 200,000 and one million bits of information for every bit of information that enters our awareness.[44] Likewise, our capacity for memory is not fully, or even primarily, within our conscious control.[45] We perceive, remember, and assess—in short, we learn—much more than we could ever process with our conscious minds. And it is not simply the quantity of information that makes tacit knowledge important. Oftentimes it also has the edge over explicit learning in terms of quality. It is frequently more robust and resilient in the face of a complex, challenging, and changing world.[46]

In the late 1960s, chemist, social scientist, and philosopher Michael Polanyi described in phenomenological terms how it is that we can have a "subsidiary" knowledge of things that never rise to consciousness. The paradigm case for such tacit knowledge, according to Polanyi, is the way we "know" our own bodies.[47] The balance and coordination we exhibit when walking, running, or jumping demonstrate that we know how to do many things without being able to explain how we do them.

---

[43] Jesse Daniels, Interview, "The Internet Can't Teach What the Social World Can," *Contexts* 8:14 (2009), <http://contexts.org/articles/fall-2009/the-internet-cant-teach-what-the-social-world-can/>.

[44] Timothy Wilson, *Strangers to Ourselves: Discovering the Adaptive Unconscious* (Cambridge, MA: Belknap Press, 2002), p. 24; Manfred Zimmerman, "The Nervous System in the Context of Information Theory," in R.F. Schmidt and G. Thews (eds), *Human Physiology*, 2nd ed. (Berlin, Germany: Springer-Verlag, 1989), pp. 166–173; Ap Dijksterhuis, Henk Aarts, and Pamela Smith, "The Power of the Subliminal: On Subliminal Persuasion and Other Potential Applications, in Ran Hassin, James Uleman, and John Bargh (eds), *The New Unconscious* (Oxford, UK: Oxford University Press, 2005), p. 82.

[45] Jeffrey P. Toth, "Nonconscious Forms of Human Memory," in Endel Tulving and Fergus Craik (eds), *The Oxford Handbook of Memory* (Oxford, UK: Oxford University Press, 2000), pp. 245–261, p. 252. See also K. Koh and D.E. Meyer, "Function Learning: Induction of Continuous Stimulus-Response Relations," *Journal of Experimental Psychology: Learning, Memory, and Cognition* 17:5 (1991), pp. 811–836. P. Lewicki, M. Czyzewska, and H. Hoffman, "Unconscious Acquisition of Complex Procedural Knowledge," *Journal of Experimental Psychology: Learning, Memory, and Cognition* 13:4 (1987), pp. 523–530.

[46] See Arthur Reber, *Implicit Learning and Tacit Knowledge: An Essay on the Cognitive Unconscious* (New York: Oxford University Press, 1993); Guy Claxton, *Hare Brain Tortoise Mind: Why Intelligence Increases When You Think Less* (Hopewell, NJ: The Ecco Press, 1997); George E. Marcus, W. Russell Neuman, and Michael MacKuen, *Affective Intelligence and Political Judgment* (Chicago, IL: University of Chicago Press, 2000), p. 30.

[47] Michael Polanyi, *Knowing and Being*, ed. Majorie Greene (Chicago, IL: University of Chicago Press, 1969), p. 183.

The French aphorist La Rochefoucauld observed that "Simple grace is to the body what common sense is to the mind."[48] Our common sense is both a product of and generator of tacit knowledge. A lack of common sense reflects an inability to grasp those lessons that human beings are predisposed to learn. We have many common senses, such as the ability to gauge distances or weights, assess visual perspective, recognize faces, and attribute goals and intentions to actors. We cannot well describe how we achieve these complicated feats of perception and assessment, no less than we can well describe how we ride a bicycle. As philosopher G.E. Moore observed: "We are all, I think, in this strange position that we do know many things . . . and yet we do not know how we know them."[49]

Tacit knowledge, whether in the form of common sense or more specialized physical or cognitive skills, might be described as a kind of experientially acquired know-how. We do not arrive in the world with knowledge of how to walk, ride a bike, or speak a language. Rather, we are born with the potential, if we are typical, of developing the muscular coordination, sense of balance, and linguistic skills that make these complicated feats possible. We are not "hard-wired" to do these things in the same sense that we are hard-wired to breathe. But we are genetically predisposed to learn to do these things given a sufficiently supportive environment.[50]

When gaining tacit knowledge, we are engaged in what Polanyi called "learning without awareness."[51] We first learn to speak, walk, and ride a bicycle, for example, without acquiring conscious knowledge of grammar, physiology, or classical mechanics. We are engaged in implicit learning (also known as implicit cognition) as opposed to explicit learning. Explicit learning in specific arenas, if it ever occurs, happens long after the respective tacit knowledge and skills have been acquired and perfected.

Developmental psychologist and educational theorist Jean Piaget experimentally demonstrated this phenomenon of learning without awareness. Piaget had children practice hitting a target with a ball tethered to a rope. Swinging the ball in a circle, the children had to let go of the rope at just the right time, so that the ball would strike the target. With practice, the children quickly learned to accomplish the task. And yet, when asked to explain to another child how best to hit the target, many children, including all the younger ones, incorrectly stated that one should let go of the rope when the ball is directly in front of the target. They had gained tacit knowledge without awareness, which allowed them to strike the target even though they could not explain this strategy to their peers.

Political theorist Michael Oakeshott worried about the danger posed by the undervaluing and undermining of tacit knowledge in education. He was particularly concerned with the cultivation of the tacit capacity for practical judgment and other complex mental capacities.[52] Like Polanyi, Oakeshott insists that tacit knowledge, which he calls "knowing how," is not limited in its domain

---

[48] La Rochefoucauld, *Maxims*, trans. Leonard Tanock (London, UK: Penguin Books, 1959), pp. 45, 67.

[49] Quoted in John Coates, *The Claims of Common Sense: Moore, Wittgenstein, Keynes and the Social Sciences* (Cambridge, UK: Cambridge University Press, 1996), p. 47.

[50] Reber, *Implicit Learning and Tacit Knowledge*. See also LeDoux, *The Synaptic Self*, p. 85.

[51] Polanyi, *Knowing and Being*, pp. 141–142.

[52] Michael Oakeshott, *The Voice of Liberal Learning* (Indianapolis, IN: Liberty Fund, 2001), pp. 49–51.

or impact to physical or perceptual skills. The tacit knowledge that allows us to make use of information and apply rules intelligently, Oakeshott insists, is learned "obliquely." Without this tacit knowledge, much of what we "know" cannot be properly utilized. Empirical evidence supports this conclusion. Students who demonstrate high levels of tacit knowledge achieve better academic grades than students who are low in tacit knowledge but equal or higher in explicit knowledge.[53]

Teaching, Oakeshott maintains, is a "twofold activity." First, it always entails the communication and transmission of information. Oakeshott calls this "instructing." In turn, it also entails the cultivation of a capacity for judgment. This skill is not gained by way of instruction. Rather, it is "imparted" as a by-product of instruction. Judgment is impossible to teach in "a separate lesson." It can only be "imparted obliquely in the course of instruction."[54] The capacity for judgment is the crucial side effect of the manner in which information is discovered, created, and shared.

Students gain an aptitude for judgment by actively interpreting their teachers' and each others' performances of thinking and judging. It "is implanted unobtrusively in the manner in which information is conveyed, in a tone of voice, in the gesture which accompanies instruction, in asides and oblique utterances, and by example."[55] The challenge, Oakeshott writes, is for the student

> to detect the individual intelligence which is at work in every utterance, even in those which convey impersonal information . . . We may listen to what a man has to say, but unless we overhear in it a mind at work and can detect the idiom of thought, we have understood nothing . . . Learning, then, is acquiring the ability to feel and to think, and the pupil will never acquire these abilities unless he has learned to listen for them and to recognize them in the conduct and utterances of others.[56]

As Guy Claxton observes, "One needs to be able to soak up experience of complex domains—such as human relationships—through one's pores, and to extract the subtle, contingent patterns that are latent within it."[57] The tacit skill of judgment, which grounds most if not all explicit knowledge, is experientially absorbed.[58]

Mark Twain counseled that we should never let our education get in the way of our learning. If formal education does not foster the acquisition of tacit knowledge and skills, then it may be gained at the expense of a deeper and more enduring form of learning. Political theorist Sheldon Wolin had this same worry. The use of standardized step-by-step procedures for inquiry and research—Wolin called it methodism—was impeding the acquisition of crucial knowledge and skills. Wolin writes: "The triumph of methodism constitutes a crisis in political education and . . . the main victim is the tacit political knowledge which is so vital to making judgments, not only judgments about the adequacy and value of theories and

---

[53] Anit Somech and Ronit Bogler, "Tacit Knowledge in Academia: Its Effects on Student Learning and Achievement," *The Journal of Psychology* 133:6 (1999), pp. 605–616.

[54] Oakeshott, *The Voice of Liberal Learning*, p. 58.

[55] Ibid., 60.

[56] Ibid., 59.

[57] Claxton, *Hare Brain Tortoise Mind*, p. 192.

[58] Oakeshott, *The Voice of Liberal Learning*, pp. 53–54.

methods, but about the nature and perplexities of politics as well."[59] What Wolin says about political knowledge and judgment applies as well to a much broader arena of social and ecological affairs, including the development of common sense in these areas. The key to averting this crisis entails acknowledging that much crucial learning occurs, to recall Oakeshott's phrase, "obliquely in the course of instruction" as students absorb the embodied thought and judgments of their teachers and their peers.

Job Preparation versus Life-long Learning

Despite all the evidence supporting the important role of embodied education for the development of crucial civic skills, wholly online degree programs constitute a growing and lucrative market. The development of this market is often justified by reference to the need to better prepare students for specific jobs, as opposed to offering them a traditional liberal arts education.[60]

Preparing students for citizenship is generally neglected in the push for online education, as is educating students, through the development of skill sets, so they learn how to learn. Yet developing students who are life-long learners, apart from its value for democracy, is a crucial need for today's economic marketplace. The Bureau of Labor Statistics reports that the average worker today stays at each of his or her jobs for 4.4 years. The expected job tenure of students now entering the workforce is about half that.[61] This means that a student leaving college today should expect to have between fifteen and twenty different jobs in his or her lifetime. In this context, the students best prepared for the marketplace are those who have developed a skill set that allows them to learn adaptively in a changing environment. Critical thinking, communication, and collaborative problem-solving skills are the foundation for such life-long learning.

While the development of such skill sets in students (for example, in the liberal arts) may not yield them salaries at their first jobs out of college that measure up to the initial salaries of students emerging from professional degree programs, the long-term prognosis looks different. Tom Auxter, President of the United Faculty of Florida, recently criticized Florida Governor Rick Scott's use of an overly simplified and strictly economic metric in his assessment and restructuring of the state university system. Concerning Scott's policy of using post-graduation salary levels as a sign of success, Auxter writes, "The salaries of liberal arts and sciences graduates do not jump ahead until a decade after graduation.

---

[59] Sheldon Wolin, "Political Theory as a Vocation," *American Political Science Review* 63:4 (1969), p. 1077.

[60] See for example, Erin Sparks and Mary Jo Waits, *Degrees for What Jobs? Raising Expectations for Universities and Colleges in a Global Economy* (Washington, DC: National Governors Association, Center for Best Practices), <http://www.nga.org/files/live/sites/NGA/files/pdf/1103DEGREESJOBS.PDF>, cited in Ashley Finley, "Civic Learning and Democratic Engagements," Paper prepared for the United States Department of Education as part of Contract: ED-OPE-10-C-0078 (2011).

[61] Jeanne Meister, "Job Hopping Is the 'New Normal' for Millennials: Three Ways to Prevent a Human Resource Nightmare," *Forbes Magazine*, August 14, 2012, <http://www.forbes.com/sites/jeannemeister/2012/08/14/job-hopping-is-the-new-normal-for-millennials-three-ways-to-prevent-a-human-resource-nightmare>.

With training on the job, work experience, and creative, critical thinking, they not only catch up ten years out; they move ahead of others. They have either much higher salaries paid for business or professional innovation, or they have jobs with important, socially valued responsibilities. If it is the latter, the salaries may be less impressive, but the contributions can be much greater."[62]

The capacity for online degree programs to cultivate the skills and dispositions for life-long learning is challenged by many educators. One professor laments in a *New York Times* op-ed, "Online education is a one-size-fits-all endeavor. It tends to be a monologue and not a real dialogue . . . But in real courses the students and teachers come together and create an immediate and vital community of learning. A real course creates intellectual joy, at least in some. I don't think an Internet course ever will."[63] It is too soon to say whether intellectual passions can be ignited and sustained through online learning. Certainly online courses composed primarily of filmed lectures that are "in the can" may present students with a single, stationary point of view that is not conducive to the development of their own intellectual passions and skills. But the standard fare in many universities and colleges—PowerPoint-driven lectures to large classes—may be equally monological and uninspiring.

Given a choice between attending canned (and quite possibly dated) PowerPoint lectures delivered to large classes in brick and mortar universities and colleges, and a state-of-the-art online education that utilizes the best that the web has to offer, it is likely that a great many students will opt for online learning. It is both more convenient and more in keeping with their daily practices of online interaction (that is Facebook, Twitter, Instagram, and online shopping). With this in mind, it is counterproductive and likely futile to resist the development of online education in the hopes of retrieving a liberal arts pedagogy limited to Socratic inquiry in small classes. Better to exploit web-based resources and technologies—including those developed for online degree programs—while redeploying and further investing in key classroom interactions for the development of crucial skills. This is the potential of the blended learning environment.

The current drive for online degree programs in many ways resembles the early dot-com boom of the late 1900s. As eager as those venture capitalists were to embrace the initial rise of web-based business, administrators and politicians today cheer online learning's promise to lower costs and increase market share. The dot-com boom of the late 1990s transformed the business landscape. Then the bubble burst. At the end of the day, there were many winners, and no small number of losers. Arguably, the market is a fitting place for high-stakes gamblers. The university is not. The difference is that the current enthusiasm for online education is not risking venture capital, but the lives and prospects of a generation of students, and the prospects for democracy.

---

[62] Education Votes, "Florida Universities Suffer Funding Crisis as Gov. Scott Ramps Up Political Games," <http://educationvotes.nea.org/2014/07/22/florida-universities-suffer-funding-crisis-as-gov-scott-ramps-up-political-games/>.

[63] Mark Edmundson, "The Trouble With Online Education," *The New York Times*, July 19, 2012, <http://www.nytimes.com/2012/07/20/opinion/the-trouble-with-online-education.html>.

Conclusion

The Agricultural Revolution led to monarchical governments; the Industrial Revolution ushered in representative governments; the Digital Revolution will likely generate significant shifts in democratic governance. It is too early to say what transitions and transformations will occur, though predictions range from the death of democracy to its full flowering. This article examined the role of higher education in providing students with the skills they require to flourish within the protean democracies of the Digital Age. To some extent, these skills are oriented toward helping students navigate and exploit the digital resources that appear in accelerating profusion. Notwithstanding all the technological novelty, and its transformative power, the Digital Age is still populated by flesh and blood human beings living within and depending upon an interconnected web of social and ecological relationships. We assert that embodied learning is key to the education of empowered citizens, and we have presented evidence supporting this claim from social scientists and natural scientists. Today, this embodied education is threatened as online education usurps more traditional forms of pedagogy, and consequently deprives students of the worldly experiences and tacit learning so crucial to sustaining human and ecological communities.

The rush to develop wholly online college degrees ignores crucial insights of centuries of humanistic and pedagogical scholarship, as well as much contemporary science. But Web 2.0 capacities, blended classrooms, and other technologies and processes made available by the internet ought to have the chance to prove themselves within a diverse educational ecosystem. With this in mind, the technologies of online higher education should be adopted when they demonstrate verifiable improvements in learning, and when it is safe to say they do not endanger educational outcomes that are key to participation in democratic societies. As there exists little evidence for the efficacy of many components of online education, and ample evidence demonstrating the loss of vital civic components, adoption of online platforms should be slow, and at scales that are safe to fail, rather than wholesale across higher education institutions. Online higher education should not be a revolution. Rather, it should be an evolution. The deployment of Web 2.0 media and technologies should be closely tied to the mandate of experiential and interpersonal skills-based education, which is key to the democratic goals of our learning institutions.

As students navigate an increasingly interconnected, globalized, and quickly changing world, they will have to exercise adaptive skills. Institutions of higher education have a mission to cultivate these skills in their students, as well as the good judgment required to deploy them well. These academic institutions will exhibit good judgment themselves when they successfully exploit the best of new technologies while continuing to nurture the natural learning dispositions of their students. Dewey maintained that our capacity for learning in complex social situations determines the resilience of our democracies. The future of democracy remains integrally tied to the quality of education.

Dewey was no defender of intellectual cloisters. As a pragmatist, he maintained that we learn best when we adaptively apply intelligence to worldly problems. We agree, and have argued here that institutes of higher education should not reject or even resist online resources. Indeed, they should creatively exploit them. But we would be mistaken to abandon the ivory tower for a hasty pilgrimage to Silicon Valley. Far better to integrate web technology and media into a classroom that builds upon, and further cultivates, crucial learning and democratic skills.

The Changing Democratic Functions of Historically Black Colleges and Universities

Clyde Wilcox
Georgetown University, USA
JoVita Wells
University of the District of Columbia, USA
Georges Haddad
Howard University School of Medicine, USA
Judith K. Wilcox
Boston University School of Medicine, USA

Abstract *Historically Black Colleges and Universities (HBCU) face the same financial pressures as traditionally white institutions, and face unique challenges that stem from historical racial disparities in funding, their historical missions and student bodies. HBCUs have served diverse democratic functions over time, but today critics on the right and left question their continued relevance. Here we review the changing democratic functions of HBCUs and argue that in an era of retreat from affirmative action HBCUs remain important to the educational opportunities of African Americans and others. We suggest some additional democratic functions that HBCUs might play in the twenty-first century.*

Introduction

An air of impending crisis hangs over the academy. With costs rising and traditional revenue streams limited, many colleges and universities face grave financial difficulties and are considering remedies that may redefine higher education. These financial problems are especially acute at the nation's historically black colleges and universities (HBCUs), where financial shortfalls threaten the continued operation of some schools, and the unique missions and student bodies of these universities limit their abilities to adopt cost-cutting moves that are common in traditionally white institutions (TWIs). In an era where TWIs use their superior resources to recruit the strongest black students, some question the continued role of HBCUs. Here we argue that these institutions perform important democratic functions.

HBCUs are defined in federal law as institutions formed before 1964 whose primary mission is the education of black Americans. Not all minority-serving institutions are HBCUs, and, conversely, not all HBCUs today principally serve African Americans.[1] Two HBCUs in West Virginia have for decades had student

---

[1] Many community colleges serve large black student majorities but were formed after 1964.

bodies that are 80% or more white, due in part to conscious decisions by the institutions.[2] Moreover, HBCUs vary in their missions and their focuses. Some, like Morehouse and Spelman Colleges in Atlanta, offer single-sex education, but most are coeducational. Some, like Howard University in Washington, DC offer a number of doctoral and professional degrees, while others offer only four-year and in some cases two-year degrees. Some are elite schools with selective admissions; others offer open admission. And some have high graduation rates, but a disappointingly large number of HBCUs graduate fewer than thirty percent of black students who enroll.[3] Generalizations about HBCUs abound, but few fit all of these myriad institutions. Administrators at HBCUs often bemoan the tendency of many observers to lump all institutions into the same category.

Why use such a heterogeneous category in an article on the democratic functions of minority serving institutions? First, we focus on HBCUs because the creation of this category in federal law has resulted in better available data for institutions that fall in this category. Second, we focus on HBCUs because they have a long and complex history of democratic functions, and the justification of their continued existence and/or support is questioned by both conservatives and liberals alike. Many HBCUs were incubators of ideas, strategies, and theories in the Civil Rights movement, and many African American students choose these institutions because of that history. But these institutions also have a history of providing college access to economically and socially disadvantaged students, and this historic mission remains central to many HBCUs. Finally, we examine HBCUs because of an irony inherent in their history: they were a fertile breeding ground for political activists who challenged the separate but equal, segregated universities and colleges in the 1970s, but their very success has redefined the role of HBCUs in the twenty-first century.

Financial Pressures and Strategies in the Academy and at HBCUs

Most American colleges and universities find their costs rising and many of their traditional revenue streams limited. As universities have added administrative staff and in many cases sought to provide additional student services, costs have increased steadily.[4] National research funding and state support for public colleges and universities have declined, in many cases sharply. Colleges and universities have responded by increasing tuition, but this has priced many potentially talented students out of higher education and left many who graduate with crippling debt loads. Soaring tuition costs raise troubling questions about the

---

[2] Shereen Marisol Meraji and Gene Demby, "The Whitest Historically Black College in America," *Morning Edition*, (October 18, 2013). <http://www.npr.org/blogs/codeswitch/2013/10/18/236345546/the-whitest-historically-black-college-in-america.>

[3] "Black Student College Graduation Rates Remain Low, but Modest Progress Begins to Show," *The Journal of Blacks in Higher Education* (2006), <http://www.jbhe.com/features/50_blackstudent_gradrates.html>.

[4] During the 2000s, faculty salaries were essentially flat, although faculty benefits increased. But one study argued that additional administrative costs were the main driver of the increase in university expenses. See Scott Carlson, "Administrator Hiring Drives 28% Boom in Higher-Ed Workforce," *Chronicle of Higher Education*, (February 5, 2014).

future democratic contributions of higher education.[5] Today there is considerable public backlash against tuition increases, and at the same time universities have also seen a decline in total charitable giving.[6]

In an effort to curb personnel costs, many institutions of higher education have sharply increased the portion of courses taught by part-time, non-tenure temporary (temps) and adjunct faculty. The *Chronicle of Higher Education* has recently launched a series of articles exploring the "adjunct explosion." The American Association of University Professors (AAUP) estimates that more than fifty percent of college and university faculty are part-time, although many work full time hours by combining part-time positions across multiple institutions – but for far less than full time faculty and without benefits such as health insurance. These adjuncts often teach a single class at a university, may share an office with several others, and are not expected to maintain substantial office hours. These temps and adjuncts do not engage in research with graduate or professional students and are less able to mentor students than are full time faculty.

College and universities have also sought to decrease personnel costs by expanding their offerings of online courses. In some cases these courses are designed to increase revenue by offering certificate programs and, in some cases, MA degrees to non-traditional students who may live anywhere in the world. In other cases online courses are designed to lower instructional costs because, once produced, they require only a few hours of grading, making them cheaper than adjuncts. Many administrators feel compelled to move into the online market, facing growing competition from the vamped up online offerings of many private institutions that now constitute twenty-six percent of all colleges and universities. The University of Phoenix boasts the largest student enrollment in America, and other vendors are crowding the market. Today twenty percent of college students take at least one course on-line, and nine percent take all of their courses online.[7]

Not all online instruction has immediate financial advantages for universities. There has been a significant push to provide free online courses to very large or to more targeted audiences. There have been online startups such as Coursera and the new MIT-Harvard initiative EdX, which help provide massive open online courses (MOOCs) to international audiences. Stanford's online course in artificial intelligence has boasted enrollments of 160,000. These MOOCs are sometimes supplemented by various types of online discussions and graded content, frequently provided by contractors. Currently MOOCs have low completion rates, and few students ultimately obtain college credit for these courses, although the practice is in its infancy. But it is difficult to yet see a good business model for MOOCs. To date, information industries that give their products away for free have found it difficult to survive.[8] But free online college content may help

---

[5] Gary King and Maya Sen, "The Troubled Future of Colleges and Universities," *PS: Political Science and Politics* 46:1 (2013), pp. 83–89; Nannerl O. Keohane, "Higher Education in the Twenty-First Century: Innovation, Adaptation, Preservation," *PS: Political Science and Politics* 46:1 (2013), pp. 102–105.

[6] King and Sen, "Troubled Future."

[7] Ibid.

[8] Henry E. Brady, "Let's Not Railroad American Higher Education!," *PS: Political Science and Politics* 46:1 (2013), pp. 94–101.

ameliorate to some extent the negative democratic consequences of skyrocketing tuition costs, for those priced out of a four-year education may be able to access college-level pedagogy.

Finally, many universities have sought to enter into partnerships with private industry, seeking to develop patents and products that might increase revenue while attracting large contributions to the university. These collaborations raise their own set of questions, including distortions to the intellectual agendas of disciplines which do not focus on developing products, and the tension between the free flow of ideas through peer reviewed publications and secrecy required in developing and protecting patents. The model of ideas as private property is somewhat antithetical to the ethos of the university, but John Mark Hansen has noted that

> the university occupies a peculiar space in democratic societies with market economies. Higher education serves the cause of democracy by fostering a more able and enlightened citizenry and the needs of the economy by producing a more skilled and creative workforce. The university likewise depends on the state and the market for its resources...that are the lifeblood of every institution of higher learning.... And therein lies the tension. The university forever has been in but not of the polity and the market. Its values are not the preferences of the powerful or the returns of its investors, or the wants of its customers. Its ideals are the Enlightenment principles of reasoned argument, systematic evidence, and judicious inference.[9]

HBCUs face the same cost constraints as traditionally white institutions, but some have an even greater difficulty justifying tuition hikes to their less-affluent constituency. Smaller HBCUs face intense financial pressure, including elite Fisk University which produced a cadre of civil rights activists in the 1950s and 1960s. Even some elite schools such as Howard University in Washington, DC are in financial trouble.[10]

HBCU's face the same fiscal squeeze as TWIs, but they have additional problems. State-funded HBCUs have never been funded at parity with TWIs, and although some states reached agreements to partially compensate for past funding inequities, subsequent state budget woes have been offered as an explanation for the failure to follow through. For many HBCUs, then, there is a structural funding issue that is directly related to past racism. It is difficult to compete today with TWIs that have had substantial funding advantages for decades.

More recently, changing eligibility requirements by the Department of Education for the Parent Plus loan program (a federally funded loan program for parents and guardians with good credit) has led to the denial of funding to more than seventeen-thousand HBCU students. Forty-six percent of students at HBCUs come from families with incomes lower than $34,000, and a substantial majority of students qualify for Pell grants. The denial of the Parent Plus loans for many poor parents has not only blocked these students from enrolling, but denied HBCUs

---

[9] John Mark Hansen, "Paying the Piper: Higher Education Financing and Academic Freedom," *PS: Political Science and Politics* 46:1 (2013), pp. 110–113.

[10] Charlayne Hunter Gault, "Hard Times at Howard U," *The New York Times*, February 4, 2014.

more than one-hundred million dollars in tuition. Some HBCUs have floated the idea of suing the Obama Administration over these rules, although to date there has been little action.[11]

Moreover, HBCUs mostly have small endowments. The total endowment of all 106 HBCUs in 2013 was $1.6 billion, less than the total endowment of just one large TWI research institution, The Ohio State University.[12] These institutions also have relatively anemic fundraising campaigns. As TWIs began to desegregate the largess of white northern liberals, HBCUs declined.[13] But as a group, HBCUs also have poor records of fundraising from alumni, despite the plethora of affluent and famous alumni that some institutions possess. Only Spelman College has a strong tradition of alumni giving, although Howard University has successfully expanded its fundraising despite a period of administrative difficulties that led to the resignation of two presidents.[14] Many alumni apparently believe that their institutions are mismanaged. Walter Kimbrough, president of Dillard University in New Orleans, refers to the "Bermuda Triangle" where students encounter problems with the registrar, business office, and financial aid office, which leaves alumni fearing that their contributions might not be used properly. Speaking at Morehouse College's commencement in May 2013, President Obama joked that "I know that some of you had to wait in long lines to get into today's ceremony. And I would apologize, but it did not have anything to do with security. Those graduates just wanted you to know what it's like to register for classes here."[15]

Faced with even greater cost constraints than TWIs, HBCUs have already moved rapidly toward hiring adjuncts, and are moving somewhat more slowly to offer online courses. But these strategies pose significant risks for HBCUs, many of whom service student bodies that have many students who are first in their families to attend college, and who have special needs for mentoring and close faculty contact. HBCUs not only provide training in science, technology, engineering and mathematics (STEM), political science, and music; their special value is in promoting Black identity, and confidence and self-esteem, qualities that are best provided by full-time faculty.[16] These institutions need full-time faculty to fulfill this mission, as many of the administrators we interviewed stated. Because these students enter with a variety of deficits discussed below, the diverse needs of HBCU students require constant monitoring and mentoring.

---

[11] Ibid.; Tyler Kingkade, "HBCUs may sue Obama Administration Over New Student Loan Rules," *Huffington Post*, March 13, 2013, <http://www.huffingtonpost.com/2013/03/13/hbcus-obama-administration-black-colleges-lawsuit_n_2869216.html>.

[12] Ibid.

[13] Gene Demby, "Are HBCUs in Trouble? An Evergreen Question," *NPR*, June 26, 2013, <http://www.npr.org/blogs/codeswitch/2013/06/25/195666060/are-hbcus-in-trouble-an-evergreen-question>.

[14] Demby reports that Howard increased its rate of alumni giving from 4 to 16% between 2008 and 2012.

[15] Ibid.

[16] Gregory N. Price, William Spriggs, and Omari H. Swinton, "The Relative Returns to Graduating from a Historically Black College/University: Propensity Score Matching Estimates from the National Survey of Black Americans," *Review of Black Political Economy* 38:2 (2011), pp. 103–130.

The Changing Democratic Functions of HBCUs

HBCUs across the country have been created for various purposes and have served various democratic functions over time. The first HBCUs were formed by northern evangelicals and other religious liberals who sought to extend educational opportunities to Blacks, in an extension of Jefferson's vision. Prior to the end of the Civil War, southern states generally banned teaching slaves to read or write. Three HBCUs were founded by missionary groups in northern states during this period: the Institute for Colored Youth (now Cheyney University) in Pennsylvania in 1837, Ashmun Institute (now Lincoln University) in Pennsylvania in 1854, and Ohio African University (now Wilberforce University) in Ohio in 1856.

After the end of the war and especially during Reconstruction, there was a rapid expansion in the number of educational institutions in the South aimed at serving Blacks. The drive for institution building came from religious activists in the American Missionary Society, the American Baptist Home Mission Society, and the African Methodist Episcopal Church seeking to provide education to former slaves, but it also was motivated by ex-slaves who saw education as the best opportunity to escape the continued and increasing indignities from some whites.[17] These organizations and activists helped fund a number of private colleges and universities in the South and border states, including elite schools such as Morehouse, Spelman, Fisk, and Virginia Union University.[18] Many of these schools initially provided both secondary and post-secondary degrees, with the latter centered on a liberal arts curriculum. In 1865, the establishment of the Freedman's Bureau further spurred the building of schools including a few important colleges and universities such as Howard University, Hampton Institute, and Atlanta University.

These early private HBCUs served to train a generation of teachers who would spread literacy in secondary and even elementary schools. They also focused on developing the moral character and personality responsibility of their students, and most also trained a generation of pastors who would provide cultural leadership to African American communities throughout the South. Morehouse College for example was once called Atlanta Baptist Seminary. These schools were funded primarily by wealthy philanthropists and benefitted from gifts of land and facilities.

If the first wave of HBCU formation was aimed at expanding educational opportunities, the second was driven, at least in part, by the logic of segregation and white advantage. Of the seventeen Southern states that received funds from the 1862 Morrill Act that established land grant institutions, only three (VA, MS, and SC) shared those funds with Black colleges and universities.[19] The passage of the Second Morrill Act in 1890 sparked a wave of public HBCUs in the South.

---

[17] Roland G. Fryer and Michael Greenstone, "The Causes and Consequences of Attending Historically Black Colleges and Universities," *American Economic Journal: Applied Economics* 2:1 (2010).

[18] Garian Clark, "*U.S. v. Fordice*: The Irony of Integration and the Elusive Goal of Equality," *Yahoo Voices*, 2009, <http://voices.yahoo.com/us-v-fordice-irony-integration-elusive-2532231.html>.

[19] Alcorn University, Hampton Institute, and Claffin University were the first HBCUs to be designated as land grant institutions.

In order for southern states to gain access to federal funds for their TWI land-grant institutions, they needed to provide funds to educate Black students. The Act denied funds to institutions where a "distinction of race or color is made in the admission of students," but maintained that "the establishment and maintenance of such colleges separately for white and colored students shall be held to be in compliance with the provisions of this act if the funds ... be equitably divided."[20] This "separate but equal" doctrine was later enshrined into constitutional jurisprudence with *Plessy v. Ferguson* in 1896.

Of course the "equitable division" of resources was never taken seriously, and thus one function of this second wave of HBCUs was to allow southern states to reap larger disbursements to support their TWIs. But the Second Morrill Act did lead to the establishment of a number of colleges that provided training in agriculture, mining, and technical trades that were previously unavailable to Blacks, and to the establishment of schools such as North Carolina A&T State University and Florida A&M University. Moreover, the "separate but equal" doctrine required that southern states allot public funds to build elementary and secondary schools for Blacks, and the rapid expansion of especially high schools in urban areas led to increased demand for Black teachers for these schools. HBCUs suddenly found a steady stream of students seeking to gain credentials to teach in these schools.[21]

During the late 1890s, a heated debate over the function of HBCUs and higher education opportunities for African Americans arose between Booker T. Washington, founder of the Tuskegee Institute, and W.E.B. DuBois, the first African American to earn a doctorate from Harvard University. Washington argued that HBCUs should focus on providing a vocational and industrial education instead of the traditional liberal arts education advocated by northern intellectuals. Speaking at a time when the Southern white establishment was reestablishing their dominance over African Americans with a mixture of political and economic power and raw violence, Washington suggested a compromise in which Blacks were allowed to pursue technical education that led to high paying jobs, but in which they did not challenge white privilege. In a famous speech at the Atlanta Exposition in 1895, he told a white audience that "The opportunity to earn a dollar in a factory just now is worth infinitely more than the opportunity to spend a dollar in an opera house." Washington envisioned large numbers of Blacks acquiring skills needed to be teachers, nurses, and skilled workers, and then accumulating economic resources necessary to build separate community institutions. He proclaimed that "there is no defense or security for any of us except in the highest intelligence and development of all."

DuBois was sharply critical of what he termed the "Atlanta Compromise." He believed that Washington ceded too much to the white power structure, and also argued that the true function of higher education was to provide a quality liberal arts education to a new Black elite who could then guide the development of the larger community—including teaching in the technical schools that Washington envisioned. He proclaimed that "The Negro Race, like all races, is going to be saved by its exceptional men. The problem of education then, amongst Negroes, must first of all deal with the "Talented Tenth." It is the problem of developing the

---

[20] Kingkade, "HBCUs may sue."
[21] Fryer and Greenstone, "Causes and Consequences."

best of this race that they may guide the Mass away from the contamination and death of the worst."

Washington believed that resistance to the white Southern power structure was futile, but even setting aside the accomodationist language that Washington believed was necessary to protect black educational institutions from white backlash, these two men offered starkly different visions of the democratic functions of higher education for African Americans at the turn of the century. Washington saw HBCUs as providing large numbers of Black southerners with the skills to earn a decent living, to attain occupational status that was beyond most African Americans, and to accumulate economic resources. DuBois instead saw the function of these institutions as providing the Black elite with the background and skills that they would need to advocate for African Americans, to contest politically with whites, and to direct further political and economic development of the community.

Since that time, some HBCUs have provided associates degrees and practical education designed to provide concrete job skills, whereas others have focused on providing a quality liberal arts education to a select student body. What Washington and DuBois shared was a vision of a university with full-time faculty who mentored and worked closely with students. Both saw the virtue of faculty who modeled success in their professions and their lives, and who would inspire students by their examples.

Half a century later, the democratic functions of HBCUs began to change again. By the 1940s, the top HBCUs were training a generation of leaders who would challenge the "separate but equal" doctrine that was anything but equal in practice. HBCU land grant institutions had received far less than their share of resources from their establishment in the 1890s until the attack on segregation launched by the National Association for the Advancement of Colored People (NAACP) beginning in the late 1930s. This in turn led to a series of legal challenges to the doctrine of "separate but equal" as applied to higher education, and education more generally.[22] The legal assault was led by Mordecai Johnson, the first African American president of Howard, Charles Hamilton Houston, who was the first dean of Howard's law school, and Thurgood Marshall, who had graduated first in his class from Howard Law in 1933. Johnson recruited a top group of Black scholars, activists, and lawyers to teach at Howard, which offered the nation's first course in civil rights law in 1938. Houston and Marshall went on to be the nucleus of the NAACP Legal Defense Fund.[23]

HBCUs provided a safe haven for the debates amongst future NAACP lawyers who challenged segregation. Beginning in the late 1930s, these leaders brought test cases to the Supreme Court that challenged the separate and unequal system of universities and colleges. In 1938, in *Missouri ex. Rel. Gaines v. Canada*, the Supreme Court ruled that Missouri's practice of offering out-of-state scholarships to Black students rather than admitting them to the white university system was unconstitutional. Although Missouri argued that the education provided by the out-of-state school was substantially equal to that offered by the University of

---

[22] Gil Kujovich, "Equal Opportunity in Higher Education and the Black Public College: The Era of Separate but Equal," *Minnesota Law Review* 72:23 (1987), pp. 29–43.

[23] John Hope Franklin and Evelyn Brooks Higginbotham, *From Slavery to Freedom: A History of Black Americans* (New York, NY: McGraw Hill, 2010).

Missouri, the Court ruled that comparison irrelevant, and ruled that the state had a duty to either admit Lloyd Gaines to the University of Missouri Law School, or to provide increase funding to Black institutions which could offer a similar education.[24] A series of more dramatic rulings followed, in which the Court ordered southern states to admit Black students to law schools and graduate schools. In 1954, the Court explicitly overturned *Plessy v. Ferguson* in *Brown v. Board of Education of Topeka, Kansas.*

By the late 1950s, many (but not all) HBCUs were providing an education that helped to radicalize students who would resist segregation and push for civil rights. Martin Luther King, Jr., John Lewis, Jesse Jackson, Thurgood Marshall, Barbara Jordan, Maynard Jackson, and Stokely Carmichael all graduated from HBCUs, as did Toni Morrison, Alice Walker, and many others.[25] But many less famous students braved harsh treatment to resist segregation and racism. Students from North Carolina A&T staged the first sit-in in Greensboro NC, and a few months later students from Wiley and Bishop Colleges sat-in at Woolworth lunch counters in Marshall, TX. In February 1968, a number of African American students from South Carolina State University were shot while protesting a segregated bowling alley. All police involved in the incident were acquitted but Cleveland Sellers, a recent Howard University graduate, was convicted of inciting to riot, and pardoned some twenty-five years later.[26] African American students from land-grant technically oriented schools and those from elite private schools alike joined together in activism: the ideological divide between Washington and DuBois no longer was a relevant predictor of politicization.[27]

But the push for desegregation in higher education had complicated consequences that have still not fully played out. With desegregation, white student enrollment increased in HBCUs, and two schools—West Virginia State University and Bluefield College—rapidly became majority white institutions. At the same time, TWIs began recruiting the best and brightest African American students, and were often able to offer significant financial incentives to lure these students away from HBCUs.

Although *Brown* ordered Southern states to dismantle their separate and unequal systems for elementary and secondary education, its implication for higher education was less clear. A series of lower court decisions endorsed state plans to merge HBCUs with TWIs in Tennessee and Louisiana, but in *Adams v. Richardson* the US Court of Appeals for the DC Circuit argued that any such

---

[24] After the ruling Gaines had disappeared, so the actual judgment was dismissed, but the precedent was crucial to later cases including Brown.

[25] H. "Rap" Brown was expelled from Southern University.

[26] Sellers chose not to have his conviction expunged from the official record, deeming it a badge of honor.

[27] DuBois claimed that "If we make money the object of man-training, we shall develop money-makers but not necessarily men; if we make technical skill the object of education, we may possess artisans, but not, in nature, men. Men we shall have only if we shall make manhood the object of the work of the schools—intelligence, broad sympathy, knowledge of the world that was and is, and the relation of men to it—this curriculum that Higher Education which must underlie true life" (cited in Franklin and Higginbotham, *From Slavery to Freedom*). But the ability of students of technically oriented HBCUs to act as men (and women) of conscience suggests a broader sense of community. See: Iris Marion Young, *Inclusion and Democracy* (New York, NY: Oxford University Press, 2000).

actions must include a plan for minority success and for the training of minority doctors, lawyers, engineers, and other professionals. The decision suggested that all plans to dismantle segregated systems should take into account the special needs of Black students and recognize the special role of HBCUs in higher education. The court ordered the Department of Health, Education, and Welfare (HEW) to establish new criteria that would mandate increased investment in the physical and intellectual capital of HBCUs.

In the long and convoluted litigation that began in 1975 with *Ayers v. Allain* and led to the ruling in *United States v. Fordice* in 1992, the state of Mississippi offered several proposed remedial measures to deal with the de facto segregation of the state's system of higher education. The state offered to merge HBCUs with branch centers of TWIs, to eliminate duplicate programs between HBCUs and TWIs, and to improve programming offerings at HBCUs. The Supreme Court found that four distinct policies contributed to the continuation of the de jure segregation of the state's institutions of higher education: different admission standards that relegated many African Americans to HBCUs instead of comparable TWIs, the unnecessary duplication of programs that were seen as a legacy of the historic dual educational system, the limited mission statements of HBCUs relative to the flagship TWIs, and the presence of eight institutions of higher education, which it saw as a legacy of state laws forbidding the mingling of the races. The decision suggested that the elimination or merger of some of these institutions was a possible remedy, but left that issue to the lower court on remand. Despite a negotiated settlement in 2001, some aspects of the case remain under litigation, long after the death of Jake Ayers, the original plaintiff, in 1985. In many states, successful negotiations to remedy the historic pattern of unequal funding have involved promises of substantial monies to be allocated to HBCUs to remedy past discriminatory funding, but such funds have not been forthcoming. State legislatures have balked at these awards, especially in a time of fiscal austerity.[28]

Meanwhile, increasing numbers of African American students now enroll in TWIs. In 1968, some eighty percent of Black students receiving bachelor's degrees attended HBCUs, but by 1976, that number had fallen dramatically to thirty-six percent. By 2010, the figure had fallen to sixteen percent, and today, only twelve percent of African Americans enrolled in bachelors programs attend HBCUs.[29] HBCUs constitute only three percent of all institutions of higher education, and thus continue to provide disproportionate numbers of degrees, but their role in African American higher education has clearly changed. In 2009, the four HBCU medical schools produced 179 African American MDs, some seventeen percent of all Black MDs that year—a great decline from the more than

---

[28] Robert T. Palmer, Ryan J. Davis, and Marybeth Gasman, "A Matter of Diversity, Equity, and Necessity: The Tension Between Maryland's Higher Education System and its Historically Black Colleges and Universities over the Office of Civil Rights Agreement," *Journal of Negro Education* 80:2 (2011), pp. 121–133.

[29] HBCUs have a somewhat higher graduation rate. If past rates hold then this twelve percent of students will earn fifteen percent or more of degrees. The graduation rate differential is well documented but not universally reported, but see Milkyong Munsun Kim and Clifton F. Conrad, "The Impact of Historically Black Colleges and Universities on the Academic Success of African-American Students," *Research in Higher Education* 47:4 (2006), pp. 399–427.

sixty percent produced some forty years earlier, but still a substantial share of all medical degrees.[30]

A string of recent US Supreme Court decisions on admission policies in public universities has limited the ability of states to diversify their student bodies at TWIs through affirmative action. Most recently in *Fisher v. Texas* the Court has remanded a case to the lower court with the order that the court search for a suitable remedy that can lead to a diverse student body but does not involve race as a criteria for admission or funding. There is a very real possibility that race-based affirmative action programs will be overturned by the Court in the future. Taken together these rulings suggest a continued importance for HBCUs, a topic to which we will return in the final section. The Court's decisions may point to decreased opportunities for African Americans to enroll in TWIs in many states, leaving HBCUs as an even more vital avenue for higher education for blacks.

HBCU Approaches to Fiscal Crises: 2014

To better understand how HBCUs have approached their financial crises, and how this reveals their continued mission, we conducted interviews with representatives of eleven institutions, although none were willing to be quoted by name for the study—which suggests the delicate nature of the tradeoffs that these institutions face. We agreed to anonymous interviews to encourage these representatives to speak frankly. We spoke to university presidents and provosts, directors of sponsored programs, and senior faculty. The institutions represented here include large and small, single-sex and coed, elite and open admission, liberal arts and institutions with graduate and professional degrees. These include Alcorn State University (Lorman, Mississippi), Fisk University (Nashville, Tennessee), Howard University College of Medicine (Washington, DC), Johnson C. Smith University (Charlotte, North Carolina), Morehouse School of Medicine (Atlanta, Georgia), Morgan State University (Baltimore, Maryland), Norfolk State University (Norfolk, Virginia), Tennessee State University (Nashville, Tennessee), Texas Southern University (Houston, Texas), University of the District of Columbia (Washington, DC), and Wiley College (Marshall, Texas).

We noted above that TWIs have sought to lower personnel costs with an explosion in the hiring of part-time, adjunct faculty, and with an increased effort to develop online curriculum. HBCUs have embraced these strategies as well; all schools reported that the number of adjuncts and online courses had increased in the past decade. But nine of ten institutions reported that their long-term strategy was to limit the use of adjuncts and online courses because they believed the special mission of their institutions required full time faculty as mentors and their students to be in residence to benefit from those mentors. HBCU administrators and faculty noted that many of their students are the first in their family to go to college, and stressed the need for faculty who are not only available to students, but who "go the extra mile" to help them. One administrator noted that "The current model of MOOCs and the replacement of permanent faculty with adjuncts are not for us! Despite the possible short term financial gains this approach will

---

[30] Association of American Medical Colleges, "Table 30: Total Graduates by U.S. Medical School and Race and Ethnicity," 2009, <https://www.aamc.org/download/321538/data/2012factstable30.pdf>.

not address the social needs of our students. Adjuncts lack long term interest whereas full time faculty has a vested long term interest." The one HBCU that is expanding online offerings more aggressively is Wiley College, which is developing a number of online courses that it will share with subscribers. Wiley has partnered with a non-profit backed by the Gates Foundation to create on-line courses using free source materials, especially designed for HBCUs. Wiley's move is a business plan to generate revenue for the college, but the resultant courses may be better designed for the average HBCU student than other online offerings.

Medical schools at HBCUs have retained their teaching hospitals, which has led to huge financial losses because they treat less affluent patients who wait longer to seek treatment and therefore face more serious medical problems. Meharry Medical School, Morehouse School of Medicine, and Howard University all retain teaching hospitals which are significant cash drains on the institutions. But administrators and faculty there are hopeful that the financial drain of these hospitals may be ameliorated by the Affordable Care Act (Obamacare). These institutions have increased their hiring of adjunct clinical faculty and some hybrid on-line/in person courses, but remain focused on full-time faculty for basic science courses and strengthening their administrative leadership by recruiting high-profile clinical directors.

Respondents from all institutions reported that the struggle to recruit the best African American students was costly, and that TWIs often had better infrastructure and were able to offer more generous financial aid packages. Several schools reported fundraising programs designed to augment financial aid offers to African American and other students. Howard University has recently launched a successful fundraising campaign to provide financial assistance to students affected by the changes in their eligibility for Parent Plus loans. One administrator worried that "The abundance of scholarship funding, modern facilities and simplified admissions utilizing social media tend to attract high achieving minority students to majority serving institutions at an alarmingly higher rate. African American parents, including alumni of HBCUs, seem to have bought into the question of the relevancy of our schools, thus devaluing the historic importance of these institutions in educating and socializing our youth."

Many schools were trying innovative approaches to fiscal crises. Recent cutbacks in federal funding for research, such as National Institutes of Health (NIH) funding for medical research, have had a disproportionate impact on HBCUs. Howard University has responded by expanding their research infrastructure by combining disciplines under one new core center. Relying on the strengths and knowledge of its constituency, the university spokesperson hopes that this collaborative effort will be a magnet for new ideas and the hub for the next generation minority students. One professor there noted "These hubs require full-time dedicated researchers and faculty in order to mentor the next cadre of elite young researchers, which temps just cannot do."

Johnson C. Smith University is seeking additional revenue by admitting more international students who can pay full tuition. There have been focused efforts by some HBCUs to recruit tuition paying international students from Africa, Latin America and Asia. Most HBCUs have also seen an influx of international students in recent years. The combination of low tuition and racially inclusive social atmosphere makes these schools a popular option for students from a number of countries.

One innovative HBCU provost summed up his strategy: "All [HBCUs] must re-imagine, re-engineer and re-structure. Costs can be cut without cutting faculty or the quality of education. Tuition increases is not a solution. The cost of recruitment of top students to HBCUs is higher than the national average. Despite the high costs for recruitment, HBCUs can lose thirty percent or more before matriculating followed by retention problems and high attrition rates. These are problems we must address quickly."

Thus HBCUs face a direr economic environment with significant constraints on how far they can go in implementing some strategic responses. Tuition increases are especially damaging to the mission of HBCUs, which enroll a disproportionate number of less affluent students, and where a disproportionate number of students work jobs to pay for college. Increased reliance on adjuncts and on-line education threatens to undermine the way that HBCUs help mentor young men and women and mold their characters, although online curriculum specifically geared to HBCUs might partially ameliorate this problem. Increased recruitment of foreign students can enhance student learning experiences but at some point would begin to undermine the historical character of the institution.

Resistance is not Futile: Integration, Assimilation, and the future of HBCUs

With a majority of African American students now attending TWIs, there is a popular debate on the continued role of HBCUs. These institutions no longer provide the only access to higher education available to African Americans, and some question the contemporary value of these institutions. Some critics suggest that integrated TWIs provide ample opportunities for African Americans to achieve quality education. One recent study has concluded that students at HBCUs earn less after graduation than similar Black students enrolled in TWIs, although another recent study offers the opposite conclusion.[31] Both studies, however, suggest that there are non-economic benefits to attending HBCUs, such as increases in efficacy and racial solidarity.

We believe there are several reasons that HBCUs remain important educational institutions and that they continue to serve democratic functions. First, most HBCUs offer educational opportunities to students with financial, social, cultural, motivational, and other challenges. These students are often the first in their families to attend college, require remedial courses, and often live at home and hold part-time jobs. Many of these students will have lived in segregated communities, attended re-segregated public schools, and have been involved in segregated churches. They may therefore find HBCUs to be safe and inspiring educational environments for them to stretch their potential, because most faculty and students look like them, and where there are many cultural resonances with their background.[32] Many students and former students of HBCUs with whom we spoke mentioned this as central to their decisions to enroll.

---

[31] Fryer and Greenstone, "Causes and Consequences"; Price et al., "Relative Returns to Graduating."

[32] Nikole Hannah-Jones, "Resegregation in the American South: Sixty years after *Brown v. Board of Education*, the schools in Tuscaloosa, Alabama, show how separate and unequal education is coming back," *The Atlantic*, April 16, 2014, <http://www.theatlantic.com/features/archive/2014/04/segregation-now/359813/>.

Marybeth Gasman of the University of Pennsylvania argues that low graduation rates at HBCUs are primarily due to a student body that faces serious challenges. "What [HBCUs] have at their core is a dedication to low-income students. That makes it harder to have higher graduation rates. If you're doing that kind of work, you're dealing with low-income students, you're tuition-driven, your alumni are not making enormous salaries and you're dealing with racism, it's a difficult situation."[33] One administrator told us of buying a dress for the valedictorian of the graduating class, a story that has many counterparts at other HBCUs. Ideally, these institutions provide a supportive environment for these struggling students, and provide them with some additional social support that might help many succeed.

Second, these institutions still award a significant portion of undergraduate, law, and medical degrees to African Americans. With the last vestiges of affirmative action under assault, the loss of Howard Law School or Morehouse School of Medicine would mean even fewer Black attorneys and doctors. Moreover, faculty and administrators at these institutions believe that their students are exposed to a set of values that prioritize caring for the poor and disadvantaged, and are likely to devote at least some of their professional careers to alleviating racial and economic disparities in access to legal advice and health care. The clinical faculty at the Morehouse School of Medicine sees more patients, and spends more time per patient, than clinical faculty at TWIs nearby. Students there are taught to see patients as embedded in family and community networks.

Third, these institutions provide an opportunity for elite Black students to study in a majority-Black institution that seeks to build self-confidence, efficacy, and leadership skills. Morehouse College proclaims on its web page its mission of "preparing young men to change the world" and notes that leadership is not about politicking, but about values. "At Morehouse, we are redefining the meaning of leadership. It's not about attaining the highest title or position, but about attaining skills such as compassion, civility, integrity and even listening. Morehouse is poised to become the epicenter of *ethical* leadership as we continue to develop leaders who are spiritually disciplined, intellectually astute and morally wise." Nearby Spelman College proclaims itself a global leader in the education of women of African descent, and states that Spelman "empowers women to engage the many cultures of the world and inspires a commitment to positive social change through service." These schools also seek to instill racial pride in the student body. Morehouse goes on to note that "Most people—even the students themselves—are awestruck by the sight of so many talented, studious and highly motivated young Black men seeking knowledge and fulfillment. New Student Orientation, when hundreds of fresh-faced freshmen march into King Chapel for the first time, is just as moving as Commencement, when they emerge, queued in a line 500-members strong, as well-trained scholars and leaders."[34]

These advantages all accrue especially when motivated, full-time faculty form mentoring relationships with students. Studies have shown that Black students at HBCUs are significantly more likely to work with a faculty member on research than are African American students at TWIs. Moreover, they are usually working

---

[33] Quoted in Demby, "Are HBCUs in trouble?"

[34] < http://www.spelman.edu/about-us> and <http://www.spelman.edu/about-us > (accessed April 12, 2014).

with an African American faculty member, who serves as a role model as well as mentor. When Thomas Jefferson designed the University of Virginia, he created a set of pavilions with classrooms, student housing, and faculty residences. He sought to make higher education more widely available, arguing that "An educated citizenry is a vital requisite for our survival as a free people." Jefferson's vision was students working and living with their professors, and benefitting from what we would now call an intensive mentoring relationship. We do not suggest that HBCUs approach Jefferson's ideal, but we do believe that the mentoring that HBCUs frequently provide cannot be entirely replicated in TWIs.

But there are broader democratic benefits to maintaining a system of HBCUs. In his book *Democracy and Association*, Mark Warren discusses various possible contributions of voluntary associations, including universities, to democratic capacities of citizens and of society.[35] Voluntary associations and especially universities provide many individual level effects that students could get from a TWI as well as a HBCU—information, efficacy, and critical skills. But HBCUs may have an advantage in allowing some students to develop political skills in a nurturing and safe environment. It is most likely easier for some students to develop the ability to speak at a critical moment making a critical argument if they are in an environment with fewer reasons to fear ridicule or animosity.

Warren also posits important public sphere and institutional effects of voluntary associations that are relevant to the future of HBCUs. First, these associations can assist with public sphere deliberations and communication by studying issues and the impact of public policy in a space that is some distance from the intrusion of state and market. HBCUs are institutions with large numbers of African American and other faculty who frequently research and teach on issues of special concern to the African American community, to inner cities, and to the poor. There are few other institutions that can deliberate more fully on issues of concern to the larger community.

Second, associations can represent either difference or commonality, depending on whether they are based on exclusive group identity or broader social bonds. Here there is a case to be made that HBCUs can do both. Clearly these institutions represent the different voice of African Americans, and as noted above frequently focus on issues of concern to the community. But HBCUs serve an increasingly diverse student body that includes international students, Asians, Latinos, and whites as well as African Americans. By involving students in these discussions across racial lines, they may well develop the kind of empathetic thinking that Iris Young has suggested can bridge differences.[36]

Finally, associations can be a location for political and cultural resistance. Here Warren posits that universities are poorly situated to cultivate resistance, but that racial and religious advocacy groups have good capacity for resistance. We have seen that many HBCUs provided the space, the intellectual milieu, the leadership and many of the foot soldiers of the civil rights movement in the 1960s. Only the Black church could possibly rival HBCUs in their contribution of ideas, arguments, and evidence that fueled that resistance movement.

---

[35] Mark E. Warren, *Democracy and Association* (Princeton, NJ: Princeton University Press, 2001).

[36] Young, *Inclusion and Democracy*.

Today, HBCUs can help build resistance to neoliberal policies and ideas that are being vigorously promoted by conservatives who question the value of a social welfare state that cares for its most needy citizens. A network of conservative donors has established centers and research institutes around the country affiliated with many TWIs. HBCUs are an interesting potential institutional location for left-leaning donors to create counterweights to these conservative centers. Because many faculty and some students at the best HBCUs chose these institutions in part because of their history of political activism, their ethos of caring for disadvantaged students and building racial and class solidarity, many HBCUs will be friendly institutions. Their increasing numbers of international students suggest that HBCUs might build not just racial solidarity but solidarity amongst disadvantaged groups. Their smaller sizes and budgets mean that smaller investments can make bigger impacts than at institutes affiliated with TWIs. In this event, elite HBCUs might take on roles that resemble their roles in the Civil Rights movement.

HBCUs can also serve as a center for resistance to cultural homogenization. Many former and current students at HBCUs speak of the value of being at a school where most people look like them, but when they elaborate it frequently comes out that they also mean where there are cultural assumptions and vocabularies that encompass art, music, dance, politics, and theology that students and faculty share. This eases communications and helps build a sense of racial identity and pride.

In the *Star Trek Next Generation* television series, the Borg are a collectivist civilization with a group mind, which assimilated species through force.[37] The Borg generally threaten each space ship they encounter with statements like "We are the Borg. You will be assimilated. Resistance is futile." Many African Americans who are HBCU graduates or even those with degrees from TWIs express the desire to avoid total assimilation into majority culture. The existence of HBCUs enables resistance to assimilation. They provide cultural reservoirs of African American history, politics, music and arts, with associated clusters of faculty to study and keep these traditions alive.

---

[37] In later iterations the Borg were given a Queen, thus transforming a more frightening soulless collective into a hive mind.

Open Admission and the Imposition of Tuition at the City University of New York, 1969–1976: A Political Economic Case Study for Understanding the Current Crisis in Higher Education

Douglas A. Medina
City University of New York (CUNY), USA

Abstract *Between 1969 and 1976 the City University of New York (CUNY) experienced two monumental policy transformations. These transformations were a result of changes in the political economy of New York City and State leading class struggles to erupt between and among groups. This article highlights two of these struggles: first, what came to be known as the "open admissions" policy, one of five demands made by students and their supporters in 1969–1970 at City College, and second, the imposition of tuition for undergraduate students in 1975–1976, a neoliberal condition set by business and political elites designed to privatize and commodify CUNY. In contrast to existing policy studies and sociology of education approaches to the study of CUNY, which are approaches limited by their ideologically liberal focus on outcomes that lead to "racial disparity" and inequality of individual achievement, an alternative class analysis is proposed that entails the concrete historical, political, economic, and ideological context of these struggles and their causes. The examination of both policies reveals an ideological struggle between meritocracy, as grounded in the individualist ideal of the American Dream and equality and democracy, as grounded in calls for inclusion, access, solidarity, and empowerment. The resulting class analysis offers a critical context for understanding the current transformation of higher education beyond CUNY.*

Introduction

The debates around the current crisis in American higher education invariably condense around policy issues related to access, affordability, and accountability, particularly as they pertain to public institutions. At both the state and federal levels, the debates center on racial disparity in access to higher education and affirmative action policies designed to address it; rising tuition costs and the decline of government expenditures going directly to colleges and universities; and the purpose of higher education in light of the tension between providing students with a liberal arts education and preparing them for the labor market—all taking place within the broader context of neoliberal policies that boost market-based solutions.

The author would like to thank Nirit Ben-Ari, Jeffrey D. Broxmeyer, Jolie M.B. Terrazas, the two anonymous reviewers, the editors, and particularly Sanford Schram for their helpful comments on earlier drafts. Any errors remain the sole responsibility of the author.

The issues that frame the current crisis and debates, however, are not entirely new. Rather they are a specific, historically grounded expression of political and economic problems that were only partially resolved in the past.[1] At CUNY, the open admissions struggle of the 1960s and the subsequent imposition of tuition beginning in 1975 represent moments in the history of the university that set the foundation for subsequent debates around democratic access for minorities, affordability, and the general mission of CUNY as a public university. Both policy reforms marked the beginning of two distinct processes that are still unfolding today: the study and analysis of the open admissions struggle as an integration experiment grounded in the (neo)liberal view of education as an individual right that minorities, particularly Blacks and Puerto Ricans, should have the right to access, and the commodification and marketization of education at CUNY.

At the heart of the open admissions struggle was the student movement that sparked a discussion about academic merit, access to a higher education, cultural and racial recognition, and inclusion of Blacks and Puerto Ricans at CUNY. Six years later, a group of New York business and political elites led the charge to craft and implement austerity measures targeting the working class. Specifically, they aimed for the public sector, including the municipal hospital system, labor unions, and CUNY by imposing tuition.

In order to understand CUNY today and the democratic potential for higher education more generally, we can usefully employ a class analysis to examine the ideologies that informed the different configurations of political power and political coalitions that existed in that time period within the context of the changing political economy and demographics of New York City. Ideologically, the open admissions reform and the demands made by the Black and Puerto Rican student-led movement for proportional representation and cultural and educational recognition were most directly influenced by the Black Power Movement. Self-determination and Black unity were powerful and influential political and ideological principles that affected the student movement in the 1960s, not only at CUNY, but other movements nationwide.

Education institutions are not neutral citadels for the production and consumption of knowledge. In contrast to the mythology of the "Ivory Tower," institutions of higher education are embedded in the totality of a society's political, economic, cultural, and ideological constructs. The pressures, tensions, and contradictions found in the broader society condition the ways that education institutions operate and the ideology that informs and influences their development. As such, the values, mission, and goals of CUNY have been a reflection of the political, social and economic needs of New York City.

We cannot fully understand CUNY's history and its defining transformations if we do not take into account a deep examination and analysis of the broader conflicts and contradictions that capitalism generates. Crucial in this examination is the social movements that were inspired by the revolutionary ideology of the

---

[1] In his examination of the relationship between educational policy and inequality, Michael B. Katz, "Education and Inequality: A Historical Perspective," in David J. Rothman and Stanton Wheeler (eds), *Social History and Social Policy* (New York: Academic Press, 1981), pp. 57–101, has argued that "policy is basically dialectical and that the failure to recognize the inevitable impermanence of institutional solutions continually undercuts their effectiveness by leaving debilitating contradictions unresolved," p. 59.

1960s and 1970s, in the case of CUNY, the Black and Puerto Rican student movement that struggled for achieving full access and racial recognition. As Martin Carnoy and Henry M. Levin explain, schools in America "are subject to direct political pressures that are conditioned by the overall conflict between capital and labor, by the changing structure of the labor market, and by various social movements seeking greater equality."[2] CUNY, as the largest urban university system in the United States (US), can serve as a relevant and useful historical and political case study of the pressures affecting higher education institutions today. More specifically, a close analysis of the ideology and motives of the political actors that directly influenced the open admissions policy and the imposition of tuition allows us to open a window into the tension created by the ideals of an academic meritocracy and democratic access.

With a few exceptions, political scientists have paid very little attention to the political and economic dynamics and pressures that affect higher education institutions.[3] In this article I will employ a class analysis that reveals the limits of the most widely available literature that has accumulated about the history of the open admissions policy and the imposition of tuition at CUNY. This literature has been generated primarily in the fields of sociology, with some works in public policy, which view the open admissions policy and the imposition of tuition from a policy-process academic perspective. This focus within the literature has led to viewing the open admissions policy as a solution to a problem of liberal democracy and the racial inequality that has existed within it, and the imposition of tuition as a reform that needs to be understood as a result of different choices that were made within a policy process framework. In both cases, I argue, a political-economic, historically grounded class analysis is an important corrective addition to understanding the current crisis of access, affordability, and accountability at CUNY and in higher education more generally. This type of analysis, for example, can help us situate and understand the ideological assumptions behind one of the most noted books to hit the mainstream today— *Degrees of Inequality: How the Politics of Higher Education Sabotaged the American Dream*, by Suzanne Mettler.[4] In this book, Mettler grounds her explanation and critique of how political partisanship is one of the primary causes for the current crisis in higher education. As an informative and trenchant analysis of the current crisis, her book is a success; it places a much-needed spotlight on a problem that is rarely discussed within the field of political science. At the same time, her focus on the narrow ideological confines of political partisanship in government as related to the ideal of the American Dream in understanding the purpose of higher education is placed in needed critical context in the following class analysis.

With this problem in mind, my analysis is guided by the following questions: What role do the social relations of production in New York play in understanding the history of CUNY and specifically the open admissions policy and the

---

[2] Martin Carnoy and Henry M. Levin, *Schooling and Work in the Democratic State* (Stanford, CA: Stanford University Press, 1985), p. 5.

[3] Robert C. Lowry and Alisa Hicklin Fryar, "The Politics of Higher Education," in Virginia Gray, Russell L. Hanson, and Thad Kousser (eds), *Politics in the American States: A Comparative Analysis* (Washington, DC: CQ Press, 2013), pp. 405–435.

[4] Suzanne Mettler, *Degrees of Inequality: How the Politics of Higher Education Sabotaged the American Dream* (New York: Basic Books, 2014).

imposition of tuition? What were the ideological assumptions that informed the most active and influential political actors at CUNY in shaping both policy transformations? What are the ideological assumptions underlying the current scholarly literature on higher education and the policy prescriptions that flow from it? And finally, what does a political-economic perspective and analysis have to offer in helping us understand the crisis in higher education today?

Using interviews, archival research, and secondary literature, the primary aim of this article is to address these questions and in the process shed light on the conflictual nature of the two major reforms at CUNY between 1969 and 1976. Starting with a brief sketch of CUNY's institutional history, this article will examine the ideological, political, and economic background of the student movement at City College, particularly during the open admissions struggle. The fiscal crisis of New York City in the 1970s, six years after the implementation of open admissions at CUNY, set the context for the austerity measures that included the imposition of tuition. Re-examining both transformational changes at CUNY through a political-economic theoretical framework will reveal the ideological assumptions that inform the existing literature about these two moments in CUNY's history.

Brief Historical Background on the Establishment of CUNY

Since its establishment, the different political and economic forces in New York City have shaped CUNY's mission, mandates, and patterns of institutional consolidation. Understanding this historical context will help us situate the transformations CUNY experienced in the 1960s and 1970s.

Established in 1847 by Townsend Harris, New York City merchant and politician, as the first tuition-free public institution of higher education in the US, the Free Academy (today known as City College) was charged with trying out an "experiment…whether the highest education can be given to the masses; whether the children of the whole people can be educated; and whether an institution of learning, of the highest grade, can be successfully controlled by the popular will, not by the privileged few, but the privileged many."[5] This experiment would later expand to include other municipal college campuses throughout the five New York City boroughs. Crucial to this experiment and vision was the plan to centralize the operations of these municipal colleges into one university system.

As early as 1936, the Board of Higher Education, along with Hunter College, "envisioned a publicly supported university in New York City" that would "offer graduate and professional training," catering to the needs of a growing population.[6] This was an understandable vision considering that by World War I American colleges were following the "university model of graduate study," according to Sheila C. Gordon, "complete with the doctor of philosophy degree as

[5] David E. Lavin, Richard D. Alba, and Richard Silberstein, *Right Versus Privilege: The Open-Admissions Experiment at the City University of New York* (New York: Free Press; Collier Macmillan, 1981), pp. 1–2.

[6] Sandra Shoiock Roff, Anthony M. Cucchiara, and Barbara J. Dunlap, *From the Free Academy to CUNY: Illustrating Public Higher Education in New York City, 1847–1997* (New York: Fordham University Press, 2000), pp. 111–112.

its capstone."[7] But it was not until twenty-five years later that New York City's municipal colleges would become the City University of New York (CUNY), so declared by the signature of then Governor Nelson A. Rockefeller on April 11, 1961 on the law creating CUNY.[8]

The context for the expansion and centralization of the municipal colleges was set in terms related to national trends as well as the political economy of New York City and state. Becoming a consolidated, centralized university was in large part a project that was inevitable, given the pressures exerted on the institution by the growing population and the needs of political elites to manage the expectations of changing ethnic and racial constituencies. Labor market needs, the promise of federal funding, international politics, and the need to accommodate demands for education beyond the Master's level, were all additional factors that led to both state and city taskforce reports that concluded that the establishment of a "city university" was necessary.

By the 1950s, the Cottrell Report, as it came to be called, identified future growth well past the 1960s and into 1970. This "Master Plan Study" was an attempt to bring to light the projected growth that the municipal colleges would face in relation to the changing political economy of New York City. According to the authors, the Cottrell Report was "based upon an intensive examination of the present municipal College plants and programs, and upon present and anticipated needs as revealed by research into vocational, enrollment and population trends."[9] For example, taking into account City College, Hunter, Brooklyn, and Queens, the four oldest and most established municipal colleges, the authors projected that the 1950 enrollment of 27,258 students would grow to approximately 40,000 in the next ten years.[10] They identified three factors "determining the need for higher education in New York City" and therefore the need for capital expansion.[11] Those factors included: the "long-term tendency of enrollments and populations" to expand and therefore leading to the need for more space; the "occupational shifts involving the expansion of certain fields"— labor market needs; and the need to accommodate the regional and local expansion and the demands for "both high vocational competence and broad general background and skill in human relationships."[12]

The Cottrell Report clearly articulated the dominant class bias on the need to expand the municipal college system to better serve the economic needs of New York City. But beyond the terrain of local, external factors pushing the municipal college system toward change, the US was also feeling the pressure of the "Soviet threat" with the launching of Sputnik in 1957. In response, the Newt Davidson Collective, a collective of anonymous faculty and administrators at CUNY, provided a critique of CUNY's bureaucracy from an explicitly Marxist perspective. "American capitalists, terrified by [Sputnik's] implications, undertook a major

---

[7] Sheila C. Gordon, "The Transformation of the City University of New York, 1945–1970," PhD, Columbia University, 1975, p. 106.

[8] Ruth Landa, "The Birth of a Modern University," *CUNY*, <http://www1.cuny.edu/mu/forum/2011/09/16/the-birth-of-a-modern-university/>.

[9] Donald P. Cottrell et al., *Public Higher Education in the City of New York: Report of the Master Plan Study* (New York: Board of Higher Education of the City of New York, 1950), p. 3.

[10] Ibid., 8.

[11] Ibid., 12.

[12] Ibid.

reappraisal and reordering of the entire educational system." "In New York," the authors explain, "[capitalists] acted swiftly and decisively."[13]

But it was not until 1958 that the call for accommodating the growing demands of the city and state would be seriously heeded. New York's governor, Nelson Rockefeller, who took office in January 1959, would take up the project of expansion, consolidation, and centralization of the state's universities, including the city's municipal college system, in a very aggressive manner. One of his first acts was to appoint a commission to study higher education in New York State. Headed by Henry T. Heald, President of the Ford Foundation and former Chancellor of New York University, the New York State Commission on Higher Education (hereafter "Heald Commission") presented over one-hundred proposals, including a call for the doubling of public and private college facilities within the decade, which would bring state-wide enrollment in 1959 from 401,000 to 804,000 in 1970.[14]

Similar to the Cottrell Report, the Heald Commission, as the Newt Davidson Collective points out, "emphasized that higher education must be made more responsive to new social, economic, and ideological needs, particularly now that 'the Russian sputnik illuminated our educational skies.'"[15] This international "threat" would catapult the federal government to offer an explicit incentive to American colleges to reach for and achieve university status. As Gordon points out, the federal government restricted funding in the form of grants to universities.[16]

But in order to be responsive and acquire the necessary financial support and legitimacy, public institutions in particular would have to be centralized and controlled by the state. The Heald Commission openly acknowledged that it would have to overcome this challenge in its proposals for expansion state-wide. "The first and foremost problem which faces the State," they said, "... is to streamline the organizational structure of higher education so that colleges and universities will be able to meet the challenge of increasing enrollments during the generation ahead."[17] This would entail the realignment of five ruling bodies of higher education, including the Board of Regents, the State University of New York, the Board of Higher Education of the City of New York, and the establishment of two new bodies: local boards of "overseers" for each public college and university and a new council of higher education advisors.[18] This amounted to "massive system-wide centralization."[19] This centralization, in the eyes of the Heald Commission, was necessary to effectively manage the overall functions of the university system in New York, including the State University of New York (SUNY).

---

[13] Newt Davidson Collective, *Crisis at CUNY* (New York: Newt Davidson Collective, 1974), p. 56.

[14] Peter D. McClelland and Alan L. Magdovitz, *Crisis in the Making, the Political Economy of New York State since 1945* (New York: Cambridge University Press, 1981), p. 458, note 85.

[15] Newt Davidson Collective, *Crisis at CUNY*, p. 57; Gordon, "The Transformation of the City University of New York, 1945–1970," pp. 109 and 112.

[16] Gordon, "The Transformation of the City University of New York, 1945–1970," p. 109.

[17] New York State Committee on Higher Education, *Meeting the Increasing Demand for Higher Education in New York State: A Report to the Governor and the Board of Regents* (Albany, NY: Board of Regents, State Education Dept., 1960), p. 17.

[18] Ibid., 17–18.

[19] Newt Davidson Collective, *Crisis at CUNY*, p. 57.

The Heald Commission report did not stop there. According to the Newt Davidson Collective, the commission report also called for the "introduction of modern management techniques to improve efficiency."[20] The Heald Commission explicitly called for the application of research and the knowledge it yields into "actual practice," similar to what industries dealing with chemicals, electronics, petroleum, and agriculture actually do.[21] What this meant was that the political and administrative elites at the state level did not think the municipal college system was meeting the "new postwar requirements of capitalist development."[22] In addition to this "vote of no confidence," the Heald Commission also called for the imposition of tuition at the municipal colleges and the absorption of the municipal colleges into the SUNY system, which had been formally established in 1948.[23] In effect, the recommendations amounted to a direct call for the end of local, municipal control, the adjustment of the curriculum to meet the demands of capitalism, and the end of free tuition at CUNY. The call for the imposition of tuition was a harbinger of things to come.

And while there were plenty of reasons for dissuading the New York City Board of Higher Education from pursuing university status during the 1940s and 1950s—including the lack of financial resources, opposition from private universities, lack of central coordination and leadership, lack of political influence, the tradition of focusing on a four-year, liberal arts education, and the lack of PhD teaching faculty[24]—the Heald Commission was an instant call to action on the part of the Board of Higher Education. Headed by Mary S. Ingraham, the board created "The Committee to Look to the Future," which explicitly and without reservations called for the establishment of CUNY and for the establishment of a research and doctoral-granting institution, as well as a new administrative structure.[25] Mayor Wagner, who was a friend of the municipal college system, immediately supported Ingraham's report. CUNY's supervision would be shifted to the New York State Regents, rather than the state university system.[26]

As Gordon points out, there were both endogenous and exogenous factors that led to the decision by the board to call for the establishment of CUNY. Among them, "the general increase in central coordination of the colleges and the specific trend toward coordination of graduate study ... ; the lack of opposition from and the diminution of the power of the private universities; the increasing availability of State aid; and the new role in general of the State in public higher education."[27] The die was cast. CUNY had taken a monumental step toward expansion, centralization, and modernization.

Understanding the political and economic pressures that were placed on CUNY, as noted by the Cottrell Report, the Heald Commission report, and the

---

[20] Ibid.

[21] New York State Committee on Higher Education, *Meeting the Increasing Demand for Higher Education in New York State*, p. 39.

[22] Newt Davidson Collective, *Crisis at CUNY*, p. 57.

[23] Ibid.

[24] Gordon, "The Transformation of the City University of New York, 1945–1970," pp. 117–119.

[25] Ibid., 126; Ruth Landa, "'The Birth of a Modern University,'" *CUNY*, <http://www1.cuny.edu/mu/forum/2011/09/16/the-birth-of-a-modern-university/>.

[26] Landa, "'The Birth of a Modern University.'"

[27] Gordon, "The Transformation of the City University of New York, 1945–1970," p. 129.

Ingraham Committee, is the historical context for making sense of the transformative changes brought about by the open admissions struggle of 1969 and the imposition of tuition in 1976.

CUNYs Transformation: 1969–1976

Throughout its history, CUNY has experienced a series of transformations in relation to its core mission and population served and to the broader political, economic, and social changes that have swept New York City, New York State, and the nation. These transformations have occurred in the context of various social, political, and fiscal crises. In 1970, CUNY radically expanded access to minorities, including Blacks and Puerto Ricans, through the implementation of the open admissions policy. And in 1976, the 129-year tradition of offering a tuition-free education to qualified students came to end as a result of a city- and state-sponsored austerity program. These transformations were primarily driven by external changes that were taking place in the political economy of New York City and New York State in particular and in the US in general. In other words, as the political economy of New York and the US changed, so did the demands placed on CUNY as an institution situated squarely within the direct control of dominant political and institutional elites.

As Sheila Gordon, a historian of CUNY, has observed, a historical analysis with a political orientation is crucial to understanding CUNY as a publicly funded higher education institution. "Educational policy," she concludes, "is public policy."[28] Taking Gordon's observation further, I explain how issues of access and affordability, admissions standards, and curriculum development at CUNY between 1969 and 1976 have been inextricable from a broader political and economic context.

As educational and political reforms, both open admissions and the imposition of tuition were subject to broader social and economic pressures. These pressures set the context in which educational and political-economic policies may and often do contradict one another. For example, the imposition of tuition in 1976 would severely undercut the primary goal of the open admissions policy, which aimed to provide universal access to a higher education—not only for Black and Puerto Rican students from New York City high schools, but also for any student who qualified under the newly created admissions standards.

The pressures, tensions, and contradictions found in the broader society condition the ways in which education institutions operate. The contradictory and conflictual elements of the two major reforms at CUNY between 1969 and 1976 were expressions of a broader process of racial and class struggle—a process that is at once an expression of deeper contradictions between the imperatives of a liberal, democratic society and post-industrial capitalism.[29] One contradiction became glaringly clear to the students who participated in the militant strike and building occupation at City College in 1969. As Henry Arce recounts, H. Rap Brown visited the City College campus and urged the students to "become aware of the contradictions." To Arce, these contradictions included the oft-cited claim by the US that it is a nation of "the grand melting pot...everybody is accepted here." Yet that was not the reality he and his comrades experienced. It was a contradiction that

---

[28] Gordon, "The Transformation of the City University of New York, 1945–1970," pp. 1–2.
[29] Carnoy and Levin, *Schooling and Work in the Democratic State.*

led him and others to ask: if there is a "free college [CUNY in New York City], why aren't more poor kids coming here . . . ?"[30] This consciousness-raising question was one of the sparks that led him and others to organize in solidarity to demand access, integration, and racial recognition at CUNY for those who had been marginalized from the institution.

Open Admissions: Militant Demands for Access and Racial Recognition

> The first time gathering with all 10 groups/cells was on the morning of the takeover April 1969. That had never been done before. All 100 of us were committed to closing the school down to bring about change that would benefit many.

> I was prepared to die for our cause if needed and I am sure others felt the same. I would say we were somewhat naïve but we were so committed to our cause. Our cause had become the most important factor in our lives and the issues that we were fighting for. I was ready to die. During the takeover, I can remember standing at the gate of City College, with all the police outside the fence and saying, "Off the pig!"[31]

Compelled and inspired by Black pride and a deeply felt sense of injustice, Jennie Trotter, quoted above, was one of the students who participated in a highly organized group that called itself the Black and Puerto Rican Student Community (BPRSC). This group orchestrated the student strike, campus seizure, and occupation with the goal of having their demands met. A detailed narrative of the City College south campus seizure and occupation is not within the scope of this article, but it is important to analyze and explain the ideology that informed and propelled the BPRSC forward.

The BPRSC drew its membership from a compendium of student organizations that included Onyx (the Black student organization at City College), the Puerto Rican Students for Action (PRISA), Search for Education, Elevation and Knowledge (SEEK, the opportunity program at the senior colleges designed to admit minority students in need of additional academic and financial assistance), and the Committee of Ten.[32] Demands for access to CUNY were fueled by the streams of radical political thought offered by the civil rights and Black power movements in the 1960s, as well as the changing political economy of New York City. As Martha Biondi observes, the student movements "increasingly framed access to higher education as a right of postwar U.S. citizenship."[33] Black student leaders like Henry Arce, Afiya Dawson, Khadija DeLoache, Charles Powell, James Small, Jennie Trotter,[34] as well as Leroy (Askia) Davis[35]—who was

---

[30] Henry Arce, interview with author, February 26, 2014.

[31] Jennie Trotter, interview with author, March 8, 2014.

[32] It should be noted that both in the mainstream media at the time and some scholarly works, The Committee of Ten and the BPRSC are used interchangeably. In this article, for the sake of consistency, I will refer to the BPRSC. See Lavin et al., *Right Versus Privilege*, p. 11; Conrad M. Dyer, "Protest and the Politics of Open Admissions: The Impact of the Black and Puerto Rican Students' Community (of City College)," PhD dissertation, City University of New York, 1990, pp. 78–80.

[33] Martha Biondi, *The Black Revolution on Campus* (Berkeley, CA: University of California Press, 2012), p. 116.

[34] Interviews with all these former students took place between February and May of 2014.

[35] Biondi, *The Black Revolution on Campus*, p. 117.

active in the militant student movement at Brooklyn College in 1966—were all deeply influenced by the classic anti-colonialist film, *The Battle of Algiers*,[36] and by authors like Frantz Fanon and his work *Black Skin, White Masks*.[37] In fact, as several students recounted during interviews, the very concept of organizing as "cells" of students, as explained by Trotter in the quote above, came directly from the film.[38] Furthermore, the broader community and labor representatives such as Harry Van Arsdale, the powerful president of the New York City Central Labor Council, supported the student movement. As one scholar of CUNY has persuasively argued, the terms and timing of the open admissions policy in 1969 were directly influenced by the militant student movement of the time.[39]

The demands placed on CUNY by the student movement were also driven by larger changes that were taking place in New York and the nation in the 1960s. Without the possession of a college credential, Black and Puerto Rican youth were shut out of the white-collar labor market. Reportedly, half the Puerto Rican population in New York City found employment in blue-collar jobs, as did twenty-seven percent of Blacks.[40] And the pressure to open the gates of CUNY was felt by its administrators. As an anonymous top administrator, close to Chancellor Albert H. Bowker, at CUNY explained,

> Bowker, [Julius] Edelstein (Vice-Chancellor for Urban Affairs) most of us … believed that the survival of the city depended on CUNY serving the Blacks and Puerto Ricans. They have no access to the labor unions, and blue collar jobs are declining in the city. Then somebody, given the growth of the Black and Puerto Rican populations, has to provide them upward mobility. The university can handle that.[41]

Reacting to this reality, the militant student movement sought and demanded access to CUNY within the context of the ideology of merit, an ideology that draws clear lines of demarcation in the process of defining who is and who is not deserving in accessing a higher education and therefore the opportunity to obtain a credential to participate in the labor market. Historically, the post-World War II economic boom—coupled with the purported, international political and scientific threat posed by the Soviet Union—led to the expansion of higher education in the US. This expansion was in large part sustained by the ideology of individual, meritocratic advancement as the primary mechanism for achieving economic and social mobility, in contrast to the labor movement's collective, class-based (and at times race- and ethnic-based) politics and organizational action that had previously dominated New York City and the nation. A good-paying, unionized job in the manufacturing sector was at one point in American history a good way for working people to achieve social and economic security.

---

[36] *The Battle of Algiers* [La battaglia di Algeri], directed by Gillo Pontecorvo (1966 [1967 US]; Italy [US]: Igor Film/Casbah Film).

[37] Frantz Fanon, *Black Skin, White Masks*, trans. Charles Lam Markmann (New York: Grove, [1952] 1967).

[38] James Small, interview with author, March 25, 2014.

[39] Dyer, "Protest and the Politics of Open Admissions."

[40] Newt Davidson Collective, *Crisis at CUNY*, 64.

[41] David Rosen et al., *Open Admissions: The Promise and the Lie of Open Access to American Higher Education* (Lincoln, NE: Nebraska Curriculum Development Center, University of Nebraska, 1973), p. 63.

The power of labor unions, however, began to wane not only in New York but nationwide. In large part the decline in labor's power was a direct result of political attacks led by business interests through Congress beginning in the late 1940s (the Taft-Hartley Act of 1947) and continuing through the 1950s and 1960s.[42] Also, as Joshua B. Freeman notes, "From the mid-1950s through the late 1960s, working class New York confronted the challenge of deindustrialization, as runaway shops and automation eroded the blue-collar job base on which its culture and power rested. Slowly but relentlessly," Freeman says, "the goods production and distribution sectors shrank."[43] Fewer jobs led to fewer union members and dues payers. In other words, the struggle for access to CUNY was not only a struggle for gaining racial recognition in one of the most important institutions in American society, it was also a class struggle led by students to position themselves to gain access to the labor market through a tuition-free education.

With the exception of the Newt Davidson Collective's pamphlet, *Crisis at CUNY*,[44] no other work explicitly examines moments of crisis and change at CUNY from a Marxist/Socialist perspective. Most significantly, the authors of *Crisis at CUNY* wrote: "We think capitalism is the root of our troubles inside and outside CUNY ... "[45] Applying this view to the open admissions policy and later the imposition of tuition at CUNY is useful for the purpose of understanding the underlying power dynamics that led to these transformational policy changes. Passed by a resolution of CUNY's Board of Higher Education in July 1969, after tremendous pressure from militant students and community supporters, the open admissions policy contained major provisions, including "a separate school of Black and Puerto Rican studies"; "admissions to some University program to all high school graduates of the City"; "remedial and other supportive services" and all with the deliberate goal of achieving the "ethnic integration of the colleges."[46] It was the result of months of militant agitation by a group of Black and Puerto Rican students—primarily at the City and Brooklyn College campuses—who coalesced to demand, not only *access* to CUNY colleges, but also to actively *participate* in the decision-making structures of the institution.[47]

---

[42] Joe Burns, *Reviving the Strike: How Working People Can Regain Power and Transform America* (Brooklyn, NY: Ig Pub., 2011).

[43] Joshua Benjamin Freeman, *Working-Class New York: Life and Labor since World War II* (New York: New Press, Distributed by W.W. Norton, 2000), p. 143.

[44] Newt Davidson Collective, *Crisis at CUNY*.

[45] Ibid., 10.

[46] Lavin et al., *Right Versus Privilege*, p. 15.

[47] In addition to the activism at City College and Brooklyn College, Lehman College, Queens College, Bronx and Queensborough Community Colleges also experienced a wave of student activism. By far, the most thoroughly covered of these is City College. For a detailed narrative of the student strike and building occupation see Dyer, "Protest and the Politics of Open Admissions." For a broader historical context of student activism, including City and Brooklyn Colleges, see Martha Biondi, *The Black Revolution on Campus* (Berkeley, CA: University of California Press, 2012). Covering both City and Lehman Colleges is Frederick Douglass Opie, "Developing Their Minds without Losing Their Soul: Black and Latino Student Coalition-Building in New York, 1965–1969," *Afro-Americans in New York Life and History* 33:2 (2009), pp. 79–108; and Newt Davidson Collective, *Crisis at CUNY*, p. 66.

The transformative changes brought to CUNY as a direct result of the open admissions policy were astounding. Enrollment ballooned and so did the university's budget, which, according to Lavin, Alba, and Silverstein, grew from sixty-seven million dollars in 1960–1961 (when Governor Nelson Rockefeller signed the bill that brought the municipal colleges under the roof of the City University) to 325 million dollars in 1970–1971, an increase of almost five-hundred percent.[48] By September 1970, the entering class was an extraordinary thirty-five thousand students, which was a seventy-five percent increase from the previous year.[49] The shape and the timing of the open admissions policy was the result of a process that was primarily managed by dominant elites within a particular set of pressures and constraints. These elites included Mayor John V. Lindsay and Chancellor Albert H. Bowker, both of whom operated within institutional, political, social, and economic constraints and pressures—more so during these moments of crisis.

In contrast to an explicitly Marxist, class struggle perspective, Lavin, Alba, and Silberstein use two "fundamental perspectives on the role of education in a society like our own" as their theoretical framework for understanding the open admissions policy and its aftermath.[50] As they explain it, "one of the views implies that the extension of educational opportunity to greatly disadvantaged groups will erode social inequalities, while the other suggests that these inequalities will carry over into open admissions and be preserved even in the face of such a change."[51] They label these "the thesis of industrialism" and the "critical perspective," respectively. The former, they explain, "emphasizes the independent effects of education," which suggests that "open admissions will help create equality of opportunity for socially and economically marginal groups." The latter, in its emphasis on "the dependence of education attainment on social origin leads to another view: higher education will adapt to open admissions by absorbing the new students in a lower track (namely, community-college vocational programs) and thereby will preserve class and ethnic privileges in the face of changes purporting to further equality of opportunity."[52] In the process of comparing and contrasting these views, they add their own perspective, which they consider to be a "different way to evaluate an educational system...".[53] They propose that we look at the "value" education adds to students. "By this yardstick," they say, "it is not the quality of students at entry or even their quality at exit that matters. Rather, it is the extent to which they change intellectually, socially, and otherwise."[54]

In their analysis of open admissions in light of these two perspectives they conclude that they "cannot subsume open admissions under either of the major perspectives on the role of education; the tension between the two cannot be solved. As is true in the analysis of educational systems more generally," they add, "each of these perspectives frames a partial and selective view of the consequences of open admissions."[55] As illuminating as Lavin, Alba, and

---

[48] Lavin et al., *Right Versus Privilege*, p. 290.
[49] Ibid., 19.
[50] Ibid., 28.
[51] Ibid., 28–29.
[52] Ibid., 37.
[53] Ibid., 38.
[54] Ibid., 38–39.

Silberstein's perspective is, they do not fully consider the role of class, ideology, and the state in explaining the role of education in general and reforms at CUNY during moments of crisis in particular.

In other words, Lavin, Alba, and Silberstein build their theoretical focus primarily on an educational policy foundation, which is removed from the deeper dynamics of the political economy of New York City and the class struggles that arise from it. But a more fundamental problem with the framework they propose to interpret and understand the open admissions policy centers on the dichotomous title of their book: "right versus privilege" in evaluating the open admissions experiment. Within the parameters of this dichotomy, they conclude their book with the finding that "while CUNY is still a more open institution than other systems of higher education, such as California's, the legacy of the fiscal crisis has been a narrowing of the mission to which the University committed itself in 1969. In the end," they find, "[CUNY] has moved closer to the older view: higher education is a privilege not a right."[56] In the context of viewing education as either a right or a privilege, which is a view already circumscribed within an educational policy context, CUNY has indeed moved toward becoming a more closed, selective public institution. This view, however, underscores the ideological and legitimating construct of viewing access to a higher education as a right: an *individual* right.

Conceptualizing CUNY as a public institution responsible for educating individuals is also compatible with the ideology of upward social mobility. As Jerome Karabel explained, "Open admissions has merely confronted elitist politics with egalitarian politics, bringing with it an educational philosophy far more persuasive than that of using our colleges and universities as agents for social selection."[57] Making an explicit connection to the broader political economy of American society, Karabel observes that "The social selection function of the university grew not so much out of educational philosophy but in response to an increasingly meritocratic economic structure. As technological developments demanded greater efficiency, the university began to *confer*, rather than just to *confirm*, status."[58]

This change, according to Karabel, "Propelled by both the needs of the economy and the ideology of equal opportunity... departed from its traditional norm of ascription, the assignment of status according to characteristics determined by birth, and started searching for students of outstanding ability, whatever their social origins."[59] In other words, this movement from "ascription to achievement" is the *sine qua non* of the ideology of merit in American society in general and in education in particular. Meritocratic ideology in education is in fact fully compatible with the liberal, democratic ethos of *individual* achievement. "The credo of meritocracy is mobility; the more the better, since everyone must rise (or sink) to his appropriate state in life," says Karabel.[60] Within this dominant,

---

Footnote 54 continued

[55] Ibid., 283–284.

[56] Ibid., 308.

[57] Jerome Karabel, "Open Admissions: Toward Meritocracy or Democracy?," *Change: The Magazine of Higher Learning Change* 4:4 (1972), p. 41.

[58] Ibid.

[59] Ibid.

[60] Ibid.

ideological box "failure in a class society is tolerable in that it can be attributed to the 'system,' but failure in a meritocracy can be blamed only on oneself."[61] The open admissions policy at CUNY opened the doors for Blacks and Puerto Ricans to the higher education credentialing process within the context of the ideology of merit: an ideology that draws clear lines of demarcation in the process of defining who is and who is not deserving of access to higher education and therefore the opportunity to obtain a credential to participate in the labor market.

The dominant class-biased ideology of meritocracy is embodied in the pressures exerted on public higher education institutions across the country to promote and sustain the credentialing process believed necessary for students to enter the labor market. That credentialing process is part of a broader ideological belief that considers education, specifically higher education, to be the primary means for mitigating the effects of poverty and inequality, and to promote upward social and economic mobility in general. Nonetheless, some studies have challenged the notion that more education is a panacea for addressing poverty and inequality.[62] In this interpretation, education has served as an ideological pressure valve for accommodating social and political discontent among the poor, unemployed, and under-employed. In other words, it has had the effect of "channeling popular protest into educational protest."[63]

At CUNY, institutional elites sought to adjust the institution's mission to accommodate the needs of the economy, particularly as it pertains to training a college-educated workforce and as a solution to poverty and inequality in New York City. In fact, as Suri Duitch points out, a University Task Force on Open Admissions identified the open admissions policy as a "maximum utilization of the City University as a 'poverty interrupter' within the City of New York."[64] Prioritizing funding for education, at CUNY in particular, instead of more broadly funding the welfare state, according to the same study, was a project by state legislative leaders going back to the 1960s.[65]

With its focus on class struggle dynamics—dynamics that have existed since the establishment of public education—this study challenges the ideology of meritocracy that exists within the liberal, democratic ethos of American society and education. The dynamics of class struggles, however, involve conflict between classes and the role of those on the bottom as well as the top need to be taken into account. The conflicts around education, further, arose within particular historical moments that were circumscribed by specific political-economic contexts. In fact, drawing from some of the "social control" literature of the time, Frances Fox Piven

---

[61] Ibid.

[62] Ivar E. Berg and Sherry Gorelick, *Education and Jobs: The Great Training Robbery* (New York: Published for the Center for Urban Education by Praeger Publishers, 1970); John Marsh, *Class Dismissed: Why We Cannot Teach or Learn Our Way out of Inequality* (New York: Monthly Review Press, 2011); Jeannette Wicks-Lim, "The Working Poor: A Booming Demographic," *New Labor Forum* 21:3 (2012), pp. 16–25.

[63] Frances Fox Piven and Richard A. Cloward, "Social Policy and the Formation of Political Consciousness," in Maurice Zeitlin (ed.), *Political Power and Social Theory: A Research Annual* (Greenwich, CT: JAI Press, 1980), p. 141.

[64] Suri Duitch, "Open Admissions and Remediation: A Case Study of Policymaking by the City University of New York Board," PhD dissertation, City University of New York, 2010, p. 153.

[65] Ibid., 153–154.

and Richard Cloward argue that "public education evolved in part as a response to popular disturbances, and that once established the public schools not only shaped what we call conforming behavior, but also helped to pattern and limit the ways in which people deviate and rebel." They go on to observe that

> As Marx and Engels knew, human behavior cannot be explained solely by the structured effects of institutional life. People do not only conform to institutional imperatives. They also react against them. They deviate from institutional imperatives. But those reactions, those deviations, are themselves formed by specific features of institutional life. Even revolutionary struggle is not an act of free intellect; like other forms of reaction, it is a product of social life.[66]

In short, they argue, "the institution of education was forged in part by a process of group and class conflict."[67] And as Carnoy and Levin observe, "educational growth in the United States was conditioned by the class conflict underlying capitalist production and the changing nature of the workplace. Schools expanded as part of a production-centered historical dynamic in which they reproduced the developing conditions of capitalist production while simultaneously responding to the demands of labor and growing school bureaucracies."[68] As is the case with CUNY, "the growth [and development] of schooling is intertwined with the changing workplace and with social demands for upward mobility and increased democracy; the tensions created by such competing demands—tensions that until recently sometimes eased by educational expansion itself—have continually shaped the role and structure of schooling."[69] The shape and content of the reforms at CUNY during this time period can be explained in terms related to this broader, historical context.

Racial and class conflict and struggle have been present in the ways that open admissions and the imposition of tuition reforms have been shaped, managed, and resolved. In fact, the open admissions policy would suffer a major blow six years after its implementation in 1976 as part of a broad attack on the public sector as a result of the fiscal crisis of the 1970s, as I will show in the next section.

The Imposition of Tuition: Austerity Measures and the Attack on the Public Sector

Understanding the imposition of tuition in the midst of the New York City fiscal crisis in the 1970s is crucial to understanding not only the dynamics of class struggle that unfolded at CUNY, but also the trajectory that started in 1959 of growing state influence over CUNY, which began under Governor Nelson Rockefeller. This trajectory culminated two decades later in the centralization of more power in the hands of the state through the creation of the Board of Trustees in 1979 and the use of the Tuition Assistance Program (TAP) to exert more control over the financing of tuition costs for students. In this respect, the work of Judith S. Glazer[70]—one of the few scholarly attempts to understand the imposition of tuition at CUNY—is useful, albeit theoretically limited because of its policy

---

[66] Zeitlin, *Political Power and Social Theory*, pp. 18–119.
[67] Ibid., 129.
[68] Carnoy and Levin, *Schooling and Work in the Democratic State*, p. 80.
[69] Ibid.

studies framework for understanding a process that was fundamentally about class struggle.

The imposition of tuition in 1976 has not attracted as much scholarly analysis as the open admissions policy. This is odd considering the impact this imposed change had on CUNY in general and the open admissions policy in particular. As one of the only works that looks specifically at the imposition of tuition at CUNY from a policy studies perspective, Judith Glazer treats opposition to it as a process of resource management and "interest groups" vying to have their voices heard. While she does contextualize her analysis within a broader political environment, she makes no mention of student militancy and struggle against the attempted tuition increases during the 1970s and the actual imposition of tuition in 1976.

In her narrative, Glazer considers the significant role played by the Emergency Financial Control Board (EFCB) and the Municipal Assistance Corporation (MAC) in the imposition of tuition—as does Lavin, Alba, and Silberstein[71]—but she does not analyze them within the broader context of the direct assault on the gains made by working-class and liberal forces in New York City during the fiscal crisis. In other words, she does not analyze the fiscal crisis and the creation of the EFCB and MAC as the "occasion for a broad reordering of city life as bankers, financiers, and conservative ideologues made an audacious power grab."[72]

Appointed by Governor Hugh Carey in May of 1975, the MAC comprised nine members, eight of which had "banking and brokerage connections."[73] Later on in September of the same year, the EFCB was formed through a legislative act, which gave it the power to "supervise the financial management of the city" and to generally manage the most important aspect of New York City's financial dealings.[74] In essence, according to Lichten, both the MAC and the EFCB embodied a "banker's coup" shifting decision-making power away from elected representatives and towards the bankers and businessmen who were members of both groups.[75]

The fiscal crisis was a crisis of legitimacy and class power. Drawing from Erich Lichten's theory of crisis, the imposition of tuition at CUNY was a historically situated political-economic manifestation of crisis and as both the product and the process of struggle.[76] As Lichten goes on to explain, "crisis may also be viewed as a social process, and not the 'natural' result of uncontrollable economic forces. Crisis is produced by human actors and is the consequence of human action within, [in the case of the New York City fiscal crisis], a definite stage of class society, with very definite relations of state, economy, class, and power."[77] Without

---

Footnote 69 continued

[70] Judith S. Glazer, "A Case Study of the Decision in 1976 to Initiate Tuition for Matriculated Undergraduate Students of the City University of New York," PhD dissertation, New York University,1981.

[71] Lavin et al., *Right Versus Privilege.*

[72] Freeman, *Working-Class New York*, p. 256.

[73] Eric Lichten, *Class, Power, & Austerity: The New York City Fiscal Crisis* (South Hadley, MA: Bergin & Garvey Publishers, 1986), pp. 129–130.

[74] Ibid., 138.

[75] Ibid., 130.

[76] Ibid.

[77] Ibid., 12.

a doubt, institutional and political elites made choices within particular institutional and structural constraints and they did so under a particular set of external pressures.[78]

Conceptualizing crisis and class struggle in this way can help us explain not only the resistance and struggle by students and other agents against the imposition of tuition in the 1970s, but also the resistance of the Board of Higher Education, which at one point resisted the imposition of tuition at CUNY. Guided by Governor Rockefeller, The New York State Board of Regents in its December 1975 report called for the imposition of tuition at CUNY, a call that the Board of Higher Education refused to accept.[79] Nevertheless, the fiscal crisis of New York City ultimately led to one of the most traumatic moments in the history of CUNY.

Conclusion

This focus on class power and class struggle is an attempt to shift attention away from individual elites' "personal beliefs" and "intentions" as primary analytical factors in defining political and institutional outcomes. To be sure, specific elites have had a tremendous influence on the evolution and transformation of CUNY. As Gordon concludes in her study of CUNY's transformation between 1945 and 1970, Nelson Rockefeller and Albert Bowker "stand out for the distinctive roles they played, without whose special style and skills the development of the University might have been substantially different."[80] So while I do not discount the influence individuals have had on the evolution of CUNY, this study places emphasis on the role played by *dominant elites as a class* that operates within a historical, political economic set of constraints, particularly during moments of crisis. These constraints in turn shaped the ways in which moments of class struggle erupted, were managed and resolved.

Understanding structural reform at CUNY today, including most recently the imposition of Pathways (a standard, general education curriculum) in 2013—requires that we understand CUNY's history between 1969 and 1976. This political-economic study of CUNY can serve as a model for contextualizing and examining policies at other public higher education institutions taken up and supported by institutional and political elites who aim to instrumentalize higher education to serve the needs of capital.

---

[78] Also see Clyde W. Barrow, "The Rationality Crisis in US Higher Education," *New Political Science: A Journal of Politics and Culture* 32:3 (2010), pp. 317–344.

[79] Lavin et al., *Right Versus Privilege*, 295.

[80] Gordon, "The Transformation of the City University of New York, 1945–1970," p. 264.

Lowering the Basement Floor: From Community Colleges to the For-Profit Revolution

Brian Caterino
Independent Scholar, Rochester, USA

Abstract *For-profit colleges have become a major force in higher education. They claim to offer a career-oriented practical education that is an alternative to community and four-year colleges. Often they fail to provide what they promise. Rather than being a new alternative, for-profits are the new basement floor of education, offering substandard educations at inflated prices. The primacy of profit motives and especially financialization means that for-profits are more like a financial instrument of neoliberal policies than educational institutions. Fueled by the reliance on federal student loans for operations expenses, educational aims are secondary to advertising and recruitment of a continuing supply of students without much regard for graduation rates. They appeal to first-generation students and recent immigrants with little information about higher education or the job market.*

For-profit education is the fastest growing sector of American higher education, rising exponentially in the last decade from 3.1% of undergraduate student enrollment in 1999 to 9% in 2009. The share of total bachelor's degrees awarded by for-profits during the same period increased at an even higher rate, going from 1% to 5%.[1] For-profits have become significant players in higher education.

For-profit colleges have been around for a long time. They arose in the nineteenth century to teach trade and business skills when the demand for skilled workers could not be met by apprenticeships. These schools appealed to lower-class students, especially women and focused on narrowly defined practical skills. For-profits expanded into professional areas throughout the nineteenth century but declined in influence as progressive era reformers sought greater regulation and professionalization of higher education. The role of for-profits was largely taken over by the new community college system. Until recently, for-profits remained a small but steady segment of college students.[2]

The rapid rise in enrollment in recent decades was triggered by two developments. The first was the so-called 90/10 Rule. Since 1972, for-profit schools have been eligible for federal funds such as Pell Grants and Federal

---

[1] David Glenn, "Annual Portrait of Education Documents Swift Rise of For-Profit Colleges," *Chronicle of Higher Education* May 26, 2011, <http://chronicle.com/article/Annual-Portrait-of-Education/127639/>.

[2] Anna Kamenetz, "The Profit Chase," *Slate*, November 16, 2005. On the history of for-profits see Craig A. Honick, "The Story Behind Proprietary Schools in the United States," *New Directions for Community Colleges* 91 (Fall 1995), pp. 27–40.

Student Loans under Title IV of the Higher Education Act. However, in the 1980s, a number of well-publicized examples of fraud and abuse of student aid and loans, especially by proprietary (for-profit) colleges, led to calls for reform. Designed to crack down on unscrupulous operators who exploited federal eligibility for aid, the 90/10 Rule stipulated that any college or university had to obtain at least ten percent of its revenue from non-federal sources to be eligible for federal student aid. If an educational institution was valuable at least ten percent of students should be willing to pay tuition to attend—a standard that was easily met by traditional colleges. This low standard, however far from protecting students from fraud, allowed for-profits to expand on a low-cost basis using the large percentage of grants and student loans.

The second factor is the shrinking funding provided to colleges and especially community colleges, which has left them struggling to fulfill their missions. Criticism of the effectiveness of community colleges has created a crisis of confidence in public higher education. Overcrowded classes, limited offerings, and loss of flexibility to accommodate older or non-traditional students in community colleges have driven students to look for alternatives. For-profits have exploited this lacuna.

For-profits have replaced community colleges as the basement floor of higher education. However the basement is not a bargain. For-profit institutions offer career training programs and career-oriented degrees funded largely by student loans without any record of success in graduation or job placement, often leaving students with huge debts. The for-profit sector is an instrument of financialization of higher education which provides substandard education and earns maximized profits.[3]

The Contradictory Mission of Community Colleges

Reflecting their progressive era roots, community colleges have always had a divided, even contradictory, mission. Community colleges were established as open access institutions. Anyone with a high school diploma or the equivalent could attend college at a low cost. This conception was an extension of the American idea of education as a public good necessary for a democratic society.[4] In its ideal state, community college education was both a vehicle to expand the democratic character of higher education, since a more educated populace would be more able to contribute to public life, and extend ideas of individual advancement and upward mobility to a larger group of students. Education was a central means of overcoming the inequality of the Gilded Age. Community colleges were to be "America's Democracy Colleges," providing pathways to advancement and success.[5] "Junior" college provided a route for transfer to four-year colleges and entrance to the ranks of professionals and managers.

---

[3] For example see Sheila Slaughter and Gary Rhoades, *Academic Capitalism and the New Economy: Markets, State and Higher Education* (Baltimore, MD: Johns Hopkins, 2009); Jennifer Washburn, *University Inc: The Corporate Corruption of Higher Education* (New York: Basic, 2006); Gaye Tuchman, *Wannabe U: Inside the Corporate University* (Chicago, IL: University of Chicago Press, 2009).

[4] Steven Brint and Jerome Karabel, *The Diverted Dream: Community Colleges and the Promise of Educational Opportunity 1900–1985* (New York: Oxford University Press, 1991).

[5] Ibid., 2.

Yet the open access mission stood in direct conflict with the second aim. Community colleges also acted as gatekeepers, sorting machines that worked to lower career expectations for the majority of its students. Thus it served to reproduce social injustice rather promote equality and justice.

The extension of the ideal of individual achievement though college education often was confronted with the reality of limited opportunity in the labor market. In the first half of the twentieth century there simply were not enough professional or technical jobs to satisfy all applicants. This conflict between aspiration and economic reality was especially apparent in community colleges where students were less qualified than four-year college students. Community colleges were left to carry out what Burton Clark, borrowing from Goffman, called the "cooling out" role in education.[6] Goffman used the analogy of the con man who lets down his mark softly after the con to describe situations in which expectations led to failure or loss and had to be adjusted, rationalized, or substituted to avoid self-degradation. Clark saw this as an acceptable function of two-year schools; they had to provide a soft landing for those who had little chance of attaining the positions for which they aimed. Community colleges had to divert students into vocational programs or two-year terminal degrees. In so doing they reinforced stratification rather than providing a route to mobility. Community colleges became tools for the management of ambition.[7]

During this period, the still mostly middle-class students attending community colleges rejected the management of expectation and viewed community college as a means to transfer to a four-year college. Few students enrolled in vocational courses. It was only in the 1970s in response to demographic changes and the recession that vocational training became a prime function of community college education.

The Neo-conservative Restoration

After World War II, managing expectations was a matter of adjusting labor to demand in an essentially smooth working society. The neo-conservatives, however, inflated management and lowered expectations into a diagnosis of the times. American society was in crisis. According to critics like Daniel Bell, the turmoil of the 1960s was due to the cultural contradictions of capitalism and not its economic structure. Like Weber, Bell saw capitalism as self-undermining. He focused, however, on the loss of moral virtue. The ascetic individualism of early bourgeois culture has turned into acquisitiveness. The work ethic was religiously anchored. Without that ethic of virtue, an unregulated individualism strives only for self-gratification. Others applied this criticism toward the political system. For critics like Huntington, the political system was becoming ungovernable. They saw the new social movement of the time as a reflection of an individualistic culture that made excessive demands on goods for the political

---

[6] Burton Clark, *The Open Door College: A Case Study* (New York: McGraw Hill, 1960); and Burton Clark, "The Cooling Out Function in Higher Education," *American Journal of Sociology* 65:6 (1960), pp. 569–576. For Goffman see Erving Goffman, "Cooling the Mark Out: Some Aspects of Adaption to Failure," *Psychiatry* XV (November 1952), pp. 451–462.

[7] Brint and Karabel, *The Diverted Dream*, p. 7.

system. Both of these lines of argument led to the conclusion that excessive individual expectations were a threat to the political, moral, and social order.[8]

Progressive education, with its emphasis on individual development, was a main target of neo-conservatives. On their reading, progressive education with its emphasis on self-fulfillment and individual freedom of the learner lacks concern for the learner's morals and work discipline. It was portrayed as a failed experiment that deviated from the tried and true principles of education that failed to educate students in the "basics." For neo-conservatives, expectations had to be lowered and social discipline reèstablished.

Community colleges became one of the main arenas in which educational culture wars were fought. The invention of "career education" by the Nixon administration was a direct attempt to establish a wide-ranging neo-conservative reform in the school system and to lower the expectations of students for higher status jobs.[9] Like Bell, Nixon officials diagnosed the problems raised by movements of the 1960s as a result of anomie. Students were not rebellious because they wanted more democracy, equality, or social justice, but because their education seemed irrelevant and meaningless. Students lacked connection to their society, resulting in disenchantment, rebellion, and delinquency. Educational programs did not prepare students for higher education or the labor market. Nixon officials aimed to transform the educational system from the ground up so that all education was career-oriented education. Nixon's reform program sought to have community colleges discourage transfer to four-year programs and stressed preparation for work. Since community colleges failed to prepare students for their (inferior) role in the workplace, they had to be reformed.[10]

Nixon's reforms were for the most part failures, but the stress on the vocational role of community colleges gained momentum during the 1970s. The "junior" college evolved into the "comprehensive community college," a mixture of diverse programs that intensified the conflicting missions of community colleges. Federal aid programs (the aforementioned Title IV) introduced in the Johnson administration, encouraged expanded access of higher education to more of the population. As a result, the demographics of community college students changed dramatically. Increasingly, community college students were part-time, first-generation students, women, older students, minorities, and recent immigrants. Today the community college population is about sixty percent female, the average age is close to thirty and about thirty percent African American and Hispanic and lower income.

Community colleges expanded rapidly to meet this demand and the availability of nearby colleges fostered greater use by these underserved groups who still saw college as a road to advancement. They sought to redeem the democratic potential of education. The increasing emphasis on a college degree as

---

[8] Daniel Bell, *The Cultural Contradictions of Capitalism* (New York: Basic Books, 1976). On ungovernability see Michael Crozier, Samuel Huntington, and Joji Watanuki, *The Crisis of Democracy: Report on the Governability of Democracies to the Trilateral Commission* (New York: New York University Press, 1975).

[9] The Nixon administration program is documented in Ira Shor, *Culture Wars: School and Society in Conservative Restoration 1969–84* (New York: Routledge and Kagan Paul, 1987). A more recent analysis of vocationalization is Henry Giroux "Neo-liberalism and the Vocationalization of Higher Education," *Workplace* 5:1, 2002, < http://www.henryagiroux. com/online_articles/vocalization.htm>.

[10] Shor, *Culture Wars*, Chapter 1 develops this theme.

a basic requirement for economic advancement was another important factor. Yet these students were also underprepared for higher education. Up to fifty percent needed remedial courses in subjects like Math and English.

Progressives embraced the new student populations. They felt that the democratization of higher education required the removal of barriers to education based on class, race, gender, poverty, or culture. Community colleges were to be the vanguard for meeting the needs of disadvantaged students, providing them a "Gateway to Opportunity."[11] Conservatives, however, wanted to channel students to work-centric training programs.

Comprehensive community colleges took on a bewildering array of institutional roles. Besides their traditional preparatory role, community colleges instituted an extensive array of vocational programs and terminal degrees which were tied directly to workforce needs. One factor was increasing competition for students; administrators looked to create a niche for community colleges in light of post baby boom declines. However this was also a response to government and business pressures for "accountability" in times of decreasing government revenues. The idea that community colleges could or should serve as a local or national economic engine had been discussed since the 1930s, but now the vocationalization of the community college took center stage. Colleges cooperated with local businesses to create programs that were narrowly focused on job training and the needs of the local workforce. Students were channeled into these vocational or workforce oriented programs, such as certificates, and terminal degrees, such as health care, that provided associate degrees in areas that had an immediate workforce linkage. In addition, community colleges took on contract workforce training industries that had no degree or certificate programs attached to them. These programs conflicted with the mission of community colleges to be a means to greater democratic education and civic activity. They construed education less as a *paideia* and more as a narrow technical skill.

The new wave of open access policies in community colleges did little to overcome the stratification of American life. Fewer students were successfully transferring to four-year colleges and the dropout rate for incoming students rose steadily. The lower paying jobs produced by vocational training did little to challenge the mission of promoting democratic education and social justice. Managing and channeling expectations had become the main task. Many questioned whether the community colleges even had a specific mission.[12]

Funding to community colleges declined as resources were stretched and the value of education (especially liberal education) challenged. By the turn of the century state funding typically amounted to only about one-third of all revenues. As Ami Zuzman notes, states have become "minority partners" in educating.[13] In 2004 revenues were twelve percent less than they were in 1989. Colleges, and especially community colleges, hired more and lower-paid adjunct faculty, which today make up about seventy-five percent of all faculty. Often, courses needed for

---

[11] J.M. Beach, *Gateway to Opportunity: A History of the Community College in the United States* (Sterling, VA: Stylus Publishing, 2011), p. 32.

[12] Brint and Karabel, *The Diverted Dream*, p. 102.

[13] Ami Zusman, "Challenges Facing Higher Education in the Twenty-First Century," in P. G. Altbach, R.O. Berdahl, and P.J. Gumport (eds), *American Higher Education in the Twenty-First Century: Social, Political, and Economic Challenges* (Baltimore, MD: Johns Hopkins University Press, 2005), pp. 115–160.

degrees were overcrowded or difficult to take. Programs have been cut and funds reallocated to programs which seem to have a more immediate payoff, such as vocational oriented ones. Operating with limited resources, community colleges have not been able to cope with the new demands of a more diverse student population. Faced with these budget cuts however, many community colleges have little chance of carrying out the mandates imposed on them from the 1970s onward. Community colleges have been subject to increasing criticism as inefficient and inadequate to the educational needs of society. Students report that the culture of community colleges discourages aspiration and achievement. They quickly learn to have lowered expectations. Discouraged in advance many students are not motivated to succeed.[14]

The Neoliberal Restructuring

Neo-conservatives sought a *restoration* of "traditional" values of work and moral discipline lost in late capitalism. Neoliberalism applies a more radical approach to reforming society. It employs a modernist sensibility for conservative ends. It seeks a radical restructuring of the economy to conform to the model of a "free-market."

Neoliberalism was not always associated with an unfettered market. In the first part of the twentieth century it was associated with ordo-liberalism, a view of the social market economy that stood between laissez faire and the welfare state. In the post-Keynesian era however, neoliberalism was equated with market fundamentalism—the view that market mechanisms are sufficient to solve economic and social problems. The Keynesian assumptions behind the welfare state, according to neoliberals, distorted the economy and led to an accumulation crisis. Inflation, rising unemployment, and slow economic growth seemed to undercut the principles of Keynesian economics. The Keynesian Welfare State was unable to sustain the growth to fund the welfare state it created.

In the eyes of neoliberals, the Keynesian welfare state failed because it restricted the workings of the free market. Neoliberal economic policies included "fiscal austerity, market determined interest and exchange rates, free trade, inward investment deregulation, privatization, market deregulation and a commitment to private property."[15] All of these are attempts to transfer power from governments to private markets. However, much of the first wave of neoliberal reforms has been based on financial innovations. Financialization has a variety of senses,[16] but for our purposes it addresses the accumulation crisis of Keynesianism, shifting accumulation away from commodity production and trade or manufacturing to financial instruments which provide return for investors.

In spite of its seeming commitment to free markets, neoliberalism is by no means a return to classical laissez faire economics. Much more than a watchmen

---

[14] Beach, *Gateway to Opportunity*, p. 60.

[15] Miguel A Centeno and Joseph N. Cohen, "The Arc of Neo-liberalism," *Annual Review of Sociology* 38 (August 2012), p. 321.

[16] A summary of various senses is found in Natasha Van der Swan, "Making Sense of Financialization," *Socio-Economic Review* 12:1 (2004), pp. 99–129.

state, government is an active agent that brings about conditions for marketizing the economy that would be unachievable without its activity. As Olson notes:

> Whereas classical liberalism represents a negative conception of state power in that the individual was to be taken as an object to be freed from the interventions of the state, neo-liberalism has come to represent a positive conception of the state's role in creating the appropriate market by providing the conditions, laws and institutions necessary for its operation. In classical liberalism, the individual is characterized as having an autonomous human nature and can practice freedom. In neo-liberalism, the state seeks to create an individual who is an enterprising and competitive entrepreneur.[17]

The state here is not a watchman. It retains a good deal of its administrative functions needed to monitor the "free market." Schooling is a good example of the new role of administration. The outcomes of neoliberal school reforms are constantly measured and shaped by government-mandated testing. The shaping of educational subjects who conform to the perceived needs of the new economy is construed; it is not a natural result of an unencumbered market.

Neoliberalism of course is not just an economic theory but a set of cultural practices. For neoliberals the welfare state creates weak and dependent individuals lacking in entrepreneurial spirit. Thus it requires a radical (conservative) reconstitution of the entrepreneurial self. This contrasts with the social democratic concept of freedom and citizenship in the welfare state. For social democrats, a developed industrial society needs a baseline of economic security. Citizens have to be shielded to some extent from market conditions over which they have little control as well as from the upheavals caused by unemployment or other systematic risks in order to develop and exert freedom and to have the ability to be participating citizens; to be sure, the welfare state was Janus-faced. Subjects of the welfare state were often treated as clients rather than as citizens and mass democracies short-circuited more widespread participation. Still, the idea that in developed capitalist societies, basic protections were a necessary element of freedom was an undeniable achievement.

Despite valid criticism of the effects of bureaucracy, we cannot simply return to notions of freedom associated with the possessive individual that were developed in the seventeenth and eighteenth centuries. That would be a regression. Neoliberal culture does not represent a return to an original form of freedom corrupted by the welfare state, rather it requires a project of social unlearning in which the lessons of the last one hundred fifty years must be reversed.

Neoliberal culture is another iteration of reactionary modernism. It intensifies the tensions between the safety and security that is necessary for self-development in industrial society and the conditions of capital accumulation, between democratic self-determination and citizen participation versus steering by the market.

With the decline of a social contract based on long-term industrial and corporate jobs, individuals face an uncertain, risky, and precarious future.

---

[17] Mark Olssen, "In Defense of the Welfare State and of Publicly Provided Education," *Journal of Educational Policy* 11:3 (1996), pp. 337–362, cited in Michael W. Apple "Creating Difference: Neo-Liberalism, Neo-Conservatism and the Politics of Educational Reform," *Educational Policy* 18:1 (2004), p. 21.

Inequality between the rich and poor increases, and mobility is stagnant if not declining. The individual of neoliberalism is not the optimistic self-interested actor of classic liberal theory but is constituted through insecurity and fear. The entrepreneurial subject is not a construct of nature but requires a kind of negative individualization, which, rather than establishing identity within a community separates the individual from connections and from public life. It might be seen as a contemporary form of reification. Richard Sennett has analyzed this, borrowing Zygmut Bauman's notion of liquid modernity. He has characterized this new constellation of subjectivity as the fragmentation (through insecurity) of everyday life in the neoliberal era. In a post-Keynesian world, permanent employment in the industrial sector is unlikely and family relationships have been even more fragmented by the demands of a world in which both parents work. Work in neoliberal times is contingent employment; it changes frequently and requires constant adaption. We learn to ignore our past identity in order to go with the flow. In short, "liquid modernity" implies both economic insecurity and social instability. Neoliberalism creates new risks which are financial, social, and ecological but distributes them asymmetrically, because the wealthy can insulate themselves from some risk and privatize the risks for the less well off. In opposition to the subject of advanced industrial society we have to negotiate a new environment in which individuals face new constraints on time based on short-term relationships and marketing of the self as a "brand" for potential economic gain. Each of these destabilizes the sense of a narrative of the self so that a continuous identity is difficult to establish.[18]

As systems of social welfare retreat and privatized systems of retirement are created, individuals are increasingly responsible for managing the uncertainties they face in life. This is the product of financialization. Life becomes an asset to be managed. However when individual investors come to enter financial markets to provide for these risks, they do so with very limited information and face volatile financial markets.[19] For the most part the effect of this is a reduction in security and an increase in inequality rather than its mitigation. Looking at this in the context of higher education, Suzanne Mettler has shown that increasing stratification of education in the neoliberal era reinforces and even deepens inequality. While attendance at college has increased for all socio-economic classes, those from the upper classes are far more likely to complete school and to graduate in a timely manner. Those further down the ladder have completion rates as low as 11–15%. "As colleges grow more stratified," she notes, "more differentiated in their accessibility to different socioeconomic groups and in what they offer them, they are generating greater inequality in American society."[20] Expectations are not simply diminished, they are reshaped and redefined.

---

[18] Richard Sennett, *The Culture of the New Capitalism* (New Haven, CT: Yale University Press, 2006). Among his many works see Zygmut Bauman, *Liquid Times: Living in an Age of Uncertainty* (Malden, MA: Polity, 2006). There is a burgeoning discussion on the notion of the precarity of neoliberal society. For example see Guy Standing, *The Precariat: The New Dangerous Class* (London: Bloomsbury Academic 2011). For a more Foucauldian reading of these processes using the notion of governmentality, see Stephen C. Ward, *Neoliberalism and the Global Restructuring of Knowledge and Education* (New York: Routledge, 2012), Chapter 1.

[19] Van der Swan, "Making Sense of Financialization."

[20] Suzanne Mettler, *Degrees of Inequality: How the Politics of Higher Education Sabotaged the American Dream* (New York: Basic Books, Kindle Edition, 2014), p. 37.

Education as a Financial Instrument

In the wake of funding shortfalls and the pressures of neoliberal policies, non-profit higher education, like governmental and public sector (non-profit) institutions are increasingly employing the models of the market. Higher education has adopted profit-making models in several ways. First, education is an arena for the accumulation of capital. Research generated at universities is used to generate profit and basic research is replaced by research for private firms aimed at developing marketable products. Second, universities have marketed intellectual property such as online coursework. Universities claim ownership rather than recognizing professors' claims to ownership of their work. In its digital form, instruction itself is a commodity.

For-profit colleges do not just financialize resources, they are financial instruments. Many are owned by venture capital or other groups whose primary aim is to make a profit and not to provide education. Their primary obligation is to shareholders and not to a public good. Earlier for-profits were loosely affiliated and independently operated small schools that provided educational services. After a series of scandals in the 1980s, fifteen hundred of the four thousand for-profit trade schools were decertified. In the wake of these scandals, a series of mergers and buyouts resulted in a concentration of the for-profit higher education industry in large firms. These streamlined and sophisticated operations were created by financial groups who used educational institutions as capital for investment and thus to maximize returns for stockholders. Investor-centered, large for-profits have become publically traded companies in the stock market owned by investment companies, and several years ago were among the hottest stocks.[21] Between 2000 and 2003 for-profits were the highest earning stocks on the market. In 2009 the eight larger publically held and privately held for-profits made $2.7 billion in profits.

For-profits generate income not from more efficient education but through enrollment (that is, by making students into a financial instrument). While Title IV aid was meant to expand access to education for the less advantaged, it has, in the hands of for-profits, become a vehicle to exploit the more vulnerable members of the student population. Student aid is, in fact, the primary source of revenue. It plays a large part in the debt crisis that has threatened to drown students, many of whom never graduate, in a sea of debt that lowers their chances for the very opportunities it promises. As one critic noted:

> Much like lenders in the subprime mortgage market, for-profit institutions find themselves in position to benefit handsomely from the debt of marginally credit worthy borrowers without bearing any accompanying risk.[22]

For-profit higher education follows the predatory practices of the larger economy. Predatory education exploits the vulnerabilities of those of lower socio-economic

---

[21] Goldie Blumentstyk, "For-Profit Colleges Attract a Gold Rush of Investors," *Chronicle of Higher Education* (March 2003). The value of these stocks has dropped in more recent years.

[22] Mathew A. McGuire, "Subprime Education: For-Profit Colleges and the Problem with Title IV Federal Student Aid," *Duke Law Journal* 62 (October 2012), p. 121.

status with promises of jobs and degrees and certificates. The system is rife with predatory practices which belie any real concern for educational processes.

An Agile Flexible Education?

Proponents of the for-profit model praise it in terms that are analogous to that of neoliberal capitalism. The new knowledge-based economy requires adaptation of capitalism to the new international order and higher education follows suit. For-profits are agile and flexible, able to adapt quickly to changing market conditions and demand for skills. This flexibility is especially important to non-traditional students who have different expectations from education. Colleges and universities must adopt the methods of modern businesses in the knowledge economy. Traditional schools are too rigid and too slow to respond to market trends. According to the Bush administration's Spelling Commission (Commission on the Future of Higher Education), traditional colleges and universities including community colleges, have become risk averse "mature institutions."[23] They are staid and conservative enterprises that are expensive and not open to innovation. Thus they must be forced to change and adapt to the demands of the new economy. They require rigorous ongoing assessment to force change. Creating the new educational structure requires not just freeing restraints but also monitoring. The demands of the knowledge economy require continual monitoring and data to assess outcomes for their efficiency and productivity. This monitoring is not simply done by corporations but in large measure by governments. Education too must be measured in terms of its productive "outcomes."

Andrew Rosen caricatures the modern non-profit university as a country club for the well off.[24] Colleges, mostly private but not exclusively so, spend exorbitant funds on luxuries, have lavish facilities, display excessive emphasis on sports and athletics, and are loaded with bird courses. Colleges emphasize social connections rather than academic achievement or job skills. Tuition has skyrocketed, according to Rosen, because of these lavish facilities.

Given this portrait, Rosen positions the for-profit as a stripped down, low-cost education which does away with the luxuries. For-profits provide a practical career-oriented education using "proven pedagogical methods" which ensures students learn. Rosen interprets this mission as a great revolution in education. Following the establishment of land grant colleges in the nineteenth century, which broadened access to education and brought with it the start of an adult education, and the establishment of community colleges which further broadened access to education, the for-profits represent the third great wave of educational expansion.[25]

Students now see education as a product and see themselves as consumers of the product "education." Adult students retuning to college to upgrade skills

---

[23] Spelling Commission on Higher Education, *A Test of Leadership: Charting the Future of Higher Education* (US Department of Education, 2006), p. xiv.

[24] Andrew Rosen, *Change.edu: Rebooting for the New Talent Economy* (New York: Kaplan Publishing, 2011); Robert M. Shireman, "'Change.edu' and the Problem with For-Profits," *Chronicle of Higher Education*, January 31, 2012.

[25] George Keller, "Foreword," in Richard S. Ruch (ed.), *Higher Ed Inc: The Rise of the For-Profit University* (Baltimore, MD: John Hopkins, 2001), p. xi.

want flexible scheduling and have little time for the "frivolous" pursuits of the campus. Like low-income students and first-generation students, they often feel like outsiders in a campus setting. For-profits target these marginalized populations who are not always satisfied with traditional education. Either they could not schedule their classes, found campuses alienating, found courses too large, or found traditional college curricula boring or unnecessary. After new grant programs were created for veterans, they became part of this target group too.[26] These groups respond favorably to a "no-frills" approach to education, one that does away with the trappings of the traditional college and focuses exclusively on jobs. In serving these groups, for-profits argue that they are extending the democratic promise of education, providing educational services that community colleges and four-year colleges have failed to provide, and making education accessible to all. Of course this no frills approach does away with other elements of higher education that serve public interests, promote a democratic society, and enhance the ability of students to understand the contemporary world. For-profits carry out no organized research and do away with full-time faculty.

In contrast to these optimistic assessments, the expansion of for-profits in the last decade has been plagued with problems, both financial and educational. There is little evidence that they have created a new role for education or provided it at an effective, low cost. They spend little on investment in "capital," human, physical, or virtual, reducing their costs but providing mediocre to bad education at tuition rates higher than comparable institutions. Costs at for-profit colleges have not generally been lower, despite the fact that for-profits spend less on instruction than non-profits. Comparing spending at four-year institutions, for-profits spent on average $2,659 per full-time student, versus $9,418 at public colleges and $15,289 at private non-profit colleges. However, lower per student costs did not translate into lower overall costs. According to a Department of Education report, "the average net price for full-time dependent undergraduates in 2007–8 was $30,900 at four-year for-profit institutions, versus $26,600 at private nonprofit colleges and $15,600 at public institutions."[27] Like many large corporations, executive salaries at for-profits are excessively high. The largest for-profits such as the University of Phoenix pay CEOs more than six million dollars. Compensation at the majority of the CEOs' thirteen large for-profits owned by Wall Street firms was over three million dollars. These hardly seem to be bonuses for the effective performance in education. Graduation rates are low and default rates high. High compensation serves to make CEOs more dependent on keeping up the bottom line of profits to please shareholders.

Far from being more efficient with money spent on instruction, it appears that for-profits destroy the very resources they need. Low wages tend to reduce the professionalism of academia and exploit an overcrowded labor market for college and university instructors. This promotes the deskilling of academic work and the casualization of labor—even more than at community colleges. Even with the glut of faculty available to teach, for-profits employ instructors with limited qualifications; courses are often standardized and prefabricated with little room

---

[26] Adam Weinstein, "How Pricey For–Profit Colleges Target Vets' GI Bill Money," *Mother Jones* (Sep/Oct 2011).

[27] Glenn, "Annual Portrait of Education," <http://chronicle.com/article/Annual-Portrait-of-Education/127639/>.

for the creativity and knowledge of the instructor. At brick and mortar for-profits, faculty report they work in cubicles, without offices.[28]

If for-profits spend little money on instruction, they spend a good deal of money on advertising and recruitment. Education is a product to be sold for profit and attracting customers is more important than the quality of the product. For-profit schools advertise heavily on television, in print media, and on the internet. For example, the University of Phoenix, the nation's largest for-profit institution, spent 1.1 billion dollars on sales and promotion in the 2009–2010 fiscal year. ITT Technical Institute spent about twenty-nine percent of its revenue of 1.3 billion dollars on advertising, recruitment, and administrative services. Although this practice has been banned, recruiters were paid a commission at some schools based on the number of students they signed up. There is little attention paid to the special needs of students or to providing them the extra time and resources they need to succeed.

On the contrary, these groups seem to have been targeted more for their precarity and vulnerability to a sales pitch. Vulnerable populations are subject to high-pressure sales pitches; recruiters are taught to appeal to the pain, suffering, and low self-esteem of potential students, stressing feelings of worthlessness in order to manipulate them into attending school. A former recruiter at Corinthian College testified that recruiters were instructed to persuade students that their life was miserable and could only be improved by enrolling at the school. They used those feelings to persuade them to enroll. Similar approaches were found at other for-profits such as ITT and Kaplan.[29]

The recent expansion of the GI Bill in the wake of 9/11 and the Iraq War has turned out to be a boon to for-profits. Current and former GIs have become major recruitment targets. For-profits have set up websites like GiBill.com and set up military recruiting bureaus to exploit this source of money. Even though they only enroll one-third of the number of vets, for-profits get about the same amount of federal aid as non-profit schools, with little evidence that they pay attention to the needs of veterans.[30]

Federal student aid makes up the vast majority of revenues in for-profit institutions. The fourteen largest for-profits report that federal student aid makes up ninety percent of their revenues, and while they enroll only about 10% of all college students, they get twenty percent of all federal aid. This excessive dependence on student aid makes it imperative that for-profits maintain a steady supply of students. For-profits operate much like the large banks which exploited federal mortgage guarantees. Student loans now look to be the next financial bubble ready to burst.

For-profit schools now account for almost half of all student loan defaults. Students from for-profits carry a high debt load and increasingly have been unable to pay them off. They are clearly not obtaining jobs that make enough money to

---

[28] <http://leiterreports.typepad.com/blog/2010/08/the-rise-of-forprofit-colleges.html>.

[29] "Harkin Calls on For-Profit Colleges to End Deceptive Recruiting Practices," Press Release, February 8, 2011, <http://harkin.senate.gov/press/release.cfm?i=330975> .

[30] Adam Weinstein, "How Pricey For-Profit Colleges Target Vets' GI Bill Money." Mother Jones September/October 2011 accessed on the web at http://www.motherjones.com/politics/2011/09/gi-bill-for-profit-colleges.

cover their debt payments. One school had an astounding seventy-seven percent lifetime default rate.[31]

Students at for-profits often bear the brunt of these problems. At the University of Phoenix, the nation's largest for-profit chain, students complained about instructional shortcuts, poor quality instruction, and abuses in recruiting. Pressures from investors to increase profits were one of the prime factors driving these practices. Recently, a group of nursing students at Excelsior University sued the college over its online nursing associates degree program, claiming it was "an educational program devoid of any education . . . " The exam was based on a test that was not only highly subjective, but also required further commitment to the program (that is, costs) to access.[32]

Quality of education issues are also reflected in the accreditation procedures at for-profit schools. For-profit colleges and universities are not accredited by the same groups that certify traditional colleges and universities. The latter are regional certification associations, the former are accredited by a national accrediting agency. These only certify for-profits or online schools. Credits and degrees from these "national" accreditation groups are not recognized by regionally accredited schools. Not only are the standards lower, but the lack of regional accreditation means that the credits and degrees earned by students are not widely recognized or accepted, and not readily transferred to colleges or universities accredited by the more legitimate regional accreditation. A student who completes a two-year certificate and decides she wants to pursue a BA may find she has a worthless degree after having spent an estimated forty thousand dollars or more for tuition. Even employers are skeptical of for-profit degrees.

These practices are not the work of a few bad apples, but are systematic features of the for-profit system. In a 2009 report by the Government Accountability Office (GAO), undercover investigators found fraud in the administration of "Ability to Benefit" (ATB) tests. These are tests of basic math and English skills that prospective students without a high school degree or general education development test result must pass in order to qualify for aid. Test answers were tampered with and fake high school diplomas from "diploma mills" were submitted.[33] In a later 2010 report, investigators found patterns of deception and misinformation in a number of schools. Attempts to pressure prospective students to enroll and other dubious marketing practices were prevalent.[34]

According to committee chair Senator Thomas Harkin, "when students are enrolled through deception or fear, they are less prepared to meet the challenges of college." Rather than offering students a better life, these types of strong-arm, emotionally abusive tactics are all too typical of schools that have little or no interest in providing students with the academic help and support they need to

---

[31] David Halperin, "Why Did For-profit College Stocks Rise after the Gainful Employment Rule was Released?" *Campus Progress*, June 3, 2011. See also Tamar Lewin, "Student Loan Default Rates Rise Sharply in Past Year," *New York Times*, September 12, 2011.

[32] Carl Straumshein, "Induced to Fail," *Inside Higher Education*, February 24, 2014, <http://www.insidehighered.com/news/2014/02/24/former-nursing-students-sue-excelsior-college-over-deceptive-or-misleading-practices>.

[33] GAO, "Undercover Testing Finds Colleges Encouraged Fraud and Engaged in Deceptive and Questionable Marketing Practices," *Governmental Accountability Office* (August 2010).

[34] Ibid.

succeed. "When these types of deceptive and exploitative tactics are used to enroll students, we should not be surprised to see high dropout and high default rates as a result."[35]

Of all these issues, the debt crisis has received the most sustained attention. The increasing use of student loans can be directly linked to the conflicting imperatives of the 1980s. While even conservatives agreed on expanding access to higher education, they were not willing to pay the costs of that expansion. The cost of education was privatized and subject to market considerations. As Jeffery Williams notes in his analysis of the post-welfare state university: "Now the paradigm for university funding is no longer a public entitlement primarily offset by the state but a privatized service: citizens have to pay a substantial portion of their own way."[36] Instead of having some time free from market constraints to concentrate on learning, students, as future entrepreneurial selves, work from the time they enter college to pay costs of education. College students face an employment situation that, while offering a better income than non-college educated students, does not provide the economic rewards it did a generation ago. The ability to live a middle-class life free from excessive debt or to become effective democratic citizens is restricted.

While these considerations apply to non-profit colleges, for-profits amplify the marketizing of education. In targeting the more vulnerable and precarious they subject students, most of whom never graduate or get a better job, to a life of hopeless debt. Mamie Lynch, Jennifer Engle, and Jose Cruz note rather bluntly:

> For-profit colleges argue that they are models of access and efficiency in America's overburdened higher education system. But instead of providing a solid pathway to the middle class, they are paving a path into the subbasement of the American economy. They enroll students in high-cost degree programs that have little chance of leading to high paying careers, and saddle the most vulnerable students with more debt than they could reasonably manage to payoff, even if they do graduate.[37]

For-profits claim the mantle of equal opportunity and greater access for underserved populations but the liberatory and democratic potentials of higher education are eliminated. The contradictory mandate of community college has become a one-dimensional one, narrowly limited to vocational and job training. Students have value only insofar as they are sources of revenue.

Defenders of for-profits often argue that the market will correct the deficiencies in for-profit higher education by weeding out those operators who provide a bad result. This argument fails on its own terms for two important reasons. First, it presumes an ideal of perfect knowledge. The market participant, fully armed with knowledge of the system, can take advantage of new opportunities or make rational choices. Students do not have sufficient knowledge about college to make a reasonable "educated" decision. Such knowledge is distributed asymmetrically. The student from a lower class first-generation background is less likely to have the cultural capital and foreknowledge to correctly evaluate colleges. Second, the

---

[35] "Harkin Calls on For-Profit Colleges to End Deceptive Recruiting Practices."

[36] Jeffrey J. Williams, "Debt Education: Bad for the young Bad for America," *Dissent* (Summer 2006).

[37] Mamie Lynch, Jennifer Engel, and Jose L. Cruz, *Subprime Opportunity: The Unfulfilled Promise of For-Profit Colleges and Universities* (The Education Trust, November 2010), p. 7.

market for higher education is already imperfect. Federal grant and aid programs were enacted to stimulate demand for education. Thus it is difficult to speak of an unfettered market in education.

For-profits appear more as another version of the sorting machine that sustains and increases inequality and stratification. To the extent that the costs of education have been transferred primarily to the "consumer," the costs and the risks of education have been privatized. This in itself works to make education both harder to obtain and makes mobility and advancement more difficult. It tends to increase rather than mitigate class and status differences. Moreover, by deemphasizing the democratic elements of education, it minimizes the development of the capacities and resources needed to effectively participate with others in public life to effect change.

In the United States (US), a college education has traditionally been seen as providing a public function. It was a source of civic education in which students found the resources to become democratic citizens and to participate in public life though social and political activities. It provided both a means of personal fulfillment and a public good. In this way it could break down class barriers. Of course the reality of higher education in the US has rarely lived up to this promise, but for-profits completely eliminate this aim. As one dean of a for-profit noted, doing social good is

> not the primary objective of for-profit universities. For-profit universities do not have as their primary mission the shaping of a more informed citizenry, or creating a more cultured population, or helping young people understand their heritage, their society, and its values.[38]

Martha Nussbaum has recently put forward a defense of the humanistic education against the increasing marketization of educational institutions. She defends a traditional humanistic ideal of education that stresses the ability to cultivate critical thinking about social issues that is crucial for democratic citizenship, and to break the bounds of established tradition. Nussbaum also stresses an education of sensibility and imagination. The ability to understand the world of others and their achievements and suffering is a necessary feature of a democratic education. If we are indifferent to others we cannot be either good critics or good persons.[39]

Left critics of this approach, like the late Bill Readings, hold that we cannot simply employ unreflectively the idea of a unified culture or educated sensibility in neoliberal times.[40] Like Lyotard's skepticism of grand narrative unified national identities, he would no doubt have looked at Nussbaum's proposal with skepticism. Reading's criticism is consistent in some respects with the discussion of the fragmentation and negative individualization of the subject in neoliberalism

---

[38] James R. Osamudia, "Predatory Ed: The Conflict Between Public Good and For-Profit Higher Education," *Journal of College and University Law* 38:1 (2011), p. 68. Also see Amy Sepinwall, "Education by Corporation: The Merits and Perils of For-Profit Higher Education for a Democratic Citizenry," in Greg Urban (ed.), *Corporations and Citizenship* (Philadelphia: University of Pennsylvania Press, 2013), <http://works.bepress.com/amysepinwall/13>.

[39] Martha Nussbaum, *Not for Profit: Why Democracy Needs the Humanities* (Princeton, NJ: Princeton University Press, 2012).

[40] Bill Readings, *The University In Ruins* (Cambridge, MA: Harvard University Press 1997).

above, but his solution, like Lyotard's, relies on a notion of dissensus that leaves us trying to rack between incompatible fields of knowledge.

The humanistic foundations of education as traditionally understood can just as easily serve to reinforce hierarchy as they can to free us from it. Thus we have to approach with caution the prevalent idea that academia provides a sphere that is isolated from market or practical considerations or that it is desirable to reconstruct that ideal as a buttress against the marketizing forces of neoliberalism (or capitalism in general).[41] While I do not think that Nussbaum intends this, I am not sure her Aristotelian framework provides an adequate diagnosis of the situation. We have to reconceive the way that higher educational institutions can provide alternatives.

We can make a further step toward a critical democratic education and incorporate some of Reading's criticisms if we include teaching about conflict and dispute, not just the great ideals of humanism. As subjects who are participants in social practices, we have experience of these social conflicts that can be brought to the fore. Many of the target students of community colleges and for-profits are from the more disadvantaged segments of society. They undergo forms of domination and oppression that can be made thematic in teaching and learning. A reflexive understanding of these conditions has to be made part of the public discussion. Gerald Graff has suggested such an alternative, arguing that we ought to teach to conflicts. What he means by that is the idea that conflict or controversy clarifies and enables students to define themselves within an intellectual world. Those from less well-off groups are, as a whole, less likely to come into college with background understandings and sensibilities that provide the resources to engage in practices in institutional settings, for example in politics. Graff notes "the vast majority of American college students don't think of themselves as insiders to the academic intellectual world."[42] Learning through conflict does not begin from the educated sensibilities of cultured individuals, it draws on the students' own troubles, and transforms them into public problems.[43] In exploring their relations to the larger social world they do not learn how to conform to the dominant culture but instead learn why they are different. For-profits only provide students with narrow technical skills and few social resources. They claim to stress so-called real-world experience but this is done at the expense of exposure to intellectual culture and to the ability to become a participant in intellectual culture. This is certainly a serious problem, even in traditional non-profit colleges where marketization and elitism are rampant. Students often see the intellectual world as a closed society whose secrets are inaccessible to them, but the situation is even worse in the for-profit world where such questions are subordinated to utilitarian or instrumental concerns. Yet we need to teach these larger skills if we are to have citizens who are more capable of assessing political arguments and avoiding obvious lies.

---

[41] A related point has be made by Nancy Fraser in her discussion of the conflicts of the neoliberal state: "Marketization, Social Protection, Emancipation: Toward a Neo-Polanyian Conception of Capitalist Crisis," Unpublished; also see Rocio Zambrana, "Paradoxes of Neo-Liberalism and the Tasks of Critical Theory," *Critical Horizons* 14:1 (2013), pp. 93–119.

[42] Gerald Graff, *Beyond the Culture Wars: How Teaching the Conflicts Can Revitalize American Education* (New York: W.W. Norton, 1992).

[43] This is C. Wright Mills' formulation in *The Sociological Imagination* (New York: Oxford, 2000).

A critical conception of education requires that educating be guided by an ideal of freedom from domination. Students become aware of the relations of power and domination that affect their lives. Rather than an unthinking celebration of American values or the magic of the market, it means understanding how historical and social forces and conflicts have shaped the lives of those students. It entails a diagnosis of the problems that face us in ending or transforming domination. This way of teaching holds out the possibility of transforming the discouragement of students into a sense that they can understand and change the situation.

Education is more than technical training. Through education individuals gain the ability to understand and transform social life and their own situation through political action. This need takes on greater urgency in a current context when education for democracy is being subordinated if not eliminated. A democratic *paideia* requires a vigorous commitment to public debate and discussion within the university and in the public sphere.[44]

The cost of public education has to be reduced. The transition to payments as a market good has not been beneficial. The ideal situation is one in which a tuition-free public higher education system is available to all. Lacking this, however, we ought to consider reducing or eliminating Title IV programs which have worked to raise rather than reduce costs and return to direct grants for universities and colleges.

---

[44] See Henry Giroux and Susan Giroux, *Take Back Higher Education: Race, Youth, and the Crisis of Democracy in the Post-Civil Rights Era* (New York: Palgrave Macmillan, 2006). The Girouxs draw their notion from Cornelius Castoriadis, "Democracy as Procedure and Democracy as Regime," *Constellations* 4:1 (1997), pp. 1–18.

Academic Conservatives and the Future of Higher Education

George Ehrhardt
Appalachian State University, USA

Abstract *Having largely disappeared from the humanities and social sciences, conservatives have become the Other in progressive discussions of higher education. Crucial to this othering is the ascription of personal faults, such as racism or a lack of interest in marginal student populations. This article presents an alternative view of academic conservative writers on higher education. Rather than focus on their policy recommendations, it focuses on their perceptions of contemporary higher education, and finds that academic conservatives (as distinct from many conservative politicians) argue for the same goals as their progressive counterparts: a strong program of liberal arts, critical thinking, and access to education for diverse student populations. It divides these writers into two broad categories for analysis: traditional conservatives and libertarians. Suggestions are provided for readers who wish to explore these ideas more fully.*

Introduction

The current crisis in public higher education is often seen as engendered by the political Right. This group of antagonists includes politicians such as Governor Pat McCrory of North Carolina who seek to reduce higher education spending and publically attack the liberal arts, corporations such as College Board or University of Phoenix that see students as profit opportunities instead of citizen-scholars, the higher-education portion of the school choice movement, and conservative pundits who attack university faculty for their political views. The cumulative effect of their opposition to public higher education prevents colleges and universities from fulfilling their mission of accessible, high-quality education.

More nuanced descriptions of the current crisis argue that it is not a Democrat-Republican divide, but the transformation of American higher education into a neoliberal system where colleges and universities have been reshaped to serve the interests of state and corporate elites.[1] Processes like the commodification of academic labor and replacement of the liberal arts with occupational training for non-elite students are designed to produce useful components for elite managers, not critical-minded citizens for a thriving democracy.[2]

---

[1] C.W. Barrow, "The Rationality Crisis in US Higher Education," *New Political Science* 32:3 (2010), pp. 317–344.

[2] Benjamin Ginsburg, *The Fall of the Faculty: The Rise of the All-Administrative University and Why it Matters* (Oxford, UK: Oxford University Press, 2011).

Both narratives, however, privilege some voices and marginalize others. In the same way that the first version valorizes the political Left generally, the second version limits resistance to neoliberal hegemony to the work of progressive academics and activists. Whether intentional or not, this circumscribes the scope of potential responses to ones emerging from a particular paradigm. Other philosophies of higher education, from the Roman Catholic arguments for the liberal arts, represented by Cardinal John Newman, to beliefs in student autonomy that motivate libertarians, all collapse into a neoliberal Other.

This article encourages readers to reconsider that exclusion. After all, progressives have neither a monopoly on caring about students as human beings nor on opposing the domination of society by a political and corporate *nomenklatura*. In this time of crisis, it behooves anyone who seeks genuinely democratic higher education to find what allies they can. This article introduces readers to the ideas of some higher education reformers who promote quality education for democratic citizens but in a way that gets them the label "conservative." As a self-professed academic conservative myself, I personally support their arguments, even if they can be overstated at times. Space limitations here, however, prevent me from laying them out for readers more fully. Instead, I hope to do two things: persuade readers that arguments they may disagree with are being made thoughtfully and in good faith, and provide curious readers with resources to explore these authors on their own.

In the previous paragraph, the term "conservative" appears in quotes because there is little agreement on what it means. Defining it is beyond the scope of this article: some say it is a personality trait, some say that it is a belief in tradition, others in individual freedom, some say it stands for small government, others say it supports an all-powerful security state.[3] The term itself has little predictive power, mostly useful as a self-claimed umbrella of a label, under which disparate groups gather to seek recruits and allies. This means that conservatives often pursue contradictory goals and policies, and the higher education arena is no exception. For the purposes of this article, though, conservative writers on education can be divided into two broad groups: libertarian and traditional conservatives.

In terms of their thinking about higher education, the crucial difference between the two approaches is how they respond to changes wrought since the 1970s. The story of that era's student protests is well known: amidst the civil rights movement, the growth of feminism, and resistance to the Vietnam War, students argued that higher education excluded those in the margins and demanded a new model. In response to these demands, academics retreated from two claims. First, they retreated from demanding that students need professors' knowledge to guide them through a broad liberal education alongside their major. Second, the claim that some knowledges and texts are more important than others became, at best, highly contested.

In terms of higher education, today's libertarians are children of the revolution. Not only do they agree with the students of the 1970s on both claims, they go one step further by taking their position to its logical conclusion. After

---

[3] The best recent survey on the American conservatives is George Nash, *Reappraising the Right: The Past and Future of American Conservatism* (Wilmington, DE: ISI Books, 2009). For a good history of the Conservative *Movement*, see: John Micklethwait and Adrian Wooldridge, *Right Nation: Conservative Power in America* (New York: Penguin Press, 2004).

dethroning the Canon, rejecting professorial guidance led universities to weaken their core curricula, eliminating required courses and explicitly calling on students to choose for themselves. Libertarian critics—and the non-university course providers they often support—insist that if students can make curricular decisions themselves, they should not be constrained to a particular format of class at a particular institution. Trapping students within a one-size-fits-all credentialing agent (the university) holds learners—especially non-traditional students—back from pursuing a more creative and rewarding educational experience. Libertarians advance progressives' rejection of the second claim as well. After all, if reading Harry Potter is as useful as reading Homer, academic claims about the value of the traditional liberal arts are ultimately based on nothing but inherited prejudice.

Traditional conservatives, on the other hand, represent the detritus of the *ancien regime*. In contrast to libertarians, they still believe in both professorial expertise and the idea that some works are more important than others; this gives them a useful perspective, with insider knowledge of higher education and a minority's skepticism of prevailing academic culture. Ironically, they ask the same questions of modern higher education as the progressive students asked of their predecessors forty years ago: what are the limits of academic orthodoxy? What is omitted and what consequence do those omissions have?

Conservatives of both stripes argue that higher education today looks more like that of the 1950s than others would care to admit. For all the talk of openness, contemporary higher education has its own (albeit new) sacred cows, and it insists on a single format for learning, one that best suits the affluent. The irony of these critiques is, of course, that many conservatives disagree with progressive visions for academia, not because they have different goals, but because they argue progressive prescriptions will not help achieve their *shared* goals.

For the record, the authors described here are not a representative survey of conservative thought generally. Only one of them could creditably be considered a neo-conservative (the group that dominated foreign policy decisions during the Bush administration). They are, instead, a sample of academic conservatives who share with progressives a belief in the value of education and inclusivity, but present alternative visions of how to accomplish those goals.

The Traditional Conservative Critique

The most interesting traditional conservatives tend to be humanities faculty. Many of them are older professors who still remember teaching the pre-Culture Wars curricula, like Donald Kagan, recently retired professor of Greek history at Yale. Others, like Tony Esolen, Professor of English at Providence College, consciously engage in Catholics' long history of humanities scholarship (it is worth remembering that much of our—conservative *and* progressive—enthusiasm for liberal arts education dates back to Cardinal John Newman's work in the nineteenth century).[4] Among academic conservatives, the leading networking

---

[4] John Newman, *The Idea of a University* (Chicago, IL: Loyola University Press, 1987 [1873]). Prominent contemporary journals in this tradition include *First Things* (more political and academic) and *Touchstone: A Journal of Mere Christianity* (more theological and aimed at a wider readership).

organization is the Intercollegiate Studies Institute (ISI), which also provides seminars for undergraduates curious about conservative ideas they do not hear at college, and a book press.

As one might expect with this demographic, one distinguishing characteristic of traditional conservatives is their abiding faith in the role of a liberal arts education for preparing citizens and developing the human spirit. Consider the following justification for the liberal arts from Kagan:

> Earlier generations who came to college with traditional beliefs rooted in the past had them challenged by hard questioning and the requirement to consider alternatives and were thereby unnerved, and thereby liberated, by the need to make reasoned choices. The students of today and tomorrow deserve the same opportunity.[5]

Like his progressive counterparts, he identifies the liberal arts with questioning— and being liberated from—pre-existing beliefs.

The crucial difference, however, between progressive and traditional conservative visions of the liberal arts lies in what happens next. In the former, intellectual liberation should be followed by transformative activism to end the structures of power that prevent a free and democratic society. Traditional conservatives, however, argue that breaking down walls is not enough; a liberal arts education must re-construct the individual as well. In the words of Robert George, Professor of Jurisprudence at Princeton and another writer in the Anglo-Catholic tradition:

> If we believe in republican democracy, as we should; if we believe in the ideal of free persons, as we should; if we believe in the dignity and rights of the individual in a regime of ordered liberty, as we should; then we must dedicate ourselves to educating young people for self-mastery.[6]

George agrees that tearing down unjust power structures is a worthy goal, as is protecting the equality and dignity of all people, but building a *sustainable* democracy requires something more. To understand his use of the term "self-mastery" as a goal of liberal arts education, one can turn to Patrick Deneen, a political theorist at Notre Dame. Defending the humanities against an encroaching tide of advocates for STEM studies (Science, Technology, Engineering, and Mathematics), Deneen reminds us why the liberal arts were once considered important:

> To understand ourselves was to understand how to use our liberty well, especially how to govern appetites that seemed insatiable. The liberal arts recognized that submission to these limitless appetites would result in the loss of our liberty and

---

[5] Donald Kagan, "Ave Atque Vale," *The New Criterion* 31:1 (2013), pp. 4–12, <http://www.newcriterion.com/articles.cfm/Ave-atque-vale-7653>. Kagan is best known for writing the standard modern account of the Peloponnesian War, but those interested in his take on higher education should read his 2005 Jefferson Lecture for a defense of studying history for its intrinsic value, not just as a canvas on which to write modern values.

[6] Carol Iannone, "Our Western Heritage: An interview with Robert George," *Academic Questions* 25:1 (2012), pp. 37–45. *Academic Questions* is a higher education-focused journal of the National Association of Scholars, the second largest academic conservative association.

reflect our enslavement to desire...To be free—*liberal*—was itself an *art*, something that was learned not by nature or instinct, but by refinement and education.[7]

This insistence on self-mastery comes from two non-exclusive sources: the Socratic tradition to "know thyself," and religious rhetoric of freeing one's self from the "slavery" of physical desires.[8] The connection between those two resolves the seeming contradiction between faith and liberal education in claims made by religious conservatives, such as in the mission statement of Wheaton College (considered the most intellectually rigorous of evangelical Christian schools):

> Wheaton College advances the kingdom of Jesus Christ through a particular kind of education. We affirm our ongoing commitment to the best traditions of liberal education at a time when many liberal arts colleges are in decline...

These religious conservatives insist that not only are faith and reason compatible, but in fact a liberal arts education—a questioning and liberating education like the one Kagan describes—allows one a deeper and richer faith.

In a twist that confounds those who see conservatism as a single tradition, this argument is the antithesis of Ayn Rand's objectivism. Unbridled greed, lust, and a hunger for power are destructive; they inevitably produce exploitation and degradation, diminishing the humanity of others. Overcoming these harmful (sinful) appetites, conservatives like Deneen and George insist, requires more than just pointing fingers at others, or at structures, it demands we look inside and control our own selves as well. Otherwise, tearing down one oppressive structure will do little more than free a new set of individuals to pursue their own greed and exploit a new set of victims.

The flashpoint between these two perspectives occurs in the question of how to balance critique with content. In the 1950s, university curricula were tilted too heavily to the content side, with students uniformly expected to study the Canon and Western civilization and marginalizing others. This prompted a call for more critique, especially from previously marginalized perspectives, which emerged in the 1970s and 1980s, particularly framed in terms of race, sex, and class.

Looking back at the lessons from thirty years under the new curricular regime, traditional conservatives argue that the pendulum has swung too far, replacing the old orthodoxy with a new orthodoxy. Professors in the ancient regime insisted that learning the Western tradition was crucial, but today's professors have their own imperative. Alan Kors, Professor of History at Penn and founder of the Foundation for Individual Rights in Education (FIRE) writes:

> Academics, in their own minds, face an almost insoluble problem of time. How, in only four years, can they disabuse students of the notion that the capital, risk, productivity and military sacrifice of others have contributed to human dignity and to the prospects of a decent society? How can they make them understand, with only four years to do so, that capitalism and individualism have created cultures

---

[7] Patrick J. Deneen, "Science and the Decline of the Liberal Arts," *The New Atlantis* 26 (Fall 2009/Winter 2010), pp. 60–68. This emphasis on self-*mastery* rather than self-*fulfillment* is common to religious conservatives like George and Deneen (both outspoken Catholics).

[8] This rhetoric is common in the New Testament, particularly in Paul's letters, but it appears prominently in Islamic writings like Qutb's *In the Shade of the Qur'an* as well.

that are cruel, inefficient, racist, sexist and homophobic, with oppressive caste systems, mental and behavioral?[9]

This is not so different, conservatives insist, from the old worry that four years was not enough time to learn all the important history and arts of the Western tradition. In the same way as student radicals objected with claims about the topics that curricula omitted in their desire to spend so much time on the Western tradition, contemporary conservatives object to today's curriculum with claims about what it omits in its desire to spend so much time critiquing structures of power.

Unfortunately, this argument is often explained away with accusations of racism, sexism, or an assumed bitterness about how academia is "being taken over by people who aren't like me." Buras offers an example of this tendency, asserting that conservatives act out of "...a fear of subverted power and undermined cultural authority."[10] Similar comments are a perennial favorite at online forums like InsideHighered.com or the Chronicle of Higher Education. Those criticisms may be true of some on the Right—this article makes no claim to be fully representative—but the authors cited here make a different argument: over-emphasis on sex, race, and class undermines the very goals that progressive education claims to pursue.

A mild form of this argument comes from the National Association of Scholars (NAS), a group of conservative historians who left the discipline's main association during the Culture Wars of the 1980s and 1990s with the goal of maintaining the Western intellectual tradition. Since that time it has focused on promoting greater structure in general education, particularly the use of survey courses instead of narrow seminars. Its position is often misread as simply accusations of "leftist indoctrination."[11] In recent years the organization has produced two studies documenting what they call an outsized role for race, sex, and class in the history curricula at Bowdin College, the University of Texas, and Texas A&M.[12] Essentially, they argue that there is too much important history to spend so much time on any one focus. The Texas report reads:

> As RCG [race, class, gender] emphases crowd out other aspects and themes in American history, we find other problems setting in, including the narrow tailoring of "special topics" courses and the absence of significant primary source documents...Teachers of American history should take race, class, and gender into account and should help students understand those aspects of our history, but those perspectives should not take precedence over all others.[13]

---

[9] Alan Kors, "The Sadness of Higher Education," *New Criterion* 26:9 (2009), pp. 9–14.

[10] Kristen Buras, *Rightist Multiculturalism: Lessons in Neoconservative School Reform* (New York: Routledge Press, 2010), p. 43.

[11] Cary Nelson, *No University is an Island: Saving Academic Freedom* (New York: University Press, 2010).

[12] Peter Wood and Michael Toscano, "What Does Bowdoin Teach? How A Contemporary Liberal Arts College Shapes Students" (2013), <http://www.nas.org/projects/the_bowdoin_project>.

[13] Richard Fonte, Peter Wood, and Ashley, "Recasting History: Are Race, Class, and Gender Dominating American History?" (2013), <http://www.nas.org/articles/recasting_history_are_race_class_and_gender_dominating_american_history>, pp. 7–8.

The report takes a list of one hundred important documents in United States (US) history compiled by the National Archives and finds that 89% of faculty teaching introductory US history classes did not assign a single document from the list. Instead, the authors find that 71% of course readings in introductory US history courses emphasized RCG topics, but only 2% emphasized scientific, technological, or environmental topics. Is it racist to suggest that a university in the American West should spare time to teach how technology and the environment shaped the region?

This version of the problem suggests that when every teacher wants to spend their classes training students to ask critical questions, students have no opportunity to learn the what and the why of structures they are to question. The NAS argues that enabling students to think critically requires they learn content first, not just criticize it. In my own introductory international relations classes, for example, I often encounter students who know that McCarthyism is bad, but can tell me little about why it existed, or even about the larger Cold War context at all. For these students, the idea of anti-McCarthyism dangles unattached and useless, because they cannot recognize how and why it might appear in other (that is, contemporary) contexts. Just to be clear, these conservatives see the value of teaching race, class, and sex, but they resist the monopolizing of the curriculum— *just as the student protestors of the 1970s resisted monopolization by the classic Canon.*

Not only does the emphasis on race, sex, and class crowd out other important topics, but it may even be directly counter-productive, argues Victor D. Hanson, a historian of ancient Greece who split his career between California State University-Fresno and his family's vineyards.[14] He suggests that the problem is its banality. Consider Homer's Achilles, he says, a literary character offering rich ground for a discussion of the all-too human emotions of pride, anger, and glory—one that can challenge students' own choices and beliefs.[15] Those discussions give students opportunities to think about their own behavior and learn the kind of self-mastery described by Deneen and George. Instead, a critical discussion can actually *comfort* students (especially women and minorities): "Ho, hum, another dead white male who was sexist and had slaves. How awful. Good thing *I'm* not like that." Kagan agrees with this, insisting that while the predominant place of sex, race, and class was appropriate once, it does not reflect modern society that has, for all its imperfections, undergone a sea change since the 1960s. What might have been transgressive once is now nothing students do not regularly see in pop culture.

Kagan's experience at Yale may not be fully representative, but they match my own experiences at a public university near the Mason-Dixon line. The fraternity I advised invited a women's studies professor to participate in an in-house lecture series; she requested they read Anne Koedt's 1970 "The Myth of the Vaginal Orgasm," hoping to challenge their assumed heteronormativity. Once the

---

[14] Hanson is currently a senior fellow at Stanford's Hoover Institute, as is Robert George (cited earlier) and many prominent conservative academics. The institute provides a platform for them to speak on policy issues.

[15] Victor Hanson and John Heath, *Who Killed Homer: The Demise of Classical Education and the Recovery of Greek Wisdom* (New York: Free Press. 1998). Many of his recent writings are partisan polemics, but Hanson's *The Other Greeks* (1999), University of California Press, Berkeley remains a compelling historical argument that the democratic values of equality and participation originated with redneck farmers in Classical Greece, not urban sophisticates.

discussion began, however, she was taken aback to hear the men reach an enthusiastic consensus: "Wow, this is great. They should have told us about the clitoris at freshman orientation." Born a decade after Koedt's article appeared, it never occurred to them to be disturbed by the knowledge that women can reach orgasm without penetration, or be threatened by the idea that some women prefer other women. Her grand plans of challenging their images of masculinity ended up as nothing more than sex column advice. So it often goes, conservatives argue, with race, sex, and class coursework.

And yet, one might reply, few students leave campus radicalized. It seems fair to ask Kagan why, if students are so exposed to these ideas, do they not react? He responds by arguing that teaching critical thinking requires questions that push against strongly held beliefs. Challenging students on issues where they lack conviction, or even worse, agree with the questioner, is like weightlifting without weights, and today's students lack any reasoned convictions against which critical dialogue can get traction. As he puts it, they come to campus with

> ...a kind of cultural void, an ignorance of the past, a sense of rootlessness and aimlessness, as though not only the students but also the world was born yesterday, a feeling that they are attached to the society in which they live only incidentally and accidentally.[16]

This is not to say that students agree with progressive ideas; rather, that few of them have strongly reasoned beliefs (some strong opinions, yes, but not coherent beliefs based in things they have learned). Sure, we can all think of memorable exceptions, but those students are memorable precisely because they are the exceptions. The silent majority of students are ill-served by current practice because we cannot liberate students who have nothing to be liberated from. In a sense, the lack of student radicalism proves Kagan's point: if criticizing current power structures was enough to radicalize students, there should be far more student radicalism than we see today.

This resonates with my own experiences of teaching Marx at a university and to a group of Christian homeschoolers. My university students generally greet Marxist critiques with boredom; most do not care enough about capitalism to have an opinion. My homeschoolers, on the other hand, predictably counter-attacked— but that is when the teaching starts: how can we read Acts 2:44–45 and reject communal ownership? How can we read Isiah 65:21–22 and not see the parallels between Marx's Labor Theory of Value and the ownership of one's work in scripture? Their pre-existing beliefs *force* my students to think critically in a way that is impossible to duplicate with unmoored college students.

For the record, in making these critiques traditional conservatives are quite aware they lost control of the Academy in the 1970s, and were decisively defeated in the Culture Wars of the 1990s. Kors acknowledges this as he articulates a common sentiment among these writers:

> The academic world that I entered is gone. I teach for my students, whom I love, and I fight for intellectual pluralism, for legal equality and for fairness simply because it is my duty to bear witness to the values I cherish, with no expectation of success.[17]

---

[16] Kagan, "Ave Atque Vale."
[17] Kors, "The Sadness of Higher Education."

Historians caution us, however, to be careful of history written by the winners. Losers often have stories the winners would rather not hear, and the experience to know when victors become the very thing they originally opposed. So it is, traditional conservatives like Kors argue, in higher education today.

The Libertarian Critique

While conservatives in the humanities tend toward traditionalism, higher education writers in other disciplines tend to a more diverse set of ideas that can, at the risk of oversimplification, be collectively labeled libertarian. In contrast to how traditional conservatives unambiguously assert the value of liberal arts education, libertarians demur. Indeed, many of their proposals give the impression that they oppose higher education in general (particularly for the less well-off). They tend to support online education and vocational programs for most students and face-to-face liberal arts education for an elite few; some suggest that college is unnecessary. Based on these policies, cynics accuse them of taking the corporate shilling to advocate policies that benefit the elite.

Libertarians counter that in reality, the reverse is true. Both progressives and libertarians agree that today's higher education contributes to inequality, but they differ about why. Progressives argue that equality demands universal access to college.[18] Libertarians counter that this argument rests on flawed assumptions about education and diversity. According to them, contemporary higher education fails its 1970s-era aspirations by locking students in a system that fails to deliver a quality education, forces students into punishing debt, and most crucially, marginalizes students whose strengths lie elsewhere.

They begin their critique by noting that the signaling function of higher education has overtaken its learning one. College has become a screening device, not a place of education.[19] As *National Review* writer Andrew Ferguson puts it:

> As higher education was democratized, a college degree became more desirable than the learning it was originally meant to signify. It was a guarantee of smarts, drive, social standing, and future prospects.[20]

In other words, while a college degree may enhance a young person's future earnings, that does not happen because the student actually learns anything. Instead, a college degree provides a *credential*, one assuring employers that the candidate meets certain minimum standards.

One reason for this, libertarians point out, is that most students do not learn very much.[21] The National Survey of Student Engagement finds that, on average, students study less than sixteen hours a week; a wider analysis finds that students

---

[18] For recent examples of this, see: Ron Brownstein, "Are College Degrees Inherited?" *National Journal Magazine*, April 12, 2014; Suzanne Mettler, *Degrees of Inequality: How the Politics of Higher Education Sabotaged the American Dream* (New York: Basic Books, 2014).

[19] George Leef, "The Overselling of Higher Education," Pope Center for Higher Education Policy Paper (2006).

[20] Andrew Ferguson, *Crazy U: One Dad's Crash Course in Getting his Kid into College* (New York: Simon and Schuster, 2011), p. 38.

[21] David Labaree, *How to Succeed in School Without Really Learning: The Credentials Race in American Education* (New Haven, CT: Yale University Press, 1999).

study less than two hours a day.[22] The same source found that a majority of college students have never taken a course requiring more than twenty pages of writing a semester. Even a sympathetic observer like former Harvard President Derek Bok agrees that contemporary higher education generally fails to challenge students.[23]

The consequences of not studying are predictable. A survey of more than three thousand students at nineteen institutions found not only *no* measureable improvement in critical thinking during college students' first year at school, but also that their academic motivation and interest in their field actually *declined*.[24] In political science, a multi-year study of graduating students shows that graduating seniors actually know *less* about American political institutions than incoming freshmen.[25] While unpleasant to face, anyone who teaches outside the few highly selective institutions knows that this image is reality—with some notable exceptions, our students do not just study minimally: assignments go unread, papers are written in a single draft the night before they are due, and social and work obligations trump academic ones.[26]

While a credentialing college may not provide a quality education, libertarians note ironically, it does keep down the *hoi polloi*. Glenn Reynolds, law professor at Tennessee and author of the widely read libertarian blog *Instapundit*, explains why students see no alternative to college:

> The major problem with [apprenticeship plans] is that college now serves largely as a status marker, a sign of membership in the educated "caste," and as a place to meet a future spouse of commensurate status.[27]

Entry into the upper echelons of American society requires a college degree, and entry to a good college—to the extent it depends on personal achievement rather than inherited privilege—depends on a particular skill set, and one that clusters among the affluent.

In fact, the gatekeeping role of higher education—not just getting into college, but the sitting in chairs and doing written homework for four more years to graduate—protects the children of privilege and prevents competition from the less fortunate. For the latter, "holding out only one valued alternative, namely a four-year college degree, to them is cruel and unethical and does more harm than good."[28]

Not only does the current system of unequal access create inequality, providing universal access—as many progressives suggest—would not solve this

---

[22] Richard Arum and Josipa Roksa *Academia Adrift: Limited Learning on College Campuses* (Chicago, IL: University of Chicago Press, 2011).

[23] Derek Bok, *Our Underachieving Colleges: A Candid Look at How Much Students Learn and Why They Should Be Learning More* (Princeton, NJ: Princeton University Press, 2006).

[24] Charles Blaich, "Overview of findings from the First Year of the Wabash National Study of Liberal Arts Education" (Wabash College, Center for Inquiry in the Liberal Arts, 2007), <http://www.liberalarts.wabash.edu/study-research/>.

[25] Intercollegiate Studies Institute, "Enlightened Citizenship" (American Civic Literacy Institute, 2011), <http://www.americancivicliteracy.org/resources/downloads.aspx>.

[26] Craig Brandon, *The Five-Year Party: How Colleges Have Given Up on Educating Your Child and What You Can Do About It* (Dallas, TX: BenBella Books, 2011).

[27] Glen Reynolds, *The Higher Education Bubble* (New York: Encounter Books, 2013), p. 36.

[28] Kenneth Gray and Edwin Herr, *Other Ways to Win: Creating Alternatives for High School Graduates* (Thousand Oaks, CA: Sage Publications, 2000), p. 40.

problem. It may even make it worse, these authors argue, because not everyone graduates. In contrast, libertarians insist, before the majority of people attempted college, there were many more ways for talented young people to succeed.[29]

In an earlier era, academics might have successfully defended a "college for all" agenda by insisting that higher education contains special truths that everyone should be exposed to, both for individual and public reasons. Unfortunately, that era is gone. The "sage on the stage" is passé, and in most schools, general education based on a fixed menu of courses that all students must take has been replaced with a smorgasbord of classes from which students may choose. There are pedagogical arguments in support of the new methods, but the key point is that they no longer support assertions that education must take place in a traditional college system (as opposed to online or elsewhere).

At this point, it may be worth clearing up two persistent misunderstandings of the libertarian position. First, they do not contest the importance of critical thinking as both a job-related and citizenship-related skill. To the contrary, they remain skeptical about liberal arts majors precisely because—as the evidence above shows—too many liberal arts majors *do not actually learn critical thinking*. The growth of pop culture in college curricula makes this even more painful—who needs to go to college to read Harry Potter? Second, their opposition to the "college for all" mantra does not stem from elitism or a neocolonial interest in oppressing the uneducated. It stems from an appreciation of human diversity and the different gifts each person possesses—forcing everyone into a one-size-fits-all system that rewards a particular kind of person disenfranchises everyone else.

Is it a coincidence, libertarians ask, that so many academics push a system that privileges the very trait (college success) that they are best suited to give their own children? On the same note, is it a coincidence also that the "college for all" agenda appears perfectly designed to enhance academics' own career prospects and status?

This brings us full circle from the 1960s and 1970s. The reformers of that era insisted on greater access to education for everyone, not just a privileged few, and their demands have largely been met. Today, more than 70% of high school students go on to enroll in college.[30] Non-selective community colleges offer *all* high school graduates an inexpensive and geographically convenient place to begin their coursework. Remedial courses are offered to help those who suffered from a failed K-12 system.

More could certainly be done to make college more affordable, but that response fundamentally misses the point that conservatives are making. Pushing students into a system that ill suits their talents and background does not empower people, it punishes them. When success in academia becomes a universal measuring stick, it privileges those who are good at academia—who tend to be the children of the elite. The alternative to cramming everyone into the same square hole, libertarians insist, is redefining "higher education" itself to become more inclusive.

It is not clear from libertarian writings, though, what form(s) that new education may take. Online education and for-profit schools have their advocates,

---

[29] Anya Kamenetz, *DIY U: Edupunks, Edupreneurs, and the Coming Transformation of Higher Education* (White River Junction, VT: Chelsea Green Publishing, 2000).

[30] Gray and Herr, *Other Ways to Win.*

but so do community colleges and traditional apprentice programs like those in Germany. This diversity is natural for libertarians: instead of recommending a unified solution, their philosophical preference is to promote diverse ideas—even questionable ones—and see which ones work.

So What?

At first glance, the need for traditional conservative and libertarian voices is not apparent. For all that they might be marginalized in academia, their plight hardly warrants action; indeed, many traditional conservatives' writings suggest they (and I) find academia quite congenial. Nevertheless, it may be time for progressives to rethink their marginalization of conservatives, because they point out unpleasant contradictions at the heart of contemporary higher education.

The first contradiction is a curricular one. Academics rhetorically disavow any "special knowledge" or core texts; all across the country, conservatives argue, general education requirements have been loosened to make the student "...the autonomous authority on the content of his education."[31] On the other hand, academics insist that students cannot become true democratic citizens without sharing their professors' critiques of existing power structures (particularly those of race, sex, and class). So which is it—do students have to take their classes or not? The contemporary self-image as possessors of special knowledge crucial to democratic society is ironic, because that is exactly how the traditional conservative professors of the 1950s saw themselves as well.

The second contradiction is a mismatch between the public goals proclaimed and the private goals achieved. Defenders of higher education funding argue that it should be subsidized because it provides a public good. In theory, this could be persuasive, but its power depends on proof that a college education actually delivers the goods, and that proof is sorely lacking. There is some evidence for higher graduate earnings, of course, but that supports the private good aspect of education—the credential. And to the extent that college only provides a private good, there is no reason to subsidize it with taxpayer money, especially since the beneficiaries of that subsidy tend to be better off than average. Counterintuitively, then, the effort to provide everyone with a college credential has actually *reduced* the justification for public funds.[32]

The third contradiction is the most pernicious. The quest to make college nearly universal—undertaken to promote equality—has protected the elite by closing off alternatives. It is no coincidence that the rise in college enrollment since the 1970s has correlated with rising *inequality*, conservatives argue. Students who might have found rewarding paths elsewhere—working or learning a trade, for example—end up paying for classes from which they gain little. For the large percentage that fail, the damage is even worse: the financial cost, the years of their lives they could have done something else with, and the psychological scars of

---

[31] Wood and Tascone, *Recasting History*, p. 371. In my experience, serving on general education committees, this centrifugal pressure may be the result of disciplinary isolation more than pedagogical purpose. Nevertheless, within the University of North Carolina (UNC) system (in which I work) there is little evidence of faculty interest in stronger core requirements (Jay Schalin and Jenna Ashely Robinson, "General Education at UNC-Chapel Hill," Pope Center Report, 2013).

[32] Labaree, *How to Succeed in School*.

failure. For the elite who grow up in good schools, with parents who teach them to sit still and read books, the system works perfectly. Trapping everyone else in college only emphasizes how much "better" they are than the underprivileged.

Successfully resolving these contradictions will be difficult. Higher funding may help with the second one, but not the other two, and generating the political will for funding will require solutions to those as well. The libertarian answer to the third problem is well known: free educators develop new forms and institutions to serve those ill-served by the current system. Not all of these will succeed; the situation may resemble eighteenth-century America, in which more than a thousand colleges were founded and more than 70% failed.[33] Sprinkled among the failures, however, were successes that rose to join the greatest universities in the world. Without the freedom to fail, libertarians remind us, those successes would not have happened.

Traditional conservatives offer a simpler solution to the first contradiction: teach. Or as Hanson puts it: "Write what others can read, stay fast in the classroom, forgo the conference, and tutor the uninitiated."[34] Academia currently rewards those who minimize teaching and research niche topics, publishing them for a small coterie of fellow academics. While research can be useful, and can inform a professor's teaching, research for the sake of research does not benefit students. Is it any wonder, conservatives ask, that taxpayers doubt that college professors provide the much bally-hooed "public goods?"

The biggest obstacle to overcoming these contradictions may be tenure-track faculty. Ensuring that colleges have a monopoly gatekeeper function protects college teachers' jobs and status. Less rigor in the classroom means fewer distractions from research. Focusing on theoretical critiques instead of informative content privileges the tenured as well. After all, anyone can teach how the constitution divides government into three branches, but only an elite can explain the hidden structures of power that lurk behind them. Tony Esolen, who translates and teaches poetry at Providence College, describes the fundamental selfishness in contemporary humanities:

> Why read at all if you are not going to accept the work on its own terms? Criticism becomes nothing more than an imposition of the self upon the poet and his art. The poet does not teach us; we teach the poet, in the same way that a schoolyard bully proposes to teach the skinny kid who can't defend himself. We ply our "theory" upon a poet who cannot answer back. We dress it with pseudo-scientific language to impress the sophomores while remaining impervious to his thought and his humanity. This is called "critical thinking," quite uncritical about itself and predictable in its results, as if a living being were pressed through a grinder.[35]

Nevertheless, career incentives push faculty ever farther from the content that sophomores need. Plum jobs and promotion require ever-increasing amounts of research, and because the material in survey courses is common knowledge among faculty, ambitious researchers must go ever farther afield.

---

[33] Ferguson, *Crazy U.*

[34] Hanson and Heath, *Who Killed Homer?*, p. 161.

[35] Tony Esolen, "The Subhumanities: The Reductive Violence of Race, Class, and Gender Theory," *Intercollegiate Review* (Fall 2013).

Those concerned about the role of adjunct instructors should think about this as well. Everyone in higher education knows how adjuncts are exploited: they teach large sections of introductory classes to generate revenue that sustains a cadre of tenure-track faculty who teach fewer and upper-division courses that match their research interests. While they may rhetorically support progressive policies, many tenure-track faculty contribute to this practice out of self-interest. Hanson makes the connection explicit in a recent editorial on student protests at Dartmouth:

> But why do very liberal universities do very illiberal things like raise their costs consistently above the rate of inflation, for which, in similar circumstances, food markets or gas stations would be chastised?...And why do universities in general depend on graduate teachers, part-time lecturers and adjunct faculty to teach many courses that are identical to those taught by full, tenured faculty at rates of compensation three times higher—in an exploitative way that Target or Costco would be fined for?[36]

Nor is this only at the Ivies. Recently, I cringed when a recent candidate for chair of my (R2) department went on at length about his plans to implement course releases for grant writing. That is exactly what neoliberal elites want from university administrators—to encourage faculty to chase external (probably corporate) money instead of teaching undergraduates; encourage the exploitation of adjuncts to deal with students while the "real" professors are doing something else.

Conclusion

Some readers may find it jarring to hear conservatives criticize tenure-track faculty for being self-interested, but that misperception underlines the diversity of "conservative" thought. In reality, conservatives problematize self-interest in many different ways. For all their support of free choice, libertarians are the first to argue that when one actor has coercive power over another, self-interest promotes exploitative rent-seeking, not mutual benefit. For their part, traditional conservatives have railed against the atomized, self-interested individuals since the Enlightenment and religious conservatives have done so since time immemorial. Unfortunately, these conservative discussions about the limits of self-interest rarely penetrate far into the public consciousness, leaving too many (on *both* sides of the aisle) with the false idea that conservatism equals unbridled self-interest.

That misperception gets to the heart of the problem. These short introductions to conservative thought on higher education may not be persuasive; certainly many of the sources cited here have been criticized in ways that go beyond the scope of this article. Nevertheless, in their writings and in their daily work, the authors cited here show their passion for education and their interest in helping all Americans, not just the elite. Readers who are serious about ensuring access to quality education for all Americans need to stop reflexively demonizing conservatives as cultural supremacists and sellouts, and

---

[36] Victor Hanson, "Our Psychodramatic Campuses" (2014), <http://pjmedia.com/victordavishanson/our-psychodramatic-campuses/>.

broaden their understanding of contemporary higher education by exploring conservative views more thoughtfully.

Transforming the Game: Democratizing the Publicness of Higher Education and Commonwealth in Neoliberal Times

Romand Coles
Northern Arizona University, USA

Abstract *This article argues that neoliberalism should be understood as a game-transformative set of practices in which the objective of each move is not only to gain the upper hand in the established game, but rather to repeatedly change the basic configuration of the game itself to further enhance its power. In the face of this assault on democratic commonwealth in higher education and elsewhere, many progressives are stuck in a primarily defensive frame according to which the objective is to resist losses and re-establish conditions that facilitate a less asymmetrical political game. This political stance harbors little democratic promise because it is insufficiently attentive to neoliberal game-transformative practices. To rejuvenate vital and mutually supportive relationships between public higher education and democracy, we must co-create a radically democratic game-transformative pedagogical and political practice in which we intensify and expand the meaning of publicness and publics. The article explores Northern Arizona University's Action Research Teams initiative as one prefiguration of this possibility.*

Introduction

The assault on higher education in recent decades is part of a broader attack on democratic commonwealth. This attack aims to privatize and undermine institutions and practices that foster capacities that are integral to active citizenship and relatively egalitarian participation in goods without which attentive and active publics become highly precarious. The United States (US) has moved a remarkable distance along this neoliberal trajectory, and as it has, people's facility with and active support for democratic commonwealth appear to have waned significantly. Many factors appear to be forming a set of negative feedback loops, punctuated only episodically by brief bouts of mobilized resistance or modest electoral pushback when the far right wing overplays its hand, thoroughly inebriated by its success. These antidemocratic loops between institutional privatization and cultural changes have engendered new conditions in which democratic actors and movements that once had significant leverage are now regularly overpowered, co-opted, and reduced.[1]

---

[1] See, for example, Sheldon Wolin, *Democracy Incorporated: Managed Democracy and the Specter of Inverted Totalitarianism* (Princeton, NJ: Princeton University Press, 2010); William E. Connolly, *Capitalism and Christianity, American Style* (Durham, NC: Duke University Press, 2008); David Harvey, *A Brief History of Neoliberalism* (Oxford: Oxford University Press, 2007).

So far, most efforts to resist the assault have been primarily defensive, seeking to restore elements of a receding status quo while leaving contemporary system dynamics and neoliberal shifts in power largely unaddressed. Moderate and progressive political constituencies often limit themselves to action frames that (at best) were appropriate to conditions that have now been displaced by neoliberal dynamics. For heuristic purposes, let us call this new situation of contest—the power dynamics, systemic tendencies, explicit and tacitly assumed rules, and modes of interaction, institutions, practices, dispositions, and scopes of aspiration and expectation—a "game," while realizing that there is nothing playful about it. While most progressives recognize that they are taking a beating in terms of politics, policies, and outcomes, they continue to play as if the basic game has not changed in fundamental ways. Meanwhile the right wing recognizes and engages in a "game-transformative practice."[2] They play a game that is radically dynamic, insofar as they seek at every turn to *change the most basic parameters of the game itself*, in ways that further enhance, intensify, and accelerate their capacities to create further transformations in the game in future moves. Compounding this catastrophe is the fact that even as the right wing engages in a game-transformative practice, they are aware that moderates and progressives will *continue to play the antiquated game*, and thus they have prepared resonant frames, images, scripts, and correspondences that track these predictable moves and imbue them with qualities like selfishness, lack of realism, elitism, and utter farce. In this context, efforts to bolster the relationships between higher education and democracy that remain primarily defensive and resistant to the idea of forging a *radically democratic* game-transformative practice will likely be swept toward the dustbin of history.

To ask how progressives, radical democrats, and moderates might save public higher education as we have known it is to risk avoiding crucial questions. Instead, we should critically interrogate and imaginatively expand the very idea of *public* education. How might we re-envision the *publicness* of education in ways that open paths for radical democratic pedagogy and movements in myriad relationships between the academy and democratic communities? How might we powerfully rejoin higher education with a complex, plural, and dynamic demos in order to create radically democratic game-transformative practices with significant promise for dismantling neoliberalism and forging powerful alternatives?

I argue that crafting such a movement calls us to create ecologies of democratic action research that combine scholarship and community engagement. Community-based action research performs what has been coined "public work."[3] *The*

---

[2] I elaborate the concept of "game-transformative practices" in *Visionary Pragmatism* (Durham, NC: Duke University Press, forthcoming).

[3] For a discussion of "public work" see Harry C. Boyte, *Everyday Politics: Reconnecting Citizens and Public Life* (Philadelphia, PA: University of Pennsylvania Press, 2005). The genealogies of community-based, civically engaged, and participatory action research pedagogy are complex and contested, yet for the purposes of this article I will use these terms interchangeably. Many strands of engaged pedagogy have been significantly influenced by Paulo Freire's, *Pedagogy of the Oppressed*, Myra Ramos, trans. (New York: Continuum Press, 1986); and Paulo Freire, *Pedagogy of Freedom: Ethics, Democracy, and Civic Courage*, trans. Patrick Clark (Washington, DC: Rowman and Littlefield Publishers, 2000); and critical pedagogy theorists such as bell hooks, in *Teaching to Transgress: Education as the Practice of Freedom* (London: Routledge Press, 1994). For overviews of participatory action research, see Alice McIntyre, *Participatory Action Research* (Thousand Oaks, CA: Sage Publications, 2007); and Ernest T. Stringer, *Action Research, Fourth Edition* (Thousand Oaks,

most profound public work hinges upon co-creating publics and publicness.[4] Institutions of higher education that nurture rich ecologies of action research become public in new senses that actively involve all sorts of communities in knowledge production around countless problems and possibilities. In the process of co-activating broader publics, such institutions would be significantly co-owned and co-guided by them in ways that include but far exceed public finance. Simultaneously, these academy–community assemblages presage forms of hopeful power for reclaiming democracy, commonwealth, and ecological resilience. After sketching some of the broad contours of this critical and generative position, I flesh it out with an engaged observer account of the community-based action research initiative underway at Northern Arizona University (NAU) and in networks across the US. In conclusion I reflect upon the broader political and theoretical implications of the work we have done at NAU during the past six years.

Corporate Assault and Contemporary Resistance

The corporate assault on higher education has been critically analyzed on many levels. Proponents of "shock doctrine" employ manufactured fiscal crises to advance transformative restructurings that are antithetical to liberal education and democracy.[5] Many have analyzed myriad forms of corporatization at work today: increasing ratios of contingent faculty to tenured faculty (contingent faculty now constitute three-quarters of the instructors at many campuses and typically receive lower wages, fewer or no benefits, no research support, and less governing power); exponential growth in the size, powers, autonomy, and compensation of technocratic administrative layers; the direction of funding to privatized construction contracts; the growth of consumer culture pedagogies; universities of "excellence" where learning outcomes are modeled according to corporate imperatives; disciplinary proliferations of quantitative assessment; and dramatic increases in tuition and student debt.[6] All of these measures operate to decrease

---

Footnote 3 continued

CA: Sage Publications, 2013). Robert Hildreth's, *Building Worlds, Transforming Lives, Making History: A Guide to Public Achievement* (Minneapolis, MN: Center for Democracy and Citizenship, 1998) articulates a practice of civic engagement pedagogy called "Public Achievement" that has influenced the movement at Northern Arizona University.

[4] Romand Coles and Blase Scarnati, "The Craftsperson Ethos and Transformational Ecotones in Higher Education," in Harry C. Boyte (ed.), *Democracy's Education: A Symposium on Public Work, Citizenship, and the Future of Higher Education* (Nashville, TN: Vanderbilt University Press, forthcoming 2014). See my contributions to Romand Coles and Stanley Hauerwas, *Christianity, Democracy, and the Radical Ordinary: Conversations between a Radical Democrat and a Christian* (Eugene, OR: Wipf and Stock Press, 2007); and Sheldon Wolin, *The Presence of the Past: Essays on the State and the Constitution* (Baltimore, MD: Johns Hopkins University Press, 1990) for more on the formation of democratic publics. See also, David W. Brown and Derek W.M. Barker (eds), *A Different Kind of Politics: Readings on the Role of Higher Education in Democracy* (Dayton, OH: Kettering Foundation Press, 2009).

[5] Naomi Klein, *Shock Doctrine: The Rise of Disaster Capitalism* (New York: Henry Holt, 2007).

[6] See, for example, Marc Bousquet, *How the University Works: Higher Education in a Low Wage Nation* (New York: New York University Press, 2008), on contingent labor and corporate investments; Bill Readings, *The University in Ruins* (Cambridge, MA: Harvard University Press, 1997), for a critique of "universities of excellence"; and Benjamin

democratic practices, reduce labor costs, increase labor docility, channel public revenues to the private sector, and discipline the next generation.[7]

Episodic responses to this onslaught include faculty invitations to critics to discuss these changes and possible resistance, student petitions and protests against tuition hikes, and graduate student teaching assistants' efforts to organize and unionize. Among the most promising initiatives is the growth in collaborative organizing among unions and adjunct faculty, such as US Steel and adjuncts in Pittsburgh, Pennsylvania, and Service Employees International Union's (SEIU) "Adjunct Action" movement that began organizing faculty at colleges in metropolitan regions such as Washington, DC, Boston, Massachusetts, and Los Angeles, California, in late 2012, and has recently begun working in eight other cities across the country. The political frame of such action focuses on issues of rights, equity, and protections.[8]

These efforts gesture in good directions toward the importance of forming broader coalitions, as the SEIU website encourages activists to recruit students and communities for support. Yet as those who have engaged in democratic organizing and coalition building know, loosely articulated ambitions to "recruit support" from diverse communities and coalitions are extremely difficult to achieve. Occasionally, other constituencies can be mobilized for comparatively brief actions, but sustained broad-based organizing requires forging a sense of shared interests and passions that have been carefully wrought by the various organizations engaged—including a sense of belonging to a shared movement of democratic action for commonwealth. This democratic sensibility is forged as we generate experiences of action together, along with narratives that gather these experiences in ways that foreground an emergent demos. Such work and action occurs not only in large dramatic events, but also through painstaking relationship building—person-by-person, institution-by-institution.

What is generally underdeveloped in resistance efforts like those above is attention to broad, deep, and powerful political experiences, frames with compelling trajectories and horizons for action, artful forms of broad-based quotidian organizing required for the long haul, and sharp strategies for cultivating grass-roots leadership capacities among wider and wider networks of organizations and individuals, and transformative reflection on the possible relationships between all of these and the basic purposes and modes of work in higher education.[9] Instead, the initiatives are typically framed as defensive reactions that seek to rescue faculty on the chopping block and at least partially reinstate earlier conditions with regard to tenure density ratios, tuition rates, salaries, benefits, rights, and protections.

Footnote 6 continued

Ginsberg, *The Fall of the Faculty: The Rise of the All-Administrative University and Why it Matters* (Oxford, UK: Oxford University Press, 2011).

[7] Noam Chomsky, "On Academic Labor," *Counterpunch*, February 28–March 2, 2014, <http://www.counterpunch.org/2014/02/28/on-academic-labor/>.

[8] See adjunctaction.org for information on the SEIU initiative, and <http://aa.drupalgardens.com> for the Adjunct Faculty Association of United Steelworkers. The Committee on Contingency and the Profession of the American Association of University Professors also does research and organizing on contingent faculty issues. See <http://www.aaup.org/about/committees/standing-committees>.

[9] See, for example, my essays in Coles and Hauerwas, *Christianity, Democracy, and the Radical Ordinary*, especially Chapters 3 and 13.

Such defensive maneuvering is indispensable. Yet in spite of the fact that tens of millions of people suffer directly from the assault on higher education, as I argue in the next section, right-wing media and political organizations have been remarkably effective at framing such resistance as the whining of inefficient profiteering elites who are eroding American values while being accustomed to special privileges that very few others receive. While such affectively saturated frames have yet to create overwhelming animosity toward higher education, they are fueling such hostility among a sizable minority of people on the right, and across a broader political range the vitriol converges with a host of other factors that appear to be taking the wind out of the sails that might otherwise support more powerful and durable movements resisting neoliberalization.

Problematizing Publics and Publicness

Tarry briefly with the "public" that is often called upon to "support" higher education. Consider a few numbers. An American Association of State Colleges and Universities (AASCU) Report on a Chronicle of Higher Education poll notes that large majorities view four-year institutions positively, with 61% affirming that the quality of public higher education is either high or very high. Confidence ratings for these institutions are similar to those that are bestowed upon the military and religious organizations, with 93% agreeing that higher education is among the most valuable resources in the US.[10]

Yet the AASCU report suggests that this confidence has an important underside, as the view that campuses are doing well is intertwined with the view that they do not need additional support. Perhaps it is at this interstice that what is said and not said in much of the media is at work, for 68% said that public institutions could cut costs without reducing the quality of higher education. Moreover, they tend to blame educational institutions themselves for rising tuition costs, as more people think the problem stems from cultures of profiteering and inefficiency than from decreasing state aid. This sense is easily inflamed and mobilized to generate hostilities toward, or devitalize support for, public funding. Though a majority support federal assistance for education, they want it to be provided to students, not the institutions themselves; and in a recent Gallup poll far more people supported reductions in tuition and fees as a way to support access to higher education (77%) than they supported increased federal and state spending (55% and 59% respectively). The predominance of an individualist economic perspective on the value of higher education shows up in a strong majority opinion (68%) that, after cost cutting, employers providing assistance to employees seeking more higher education is the best way to address problems of access. All of this suggests a situation in which budget crises may easily be manipulated to reduce spending for higher education.[11]

---

[10] This and all other references to the AASCU report are from the American Association of State Colleges and Universities, "Connecting Higher Education, Public Opinion, and Public Policy," *Policy Matters* 2:9 (2005), pp. 1–4, <http://www.aascu.org/uploadedFiles/ AASCU/Content/Root/PolicyAndAdvocacy/PolicyPublications/Connecting%20Higher %20Education%20Public%20Opinion.pdf>.

[11] Valerie J. Calderon and Preety Sidhu, "American Want Cost Cuts, Employer Help to Fund Education," *Gallup Economy*, May 2, 2013, <http://www.gallup.com/poll/162158/ americans-cost-cuts-employer-help-fund-education.aspx>.

The AASCU report suggests that the public's somewhat diminished sense of the public purposes of higher education (compared to career preparation) contributes to the drop in support for public funding. To counter this trend, they urge those in the academy to ramp up messaging and studies that emphasize the public purposes and impacts. It is worth tarrying more with the public's declining sense of higher education's "publicness," for when we take in the full scope of the problem, the need to explore paths of political and pedagogical possibility that far exceed messaging becomes apparent.

Peoples' diminishing sense of the public purposes of higher education stems from many different factors: Career preparation and jobs are featured far more often in media discussions of higher education. University administrators, faculty, public officials, and corporations often frame the value of education in terms of enhancing US job-competitiveness far more often than they frame it as integral to vibrant democratic citizenship. The Obama administration's "costs compared to employment outcomes" frame in its College Scorecard exemplifies this economistic consumer paradigm.[12]

Yet the problem is also lodged in the overall orientations and micro practices of the academy. A pervasive consumer culture reconstitutes these practices as students and parents often approach course and major options as shoppers, selecting items on campuses that look more and more like shopping malls. As student–teacher ratios increase, students frequently find themselves in large lectures, subject to what Paulo Friere called "banking education," in which information is deposited into young minds disciplined to receive it uncritically and in relative isolation.[13]

Further diminishing our sense of the publicness of higher education is that many forms of knowledge produced in the academy have strongly technocratic characteristics focused on how to manipulate people and things. Even when these forms seek to foster "service," they often nurture practices that are devoid of genuinely dialogical public relationships with their "clients," "customers," and "stakeholders." Those often subject to technocrats are likely to feel ambivalent about the institutions that produce them.

One might think that cultures conducive to democracy would thrive in disciplines associated with critical theory, humanities, and social research, especially given the legacies of democratic struggle around gender, race, sexuality, class, and nation that have significantly marked this terrain. Yet the fields of critical theory, humanities, and social research generally tend to be far better at generating critique, cynicism, and despair than they are at imaginatively exploring powerful democratic responses to the problems they identify—let alone engaging with the knowledge of organizers, activists, and members of myriad communities and emergent publics involved in specific organizing efforts and movements.

Hence, many factors converge to undermine the "publicness" of higher education and the "support" it might garner. Moreover, because all institutions that support educated citizenship—such as K-20 education, public libraries, public spaces, public media, public research—are undergoing similar cuts,

---

[12] < http://www.whitehouse.gov/issues/education/higher-education/college-score-card>.

[13] Freire, *Pedagogy of the Oppressed*, Chapter 2.

pressures, and transformations, the manifestations, capacities, and potentials of the "public" have been profoundly debilitated. What would it mean, then, to generate "public support" for the "public purposes" of higher education in a world where the latter are anemic and "publics" are so often largely constituted as manipulated correlates of corporate-political-media resonance machines? Can there be *public* senses or *public* purposes *without democratically reflective and active publics*? If not, might not the vitality and resilience of public education and democratic publics be more intimately intertwined than appeals for the latter to support the former would indicate?

I suspect there can be neither genuinely public higher education, nor serious public support for it, without robust democratic publics. At the same time, given that higher education is (in spite of everything) still one of the comparatively most free spaces in our polity, it is likely that such institutions must play an important role in nurturing the emergence and resilience of robust democratic publics—if there are to be any. If these things are true, then the future of both public higher education and publics would be intimately intertwined in ways that call us to reimagine and recreate pedagogy and politics *at this co-generative intersection*—far beyond what the rhetoric of "public" "support" for "public education" would have us believe and do. Thoughtfully enacting these entanglements, we might forge game-transformative practices capable of revitalizing democracy and higher education. Civic engagement pedagogies and community-based action research are integral to manifesting this possibility.

Becoming Publics and Transforming the Publicness

Generally, "publics" and "publicness" are so anemic that calls for "support" typically conceal the very questions we would need to address to avoid repeating impotent and predictable patterns with little democratic promise, while plutocratic powers develop potent game-transformative practices to dismantle and manipulate all manifestations of the demos. Strategies operating primarily within the frame discussed above are unlikely to do more than occasionally slow the rate of decline or establish precarious (though crucial) protections against some of the worst. More hopeful might be a perspective that discloses the possibilities for and necessity of transformatively co-generating democratic publics and the publicness of higher education at myriad intersections where people within and beyond the academy gather to generate knowledge, practices, and action in response to the problems of our time.[14] At these intersections we might cultivate *both* new modes of pedagogy and scholarship that are indispensable to democracy, commonwealth and a planet under siege, *and* new modes of power capable of fighting off the neoliberal assault and reconstituting higher education and politics.

---

[14] See essays in Harry C. Boyte, *Democracy's Education* and Romand Coles, "It's the 'We', Stupid," or "Reflections toward an Ecology of Radical Democratic Theory and Practice," *Theory and Event* 16:1 (2013). See also, Romand Coles, "Environmental Political Thought and Action Research Teams," in Teena Gabrielson, Cherly Hall, John Meyer, and David Schlosberg (eds), *The Oxford Handbook of Environmental Political Theory* (Oxford, UK: Oxford University Press, forthcoming 2015); and Romand Coles, "The Promise of Democratic Populism in the Face of Contemporary Power," *The Good Society* 21:2 (2012), pp. 177–193.

If reflective, active, and dynamic publics are scarce, stressed, and anemic, there are nevertheless significant possibilities. The AASCU report mentioned above is suggestive in this regard: Large majorities think it is "very important" or "important" that higher education "prepare students to be responsible citizens," "help elementary and high schools do a better job teaching children," "offer broad-based general education to undergraduates," "teach students to get along with people from different backgrounds," "prepare students from minority groups to become successful," and "provide useful information to the public on issues affecting peoples' daily lives." Yet we are led astray when we interpret such polls primarily as evidence of "preferences" (ultimately *consumer*, even if for public goods) that can be mobilized for "support." Things become more promising when we read them as *opportunities for co-generative political relationships*.

By such opportunities, I have in mind especially collaborative action research, public work, and political action engaged with quotidian problems in everyday life. What if we read peoples' hunger for a better world in relation to education, relationships across difference, the lives of minorities, responsible citizenship, and the need for human beings who are broadly educated, to be an invitation to form working publics to co-creatively generate new knowledge and action around myriad problems? What if we responded to these invitations by forming action research teams around questions such as: How might we engage children and youth to become active learners and agents of change in K-12 schools? How might we co-create hospitable and just communities with immigrants in search of better lives? How might we develop strategies for retrofitting energy efficient homes that reduce utility bills and greenhouse gas emissions while stimulating a green economy? How might we cultivate a vast capillary network of productive and educational gardens in schools, neighborhoods, and back yards that enhance food security and food justice while nurturing widespread aspirations for an alternative agricultural system? How might we work to conserve scarce water and distribute it in ways that are just? How might we create networked centers for cooperative, sustainable, and community-based enterprise? How might we learn creative ways of pursuing broad-based organizing initiatives? How might we resist carbon-based energy and catalyze investment in a renewable distributed energy that democratizes power and helps avert some of the worst aspects of planetary climate catastrophe?

Action research is a relational approach to generating knowledge, practices, communications, and powers necessary to respond effectively to challenges like these and countless others. When done well it is not a form of what commonly flies under the rubric of "service learning" *for* communities, but rather a form of deep democratic engagement *with* communities.[15] It is not a practice of

---

[15] Here I employ "service learning" heuristically as the self-descriptive term used by many programs on campuses across the US that frequently create opportunities for service that are short-term, "one-off," construed in ways that accent "volunteers" "helping" communities, non- or minimally-dialogical, focused on symptoms rather than systems, and avoid questions of power and politics. Such programs are widespread and proponents of "civic engagement" and democracy education often distinguish their work from such service by emphasizing the need for public work and action research that builds long-term relationships, co-creates practices that are explicitly reciprocal and developed through ongoing dialogue, seeks to address the systemic conditions that generate problems,

"applying" academic knowledge, but rather of bringing various kinds of academic knowledge into dialogue with various kinds of knowledge in broader communities and listening well, to produce new forms of knowledge and practice that greatly exceed the sum of their parts.

Faculty often initiate action research because they think it can make a valuable contribution to knowledge and specific communities, and because they think it may enhance their pedagogical practices. Beyond myopically professionalized disciplines, faculty who are involved in action research often rediscover and rekindle the deeper public purposes that initially drew them to pursue academic vocations. Simultaneously they frequently generate new vitality in their disciplines as they enter knowledge created there into broader conversations. Many students, especially those who are "first generation," gain a sense of excitement and pertinence in their studies that can be far more elusive in traditional classrooms and pedagogies. Many people in diverse communities gain a new sense of the value and power of their own forms of knowledge, as their insights informatively enter the mix with scholars. Most of us deepen a respectful sense of others as potential collaborators who solicit our modesty, curiosity, and ears—as well as our voices, insights, and agonistic provocations.

Now imagine the following scenario: Beyond the ventures of a few idiosyncratic faculty or tiny programs, hundreds of campuses begin to catalyze dozens of action research teams in which students, faculty, and a multitude of community partners join together in a process that involves both *becoming publics* (engaging in relational networks of bodies, imagination, knowledge, aspiration, practice, action, collective experimentation, and power that tend to common goods and the vitality of democracy itself) and becoming *public beings* (beings whose sensibilities and capacities render them attentive to and reflectively engaged with questions of commonwealth and freedom). As this happens, the *publicness* of higher education undergoes a radical reformation that rejuvenates the deepest aspirations of democracy: publicness becomes a mode of pedagogical being and begins to transform the cultures and relational networks of institutions of higher education and related communities.

The public purposes of higher education are revitalized, transfigured, and multiplied, and so too are our pedagogical modes of pursuing such purposes, as new and hybrid publics are catalyzed and the ecology of practices in which faculty

---

Footnote 15 continued

frequently aims to cultivate grass-roots democratic power, and understands democracy not simply as a volunteer activity but rather as a practice that ought to shape the public character and purposes of our working lives—including curricular and co-curricular activity and scholarship. See, for example, Harry C. Boyte and James Farr, "The Work of Citizenship and the Problem of Service Learning," in *Experiencing Citizenship: Concepts and Models for Service Learning in Political Science* (Sterling, VA: Stylus Publishing, 1997), pp. 35–48. Nevertheless, much of the scholarship on service learning is more sophisticated than what one often finds in many campus service learning initiatives. Indeed, some of the best work on service learning is very close to the theory and practice of civic engagement. There is, as Barbara Jacoby describes, a "spectrum of service learning experiences" and conceptual frameworks that range from the service learning paradigm sketched above to those that have substantial kinship with what I am calling civic engagement. See Barbara Jacoby and Associates, *Service Learning in Higher Education: Concepts and Practices* (Hoboken, NJ: Jossey-Bass, 1996); and Dan W. Butin, *Service Learning in Theory and Practice: The Future of Community Engagement in Higher Education* (Basingstoke, UK: Palgrave Macmillan, 2010).

and students are immersed diversifies to include dialogue, public work, and political action within and beyond the walls of the academy. Simultaneously, as members of broader communities collaborate in action research, they begin to gain a strong sense of connection to higher education. They become invested in it in ways that far exceed their taxes. Insofar as they are integral participants in guiding action research initiatives, they gradually acquire a sense of participatory governance in and ownership of these processes and—ultimately—institutions of higher education more generally.

In the process sketched in this scenario, one might say that we would co-creatively develop new ways of thinking with diverse people that are *both visionary and pragmatic*, rather than either myopically pragmatic or so ethereally disconnected from the world as to preclude all possibility of meaningful return. We would cultivate relationships, purposes, and transformative agency in relation to the suffering and possibilities of people, places, and the planet. In so doing, we would likely regenerate powerful, reflective, imaginative, and durable support from broader publics—precisely because we have engaged in becoming public and catalyzing publics and publicness *with* them. They would likely support higher education, then, not as a provider of services, but as an institution with which they are actively implicated in relationships of reciprocity that are complex, plural, dynamic, full of tensions, and creating paths that lead beyond pervasive patterns of devastation. *These* sorts of publics would likely rally powerfully to defend higher education as a good in common, and they would be a formidable force against efforts to privatize, instrumentalize, or annihilate this and other forms of democracy and commonwealth.

These sorts of publics would be involved in an explicitly game-transformative practice in which they would, in each iteration of their pedagogy and politics, seek to co-create modes of relationship, knowledge, work, action, and institutional change that enhance their comparative power to further *democratize the political game itself*—so as to enhance their hand in future rounds. In each iteration they would seek to develop what Paulo Friere called "generative themes"—repeatedly radicalizing paths of inquiry and practice that link specific work and action with broader and broader systemic patterns of power and transformative possibility.[16]

A nice fantasy, you might say, yet so far beyond the realm of contemporary possibility as to be worthless—even ludicrous. In a context where the dismantling assaults of neoliberalism repeatedly put faculty and students on the defensive, how would we gain a hold that might enable us to muster powers capable of challenging global capitalism and moving in this direction?

One cannot say for certain, yet the scenario I have just sketched is not constructed ex nihilo, but rather as an evolving product of "living theory" generated in the crucible of my own and many others' involvement in a growing movement for democratic education that has become increasingly powerful in Northern Arizona during the past five years, as well as in other campus-community networks.[17] From conversations with numerous people who are

---

[16] Friere, *Pedagogy of the Oppressed*, Chapter 3.

[17] For example, many of these ideas are part of the exploratory conversations I have witnessed and participated in, in national civic engagement networks such as the American Democracy Project, the American Commonwealth Partnership, Kettering Foundation, and others.

engaged in this initiative, it appears that there are tendencies toward the emergence of this larger scenario that are immanent in individual and small group initiatives in action research. These tendencies sometimes appear to develop as follows. Faculty (and students and community members) first initiate action research pedagogy and scholarship because of a sense of the intrinsic value of such practices for contributing to significant knowledge, compelling pedagogy, and public goods. Not infrequently, the results of these first ventures far exceed anticipations, as students become fired up about learning and public involvement, important knowledge is generated, and relays of reciprocal empowerment are generated among members of the academy and members of broader communities. The excitement generated then draws others to become involved in similar initiatives, sometimes forming civic engagement clusters. Those involved in such work become increasingly *political, both* in the sense that their passions for and interests in public goods and publics amplify, *and* in the sense that their collaborative research work often involves them in *strategic* thinking and action as they seek ways to advance these goods and publics. As our strategic sensibilities and capacities increase, when we find ourselves in the shrinking boxes of the neoliberal academy and the broader polity, we begin to creatively direct these modes of reflective action toward the pedagogical-political-economic contexts that are generating de-empowering dynamics. As we search for relationships, multiple constituencies, practices, and paradigms that might enable us to change these conditions, the new networks, pedagogical modes, and political aspirations formed in our action research initiatives suggest powerful possibilities for revitalizing a democratic movement for commonwealth in which transformed institutions of higher education can become vital catalysts and co-creators. From there it is but a short step to the sort of analysis I have developed so far in this article.

Of course, there are many ways in which such tendencies can be—and sometimes are—truncated: They can be captured in a narrowly institutionalized "program" that devitalizes aspirations for broader institutional, cultural, and political change. Or they can be drawn back toward depoliticized modes of service. Or individuals, programs, and campuses can remain isolated, and thus fail to develop expansive senses of possibility. Or we can become mired in neoliberal practices such as unending "assessments" that exhaust and divert us; "results-based planning" strategies that fragment holistic efforts and demand immediate results; "best-practices" strategies that stem the tides of creativity and imagination; and so forth. Yet the potential paths of development discussed above manifest repeatedly, can be actively nurtured, and generate positive democratic feedback loops that are worth exploring. Sometimes the latter enable us to play parts of the neoliberal game in ways that enhance our hand, as I discuss below. For many of us, these positive feedback loops and dynamics are instilling a sense that action research and democratic engagement pedagogies are *both* intrinsically valuable *and* integral to an emergent strategy for broader transformation in higher education and the polity. To gain a further sense of this possibility it is worthwhile telling the story of the movement for democracy that is developing at NAU.

Engaged Observation of NAU's Movement for Democratic Education

I moved from Duke University, in Durham, North Carolina, to Northern Arizona University, in Flagstaff, to explore possibilities for generating democratic and ecological transformation at the intersections between NAU and broader communities in the region. As the housing bubble burst at the start of my first semester, I began to do hundreds of what community organizers call "one-to-one relational meetings." Beyond chit-chat, in one-to-ones you seek to understand what really makes a person tick: their passions, sense of purpose, most significant relationships, deepest commitments, their dreams—their sense of self, community, and urgency. As the director of the Program for Community, Culture and Environment, I was able to spend a lot of time meeting with people, so I quickly got to know the campus and community well, as I sought ways to understand and creatively navigate the labyrinth of problems and possibilities; the aspirations of long-standing organizations, as well as emergent groups and movements; the networks of power, relationships, and public affect through which NAU and Flagstaff lived, breathed, and moved.

As the economy plunged into the Great Recession, campus and community budgets suffered severe cuts amplified significantly by a right-wing legislature that was hostile to higher education, corporate taxes, and nearly all things public. Seizing the moment, the legislature began intensifying a particularly vitriolic phase of culture war. Undocumented immigrants were ground zero for this assault, but the LGBTQ community, proponents of sustainability, ethnic studies, education, and gun control—and even moderate Republicans, all came under strong attacks that continue to this day. I note these things in order to emphasize that the conditions in which NAU's movement for democracy education emerged were extremely challenging—the number of tenure lines was reduced, adjunct hiring increased, class sizes grew, workloads increased, the daily news was extremely discouraging, and the affective ambience on campus (and off) was largely one of heightened anxiety, despair, cynicism, defensiveness, and powerlessness.

Nevertheless, as we began proliferating one-to-one and small group meetings, a constellation of possibilities for a pedagogical movement for democracy, social justice, and ecological sustainability gradually emerged. In the fall of 2009, we launched an initiative lead by the Program for Community, Culture and Environment (CC&E) in collaboration with the First Year Seminar Program (FYS) and the Masters of Sustainable Communities Program (MSUS), in which students in an MSUS core course served as "facilitators" of action research teams (ARTs) made up largely of students in my FYS course. Students opted into one of the following ARTs: public achievement (coaching teams of K-12 students on the theory and practice of grassroots democracy), weatherization and community building, immigration, water conservation and rights, urban gardening and alternative agriculture, food security, and public spaces for civic engagement. We partnered with several community organizations, including Killip Elementary School, the Sustainable Economic Development Initiative, Friends of Flagstaff's Future, Foodlink, Northern Arizona Interfaith Council, and the Sunnyside and South Side Neighborhood Associations. During that semester, we participated in and catalyzed myriad projects: we coached teams of children in democratic organizing, organized with the immigrant community against abusive policing and for just democratic relationships among citizens and undocumented people, began working in urban gardens, held forums that led to action plans for a sustainable café, began community organizing around residential energy efficiency, and hosted an educational and celebratory event that drew five hundred people to what long-time residents said was the most diverse large gathering Flagstaff had ever had. Most involved ended the semester very enthusiastic about the emerging transformative possibilities, and the ARTs continued into the next semester, largely led by graduate students, faculty, community partners, and some undergraduates who stayed involved informally after the first semester.

A vortex of excitement gathered next fall, as the FYS program recruited more faculty to offer seminars connected with the ARTs, the MSUS program doubled its incoming class and provided more facilitation and mentorship (aided by stipends from CC&E), and our collaborations with community groups strengthened. Each year since, the number of FYS-ARTs courses has grown, as have enrollments of first-year students engaged in the ARTs, which totaled 450 in fall of 2013 and are expected to nearly double that in the fall of 2014. Many new ARTs have been added to the mix, including K-12 School Gardens, Queer and Ally, Hot Topics (hosting forums for civic discourse on contentious issues), Total Liberation (on intersections between animal rights and other forms of struggle), New Economy NAU (on social entrepreneurship and cooperative, sustainable, and just economics), HEALTH, and Art Through All Mediums (on the intersection of artistic performance, social justice, and personal issues). Many of the ARTs have developed sub-teams focused on different modes of public work and political action in relation to the problems they address. For example, the Immigration ART engages in humanitarian work on border issues with No More Deaths, broad-based community organizing strategies with Northern Arizona Interfaith Council, radical abolitionist democracy visions and strategies with Repeal Coalition, and educational events with a variety of campus and community partners. Other ARTs have multiplied their sites and projects. Public achievement has expanded to Kinsey Elementary and Kinlani Border Town Dormitory for students from Native Nations attending Flagstaff High School. The latter effort has a particular emphasis on traditional ecological knowledge, leadership, and indigenous environmental justice. Other ARTs have branched out to engage additional issues, such as when the Weatherization and Community Building Action Team (WACBAT) formed Divest NAU, affiliated with 350.org's campaign against climate change, and Stoking the Fires of Democracy for a Visionary Flagstaff, for intensifying civic engagement and voting. The number of partnering organiz-ations and social movements has burgeoned, and it is fair to say that the ARTs movement is an energetic participant—or catalyst—in most of the major initiatives in Flagstaff for sustainability, social justice, and grass-roots democracy.

While initial funding for faculty and graduate student involvement in this initiative came from the three programs that formed the core leadership, we have since gained substantial funding from the NAU President's Innovation Fund, a Dean's Faculty Development Grant, the National Science Foundation (on climate change science, regional and cultural contextualization, and civic engagement), the Arizona Technological Research Investment Fund (for alternative food economy research), J.P. Morgan-Chase Foundation, Kettering Foundation, and more. The strange heterogeneity of our funding sources reflects an emergent organizing philosophy that seeks to assemble a vast array of tools for transformation, as well as a supple trickster dexterity in our use of them: from collaborative research and public work on myriad specific projects; to broad-based networking; to education and outreach projects; to education and training on multiple modes of community organizing; to searching discussions of critical and radical democratic theory; to voter registration; to hosting public forums; to advocacy and testifying before various representative institutions; to radical street protests (often enough we remove our institutional hats for these); to forming a center for community-based solidarity economics; to dramatic performances and artistic interventions; to fostering collaborations with public, private, and non-profit partner institutions in ways that seek to magnify and modulate the capacities of each to create change; to seeking state-level revolving loan funds for residential energy efficiency retrofits in conjunction with community organizing; to convivial practices of slow food and gathering at farmers' markets; to daily liturgies of tending to and creating resilient gardens; to coaching children and youth in the arts of grass-roots democracy; to creative uses of the internet, social media, and video; to petitioning; to engaging in continual conversations about how to push democratic pedagogy and organizing in directions that further enhance our transformative power; to inviting speakers engaged in initiatives elsewhere.

We push and pull each other to adhere to an understanding of democratic education and politics as *most especially about the recursive question* of how to create democratic transformation, and this involves endless experimentation with multiple modes and objectives, as well as exploring the implications of creatively combining them in ever-new ways. This enables us to keep from falling into a single dogma, and it provides a very broad array of access points for—and possibilities capable of—engaging many different kinds of faculty, students, and members of the broader community who range across a wide portion of the spectrum of differences. Those involved oscillate between periods characterized by relatively convergent senses of how these differences might fit together, and periods characterized by agonistic struggles among those who accent different modes, directions, and visions. We try to remind each other that both are necessary for the jazz-like improvisational patterns of democratic pedagogy and political action. For as Sheldon Wolin reminds us: "Democracy is wayward, inchoate, unable to rule yet unwilling to be ruled. It does not naturally con*form*. It is inherently formless." Or, dynamically multiple in it forms: "Democracy, far from evoking images intimative of monochromatic, mass society, is diverse and colorful. Democracy is unique in being related to all constitutions; it is not so much amorphous as polymorphous."[18] We affirmatively appropriate Plato's sardonic characterization of democracy as "an emporium of constitutions"[19] out of a growing sense that we can and must co-creatively-if-cautiously engage many different processes in our efforts to instigate transformative practice. Or, as Ani Difranco puts it, "every tool is a weapon, if you hold it right."[20] We are becoming shape-shifters, repeatedly re-learning arts of radical democratic shape-shifting.

In addition to the many modest yet very significant "successes" we are achieving in relation to the different ARTs, *the deepest public work we are doing is the*

---

[18] Sheldon Wolin, "Norm and Form: The Constitutionalizing of Democracy," in Peter Euben, John Wallach, and Josiah Ober (eds), *Athenian Political Thought and the Reconstruction of American Democracy* (Ithaca, NY: Cornell University Press, 1994), p. 50.

[19] Plato, *Republic*, trans. G.M.A. Grube (Indianapolis, IN: Hackett Publishing, 1975), 8.557d.

[20] Ani Difranco, "My I.Q.," *Puddle Dive*, Righteous Babe Records, 1993.

work of co-generating vibrant publics: activating and organizing students, faculty, community members, organizations, and social movements into sustained democratic pedagogical and political relationships and engagements. The fires of democracy are indeed being stoked, and though we are aware of how far we have to go, we are also excited about how far we have come—and the *journey*. Poised on this difficult yet exhilarating edge, growing numbers of people and organizations are forming publics, becoming public, affirming transformative publicness, and engaging in incipient practices of co-guiding, and co-owning these emergent practices of democratic education.

One vital measure of these *immeasurable* phenomena can be seen with respect to first-year students engaged with the ARTs. NAU students have very high dropout rates, with roughly 27% of first year students leaving NAU before the second year. A recent assessment study of the FYS-ARTs, found significant increases in retention rates from the first to the second year among students who take one such seminar. Minority students who took a FYS-ARTs course showed increased retention rates of 17%; women's rates increased 9%; overall rates were up 7%.[21] These findings strongly suggest that students who connect their education with public engagement, purposes, and agency not only "turn on" to education, but are also not as likely to "turn off." Many of us involved in this work are sensing similar effects on the interest, enthusiasm, scholarship, and resilient involvement of faculty, graduate students, and community members. Many are developing a taste for the practices of democratic pedagogy and politics.

Yet even as these numbers are very promising and suggestive, they also raise important questions about the complicated political relationships between neoliberal governance and radical democratization efforts struggling to gain a transformative hold in the academy. The economization of everything is one of the central manifestations of neoliberal power, and (as noted above) this process proceeds through dense pragmatic logics of "efficiency"; ceaseless fracturing of holistic practices into separated micro-goals, strategies, and modules in processes of "results-based planning"; establishing "best practices" that normalize and suppress deviance; subjecting everyone and everything (and every small component of everything) to ever-more frequent "assessments"; and increasing the stakes of such assessments in ways that suppress experimentation (especially among precarious faculty) for fear of negative consequences anytime there is a "failure."[22] Such modes of governance are having a profound impact on power, culture, and subjectivity in most institutions of higher education. They are integral

---

[21] Michelle Miller, "Assessment Report for AY 2012–2013 First Year Seminar/ FYSeminar-ARTs," The First Year Seminar Program, Northern Arizona University, May 2013. The study carefully controlled its comparison sample in order to avoid "propensity biases," according to which those who self-selected into the FYS-ARTs might be expected to have higher rates of retention on this basis alone. To avoid such bias, FYS and non-FYS student samples were matched and equivalent on the following characteristics: ethnicity, gender, AZ residency, FAFSA/PELL eligibility, attended previews, high school deficiencies (Math, English, Lab Science), declared college, ACT/SAT scores, high school CORE GPA, and student success inventory (six scales).

[22] See, for example, Wendy Brown, "Governmentality in the Age of Neoliberalism," Lecture at Pacific Centre for Technology and Culture, March 18, 2014, <http://pactac.net/ 2014/03/wendy-brown—governmentality-in-the-age-of-neoliberalism/?utm_content= buffer42fee&utm_medium = social&utm_source = facebook.com&utm_campaign = buffer > .

to neoliberal game-transformative practice. The Arizona Board of Regents propels this process with new outcome-based funding metrics that tie public funding of universities to retention and graduation rates rather than enrollment numbers.

NAU's ARTs movement has always played a delicate "trickster" game with respect to neoliberal governance, accessing pockets of funding by hypothesizing that engaged pedagogy would have a major positive influence on the rates to which state funding is pegged. By using the trope "trickster" game I imply, not that we are behaving dishonestly, but rather that we are playing one (neoliberal) game very well, primarily in order to institute a transformative counter and alternative practice that is much more important to us. It is not that we do not care about retention and graduation rates—far from it—but that we care about radical democracy, sustainability, and social justice far more, and primarily value these rates within this transformative frame.

As the assessment studies confirm our wager, very substantial funding is beginning to roll in, including significant allotments for graduate student assistantships, undergraduate peer teaching assistantships, support staff, numerous full-time faculty lecturers teaching ARTs seminars, and (this year) two tenure-track positions shaped by our work (one in community-based sustainable economics, and one in community-based sustainable agriculture).

One way to look at these allocations of funding is that they are mostly utilizing underpaid precarious labor—undergraduates, graduate students, and non-tenure-track lecturers. There is significant and profoundly frustrating truth to this. At the same time, all of these people are self-consciously inhabiting these significantly exploitative spaces in order to transform the structures of power that have created them, in classrooms, the broader campus, the community, and far beyond. And there are significant and growing spaces for creative freedom and democratic agency. Undergraduates can pursue a newly established civic engagement minor while getting paid to work ten hours a week as peer teaching assistants, so by the end of their time at NAU they acquire a rich body of theory, empirical scholarship, and organizing experience pertaining to engaged democracy. The organizing acumen of faculty has manifested in a successful initiative to reduce teaching loads for FYS-ARTs faculty from 4/4 to 3/3, to allow time for the organizing work of civic engagement. Recently FYS-ARTs faculty constituted themselves as a (now recognized) faculty steering committee to gain more power in relation to the conditions of their work. Similarly, graduate and undergraduate leaders in this movement meet once every two weeks to discuss, debate, dream, challenge, expand, and modulate the practices and directions of the ARTs initiative.

Hence, while the pressures of neoliberal governance are strong and exhausting, we are crafting many spaces and practices that enhance the powers of game-transformative democratic movements in higher education (and beyond). As we do so, we are simultaneously expanding and deepening myriad democratic publics and the publicness of the university and many of its community partners. We are creating knowledge and practices for the public work and political action of a robust democracy dedicated to cultivating and protecting complex, plural, and dynamic forms of commonwealth. Increasingly, others are taking notice and our work is beginning to have broader impacts. On campus, several supportive deans and faculty leaders have formed a Consortium for Civic Engagement that seeks to advance kindred efforts. Nationally, NAU's example is beginning to stimulate deep reflection in networks for democratic engagement such as the Kettering Foundation, the American Commonwealth Partnership, Imagining America, and their partnering institutions, where kindred initiatives are emerging.

Concluding Reflections

It is not difficult to imagine ways that such efforts might be assimilated into forms of neoliberal governance that often proliferate precisely in the name of collaboration, participation, consensus-building, and stakeholder teamwork. Yet based on the past five years at NAU, it is also not difficult to imagine that a crafty demos educated in the arts of public work and political action might inhabit some of the spaces of this insidious form of power in trickster ways that enhance radical democratic capacities that far exceed these modes of governance and magnify our powers to resist the neoliberal assault while midwifing alternative possibilities. If radical democrats can continue to deepen and cultivate critical agonistic as well as collaborative impulses, it is conceivable that growing networks of campuses and other institutions seeking to promote democratically engaged education, work, and action, might proliferate these capacities and powers far and wide within the next decade.

Under such circumstances, we can then imagine that regenerated publics, recognizing and valuing a revitalized publicness of higher education in which many are engaged, might muster potent resistance in response to intensified neoliberal incursions that often happen during manufactured or real crises. Shock doctrine political economy is powerful precisely because it oscillates between maneuvers to dramatically dismantle publics, public goods, and publicness, on the one hand, and maneuvers of quotidian capillary governance, on the other. By analogy, those engaged in the democratic productions of knowledge, work, and action sketched above might learn the arts of *combining* quotidian capillary practices and powers of democratic engagement with dramatic displays of shocking resistance (such as strikes, sit-ins, protests, aesthetic staging, and disruptive forms of mobilizing and organizing), in ways that similarly reinforce and advance the systolic-diastolic movement of game-transformative democratization. Developing action research education initiatives that encourage students, faculty, and community members to creatively and carefully learn and invent arts of powerfully interweaving these different political modes is, as I have suggested, integral to this struggle for the democratic future of higher education and our polity.

Surely the challenges to such a strategy are substantial, to say the least. Yet the evidence from the first five years of the movement at NAU strongly suggests that a democratic movement based in higher education-community action research networks can make rapid and substantial headway against mighty odds. Everything hinges on not getting stuck in political and pedagogical frames and modes that are primarily reactive—aiming merely to critically identify and defend against the mounting losses accrued in a neoliberal game-transformative practice that is undermining higher education, democracy, and just commonwealth at ever-increasing rates. Surely such defensive politics is a necessary *part* of what any progressive movement must enact. Yet above all we must begin to conduct a different kind of political practice, namely, one that seeks to alter the very terrain and mode of struggle by generating newly transformative and mutually implicated forms of publicness, publics, and public goods with substantial powers and promise to undercut key dimensions of the neoliberal assault; to use other dimensions of neoliberal infiltrations of our institutions in trickster ways that advance democracy by co-opting it through aikido moves precisely where it is designed to destroy us; and most of all to cultivate a vast assemblage of alternative democratic practices that prefigure, build, and empower a radically reformed democracy worthy of the name.

The task of higher education today—to slightly modify activist-scholar Marshall Ganz's employment of twelfth-century Jewish scholar Moses Maimonides' phrase—is to develop practices of learning, teaching, relationship, and action that devitalize our enthrallment to the mythic "necessity of the [neoliberal] probable" and revitalize a fine-grained and expansive sense of the "plausibility of the [democratic] possible."[23] The theory and practice proposed in this article are intended as a contribution to this perennial project.

---

[23] In "What is Public Narrative?," Working Paper, 2011, p. 5, <http://marshallganz. com/publications/>.

Index

INDEX